Germany and Austria 1814–2000

MODERN HISTORY FOR MODERN LANGUAGES

Mark Allinson

Hodder Arnold

A MEMBER OF THE HODDER HEADLINE GROUP

LONDON

Co-published in the United States of America
by Oxford University Press Inc., New York

In memory of Susan Sheridan

First published in Great Britain in 2002 by
Arnold, a member of the Hodder Headline Group
338 Euston Road, London NW1 3BH

http://www.hoddereducation.co.uk

Co-published in the United States of America by
Oxford University Press Inc.,
198 Madison Avenue, New York, NY10016

British Library Cataloguing in Publicatiion Data
A catalogue record for this book is available from the British Library

Library of Congress Cataloging-in-Publication Data
A catalog record for this book is available from the Library of Congress

ISBN-10: 0 340 76022 2 (pb)
ISBN-13: 978 0 340 76022 2

2 3 4 5 6 7 8 9 10

Production Editor: Wendy Rooke
Production Controller: Martin Kerans
Cover Design: Terry Griffiths

Typeset in 9.25 on 13 Lucida by Phoenix Photosetting, Chatham, Kent
Printed and bound in India by Replika press

What do you think about this book? Or any other Hodder Arnold title?
Please visit our website at www.hoddereducation.co.uk

Contents

Maps

Preface

The last twenty years have witnessed a general broadening of the curriculum of numerous German degree programmes to include historical and political training alongside the key language and literature elements. For the many students who have not previously studied history, the prospect of embarking on a different discipline may appear daunting. The purpose of this book is to provide non-historians with a clear introduction to events in the German-speaking world during the last two centuries, while also highlighting some of the unresolved issues and controversies. A book of this size cannot, of course, cover all the ground and answer all the questions. As an introductory text for students who have not previously studied German history, nor is this the place to reveal new evidence or to propound a new reading of the subject. However, I hope that this introduction will provide readers with a firm foundation to pursue themes and questions in greater depth in other, more specialised historical texts. A further aim is to introduce students of modern languages to the historical terminology they will encounter in German-language sources.

Determining the parameters for a broad overview of 'German' history is anything but straightforward, as Germans – that is native speakers of the German language – have always lived, and continue to live, in a multiplicity of states, an issue this book attempts to address by including as broad a coverage as possible. The division of Germany after 1945 into two opposing states – the capitalist *Bundesrepublik Deutschland* (Federal Republic of Germany, FRG) in the west, and the eastern, communist *Deutsche Demokratische Republik* (German Democratic Republic, GDR) – is perhaps the best-known illustration. More than a decade after the GDR's collapse, the legacy of division still dominates much of German political and social life, and is central to many courses on German literature, society and politics. Consequently, this book considers the history of both German states in the post-1945 period, and the difficulties of the unification process since 1990.

However, German divisions have a much longer history. Whereas many nation states (like France and Spain) were well established by the early nineteenth century, by contrast Germany had always been a rather vague construct, comprised of numerous separate states and with little national sentiment. When Germany's political unification was first achieved in 1871, the new state excluded the Germans of Austria who had for centuries occupied a key position in German affairs. In 1918, after the First World War, it briefly appeared that Germany and Austria might be united again, and a short-lived *Großdeutsches Reich* ('Greater Germany') was created under Adolf Hitler in 1938. However, the collapse of Hitler's attempt to establish German world dominance by force ensured that Austria and the eastern German provinces would no longer be included in 'Germany'. Modern Austria now considers itself entirely separate from Germany, even quite foreign; yet the unifying force of the German language continues to foster cultural links and exchanges between the two countries. One can still speak of a German *Kulturnation* (cultural nation), which arguably overarches both states. Students of German are students of the language, culture and politics of both Germany and Austria, and this book therefore includes Austrian themes within the main narrative where appropriate, and within separate sections of text for other historical periods.

While Germany and Austria have parallel histories which have sometimes intersected during the past two centuries, the same cannot be said of Switzerland. Switzerland had effectively separated from the political development of the other German states by 1499, and thereafter established quite different traditions. At no point during the creation of a united German state did a 'Swiss question' emerge. Though the literature and culture of German-speaking Switzerland have been an important influence on the German *Kulturnation* (notably through writers such as Friedrich Dürrenmatt, Max Frisch and Robert Walser), a consideration of the very different course of Swiss history falls outside the scope of this book.

To place German and Austrian history in context, each chapter includes an overview of developments in European and world history, and a timeline of the key events for quick reference and orientation. The maps in the book have all been drawn to the same scale and have an outline of the borders of modern Germany and Austria for ready comparison with the changing borders of the political states which existed in this part of central Europe. Each chapter contains further features: special inserts give more information about specific institutions, concepts or personalities, which may have importance beyond the period covered by the chapter – bold references in the text and index indicate these inserts. There are also key historical texts in German, and questions to provoke further debate and study using the literature recommended at the end of the book and other texts besides. German terminology is used for institutions and ideas wherever appropriate; these terms are also listed in the index/glossary at the end of the book.

A book of this introductory nature does not require a full academic apparatus of footnotes and references, but a list of suggested further reading is included. Most of these titles should be fairly accessible to the non-specialist, but each of them in turn provides references to more detailed works.

The idea for this series of books was conceived by Elena Seymenliyska; she and Eva Martinez at Arnold have patiently nurtured the book from proposal to publication, and I am indebted to them, to the production editor, Wendy Rooke, and to the copy-editor, Jane Raistrick. I should also like to thank the German History Society for creating a flourishing forum for debate and reflection (particularly in its journal, *German History*) on the issues covered by this book, as well as my colleagues in the German Department at the University of Bristol for allowing me a vital sabbatical term to complete this work, Sharon Behan and Bertha Garrett for shouldering much of my administrative work, Nils Langer for the fairtrade coffee, and the students who have followed my courses in Bristol for their enthusiasm for German and Austrian history.

Mark Allinson, Bristol, November 2001

Abbreviations

BRD	*Bundesrepublik Deutschland*
CDU	*Christlich-Demokratische Union*
CPSU	Communist Party of the Soviet Union
CSCE	Conference on Security and Cooperation in Europe
CSP	*Christlichsoziale Partei*
CSU	*Christlich-Soziale Union*
DAF	*Deutsche Arbeitsfront*
DAP	*Deutsche Arbeiterpartei* [forerunner of NSDAP]
DBD	*Demokratische Bauernpartei Deutschlands*
DDP	*Deutsche Demokratische Partei*
DDR	*Deutsche Demokratische Republik*
DFD	*Demokratischer Frauenbund Deutschlands*
DKP	*Deutsche Kommunistische Partei*
DM	*Deutsche Mark*
DNVP	*Deutschnationale Volkspartei*
DSF	*(Gesellschaft für) deutsch-sowjetische Freundschaft*
DVP	*Deutsche Volkspartei*
DVU	*Deutsche Volksunion*
EC	European Community
EDC	European Defence Community
EEC	European Economic Community
EU	European Union
EWG	*Europäische Wirtschaftsgemeinschaft*
FDGB	*Freier Deutscher Gewerkschaftsbund*
FDJ	*Freie Deutsche Jugend*
FDP	*Freie Demokratische Partei*
FPÖ	*Freiheitliche Partei Österreichs*
FRG	Federal Republic of Germany
GDR	German Democratic Republic
GDVP	*Großdeutsche Volkspartei*
KB	*Kulturbund*
KPD	*Kommunistische Partei Deutschlands*
KPÖ	*Kommunistische Partei Österreichs*
LDPD	*Liberal-Demokratische Partei Deutschlands*
LiF	*Liberales Forum*
LPG	*Landwirtschaftliche Produktionsgenossenschaft*

MfS	*Ministerium für Staatssicherheit*
NATO	North Atlantic Treaty Organisation
NDPD	*National-Demokratische Partei Deutschlands* [GDR]
NÖS	*Neues Ökonomisches System*
NPD	*Nationaldemokratische Partei Deutschlands* [FRG]
NSDAP	*Nationalsozialistische Deutsche Arbeiterpartei*
ÖVP	*Österreichische Volkspartei*
PDS	*Partei des demokratischen Sozialismus*
RFB	*Roter Frontkämpferbund*
RFKP	*Reichs- und freikonservative Partei*
SA	*Sturmabteilungen*
SAP	*Sozialistische Arbeiterpartei*
SDAP	*Sozialdemokratische Arbeiterpartei*
SED	*Sozialistische Einheitspartei Deutschlands*
SPD	*Sozialdemokratische Partei Deutschlands*
SPÖ	*Sozialistische Partei Österreichs (after 1991) Sozialdemokratische Partei Österreichs*
SS	*Schutzstaffeln*
USA	United States of America
USPD	*Unabhängige Sozialdemokratische Partei Deutschlands*
USSR	Union of Socialist Soviet Republics
VdU	*Verband der Unabhängigen*
VEB	*Volkseigener Betrieb*

Prologue: Germany before 1814

Only three average human lifespans – a mere seven or eight generations – separate us from the early nineteenth century. In that time almost everything which was familiar to the Germans of 1800 has been thoroughly and repeatedly transformed. Yet even as the nineteenth century dawned, the German-speaking world had already embarked upon an era of profound change which encompassed political, economic and social life.

For centuries most Germans – with the notable exception of the Swiss – had lived within the 'Holy Roman Empire', the *Heiliges Römisches Reich deutscher Nation*. This medieval construct, which derived its legitimacy from a theoretical continuity with the Roman Empire of antiquity, consisted in practice of a large number of separate states loosely bound together under the central authority of a *Kaiser* (emperor). In 1800, the *Reich* still comprised a bewildering variety of these states. Alongside the important northern Kingdom of Prussia (*Preußen*) under the Hohenzollern dynasty, and the extensive territories ruled by the Habsburg family to the southeast (which extended into modern Hungary, Romania and beyond, but can conveniently be termed Austria), were middle-ranking princely states like Bavaria (*Bayern*); *Großherzogtümer* (grand duchies) and *Herzogtümer* (duchies); *Fürstentümer* (small principalities); a number of *Reichsstädte* (free imperial cities) run by merchants and noblemen; bishoprics and archbishoprics, states in their own right ruled directly by the church; and more than a thousand territories, often tiny, ruled by *Reichsritter* (imperial knights) who traced their family rights to the early middle ages. Each of these rulers, from the powerful kings of Prussia to the most insignificant of the *Reichsritter*, claimed full power over his (and occasionally her) own territory, with the *Kaiser* holding only nominal power over them all.

Thus, unlike France, Britain and other countries which had already developed into centralised nation states by 1800, the German lands remained politically fragmented. There was no single German citizenship within the *Reich*, nor any central German capital city to rival London or Paris. The term *Deutschland* referred to a geographical area of central Europe with no fixed borders rather than to an established political state. While the unified European nation states were building world empires in the eighteenth century, no German ruler was yet strong enough to embark on such a project.

The principles of German political power and organisation were still predominantly dynastic. Most territorial boundaries within 'Germany' did not respect natural geographical limits, still less any coherent popular sense of identity based on dialect or common interest. An individual principality might cover a number of geographically separate areas, divided from one another by many miles and linked only by the rule of a single prince. Within the boundaries of a single state it was common to find towns, villages or stretches of farmland or woodland which belonged to another prince, or perhaps to one of the bishoprics or *Reichsritter*. Important cities within a duchy often enjoyed the status of a *Reichsstadt* answerable only to the emperor and outside the surrounding principality's jurisdiction. Equally, a single town might be divided between two or more princes. If one princely line died out, its territories might be absorbed by another branch of the family and integrated into a state elsewhere in the *Reich*. Wars, marriages and treaties between the princes could lead to similar outcomes, and for example enabled the growth of the Prussian state. Yet an important ruler was generally obliged to respect the different laws, rights and customs held by each of the separate territories he or she acquired, ruling more as the prince of a number of different states than as the lord of a single state. Furthermore, a number of the German princes ruled over subjects of other nationalities (notably Czechs, Poles, Hungarians and Italians). Some of these non-German populations lived within the borders of the *Reich*; conversely, some Germans were outside the *Reich*. The two most powerful dynasties, the Austrian Habsburgs and the Prussian Hohenzollern, both ruled extensive territories to the east of the *Reich* in addition to their lands within the *Reich*. In short, Germany's territorial and political structures were a jumble of jurisdictions which had turned the map of central Europe into a colourful patchwork quilt, summed up in the term *Kleinstaaterei*.

Much of Germany's political history had for centuries centred on the struggle for power between the rulers of the individual territories and the *Kaiser* (elected for life by the most important princes of the *Reich*, the *Kurfürsten* (electors), but almost always a member of the Habsburg dynasty). By the mid-seventeenth century at the latest this battle had been decided in the favour of the rulers of these smaller states. As a source of real political power, the overarching *Reich* had become a dead letter, with neither the right to impose central rule, nor the administrative machinery to enforce the will of the *Kaiser* on the individual states. The *Kaiser* was left with little more than moral and symbolic authority. Instead the Habsburgs concentrated – like other ambitious rulers – on building and extending their power in the lands they held themselves by right. Only one dynasty – the Hohenzollern – was strong enough to compete with the Habsburgs for power and influence in German politics.

Most Germans' principal allegiance at this time was to their local ruler rather than to the German nation, a concept which had not yet firmly taken root in 1800. Particular local concerns were paramount in this system, and 'particularism' remained a potent counterpoint to nationalism well into the twentieth century. The federal systems present in the modern German and Austrian republics, in which the central state power is shared with, and checked by, the constituent regions of each country, are a direct political legacy of the regional autonomies in the Holy Roman Empire.

The old *Reich* retained, however, the important task of resolving conflicts between its member states and of protecting the rights of one ruler against the claims or threats of another. In this sense, the *Reich* was vitally important to the *Reichsritter*, the *Reichsstädte* and the smaller principalities, since the authority of the *Kaiser* and the convoluted constitution of the *Reich* protected them from being swallowed up by their larger neighbours. Similarly, craftsmen, town dwellers and even peasants whose traditional rights were infringed by their local ruler could call on the imperial courts for protection and the restoration of the status quo. As the *Reich* guaranteed the framework within which all the states could flourish, and as no ruler could expect to flout the imperial constitution without simultaneously undermining his own legitimacy, the *Reich*'s power was greater than its weak structures would suggest. But historians are generally agreed that this was principally a power to hinder change and preserve the old order rather than to innovate and give a lead in responding to changed circumstances.

In 1800, many of the contours of modern political life had yet to emerge in the German states. Political parties, or even political pressure groups and trade unions, were yet to emerge. In particular there was still little or no semblance of democracy. The imperial parliament, the *Reichstag*, was a forum strictly limited to the rulers of the individual states or their personal representatives; there was no elected body to represent their subjects. Parliaments (*Stände*, often known in English as 'estates' or 'states') existed in many of the individual territories, but generally represented only the hereditary aristocracy, the clergy and the richest citizens. In the princely states, these *Landtage* (their most frequent name) were usually called only to agree to the ruler's tax plans, and had no rights to initiate their own legislation.

However, as a result of reforms in many states in the late seventeenth and eighteenth centuries, even these rudimentary representative bodies had lost much of their limited power by 1800. With the growth of stronger regular armies, some princes had imposed taxation without the agreement of the estates. In the age of 'absolutism', monarchs also attempted to rid themselves of the restrictions placed on their rule by institutions such as the nobility and the church, and to collect taxes more efficiently by building a stronger, streamlined bureaucracy. Central to these schemes was the establishment of a common legal system which would cut across the myriad local privileges and exemptions within each state. The two largest states, the Habsburg Empire and Prussia, both attempted to codify and unify their legal systems in the last decades of the eighteenth century. Similarly, the Habsburgs acted to restrict the powers of the church in their own lands. Meanwhile, more rational central government structures were established to coordinate the monarch's rule among his or her different provinces, and a new class of specially educated and trained state servants, independent of the landed aristocracy (though in practice often drawn from its ranks), emerged to ensure that government policy was put into force and that taxes were correctly collected. These *Beamten* received a privileged status to ensure their loyalty to the crown.

The degree of success in these moves towards greater administrative efficiency varied between the different states, and was limited in both Prussia and the Habsburg domains by concessions to noble opposition. Nonetheless, the notion of the state as a dynastic fiefdom, the personal property of its ruler, slowly gave way to new notions of the state as an institution in its own right. Though the monarch's right to reign remained undisputed, administrators and bureaucrats began to play an increasingly independent role alongside the traditional forces of the crown and the hereditary nobility.

While these changes were designed to cement monarchical power, a further motivation for change was the thinking of the **Aufklärung** (Enlightenment) and the desire to create a more rational societal order. The educated *Beamten* were foremost in driving forward change from above. A legal system based on equality and the removal of ecclesiastical privileges certainly fitted this pattern, but so too did religious toleration and wider access to education. In states such as Prussia, whose rulers adopted Enlightenment ideas, a form of 'enlightened absolutism' emerged, in which the concept of government for the welfare of the whole state rather than the privilege of the ruling caste became popular. Such thoughts did not, however, extend to permitting the populace to participate in decision making, and where such policies evolved, their principal motivation was still to strengthen the state, for instance by neutralising potential opposition from persecuted religious groups.

Nonetheless, the remaining powers of the *Landtage*, noble opposition and the stultifying structures of the *Reich* hindered most radical reforms to state and society before 1800. Economic structures proved particularly impervious to change. Despite the slow advance of more modern manufacturing techniques, the establishment of the first small factories and the emergence of cottage

---

Aufklärung ('Enlightenment')

The 'Enlightenment' is a fairly loose term to describe a broad revolution in science, philosophy and the arts during the seventeenth and eighteenth centuries. Scientific discoveries began to cast doubt on the superstitious beliefs of medieval Christian Europe and to suggest that the universe ran according to regular scientific laws. Philosophers similarly queried the apparently irrational organisation of society and proposed legal and constitutional systems in which the people's interests, rather than those of a divinely appointed prince, were paramount.

manufacturing industries in the rural areas, trade remained dominated by the guild system. In each town, a guild for each craft or trade held a protected monopoly and regulated the admittance of new qualified craftsmen to its ranks. On the land, too, peasants remained largely subservient to the aristocratic landowners. Some peasants were serfs, legally bound to the land they worked; others rented land or held it on a hereditary lease in return for service in the feudal lord's fields. In Prussia, by 1800 peasants had only been freed from these feudal requirements on the estates owned personally by the king; in the Habsburg lands the *Kaiser*'s attempts to emancipate the serfs were largely thwarted by noble opposition. Throughout the *Reich*, the aristocracy retained extensive rights, for instance to run the local administration, policing and judicial systems.

Undoubtedly the greatest impulse for change came from abroad. The effects of the French Revolution, which broke out in 1789, would sweep away the old *Reich* and many of the traditional German statelets, and initiate more sweeping reforms. The French Revolution resulted from a diverse set of conflicts within French state and society, ranging from noble and merchant opposition to the king's autocratic rule, to the peasantry's refusal to continue tolerating poverty and oppression from their feudal lords. In the first phase of their revolution, the French instituted the principle of equality and tore away the remaining anomalies of the medieval era, breathing life into the guiding principles of the Enlightenment. In Germany these developments were generally welcomed by the educated classes (still a very small proportion of the population), who initially perceived no threat from these developments to the political and social order in the German states. Indeed, France seemed to be copying the reforms which enlightened German princes had already introduced. There was little enthusiasm for revolution in Germany among the educated nobles and merchants, since these groups felt they were already instrumental in the processes of change. While rural and urban revolts broke out in several German states in the immediate aftermath of 1789, nowhere were the grievances as strong as in France, whose peasantry had never enjoyed the basic legal rights that were common in much of Germany. Furthermore, unlike the centralised French state there was no single focus for German protesters. Where uprisings occurred they were directed at circumstances within the individual states, and naturally limited by the boundaries of these states. Finally, the excesses of absolutist rule in France were practically impossible in the imperial German system where the *Kaiser*, the princes, the towns and the law courts regulated and limited one another.

The initial enthusiasm of educated Germans for the apparently liberating principles of the French Revolution was quickly dampened. The year 1792 saw the first incursions into the German states by French armies, driven by a desire to export the revolution to peoples still oppressed by monarchical rule, and to preempt any military alliance by the European rulers to crush republicanism. In the process the French government hoped to unite the French nation behind a military campaign.

The French armies won speedy victories in western and southern Germany. The *Reichsritter* and the ecclesiastical territories which had dominated the political landscape in these areas were swept away under French occupation. The fragility of the *Heiliges Römisches Reich* and the absence of a common sense of German nationality became apparent when Prussia abandoned the anti-French alliance in 1795, unwilling to defend the small states in the west. Following further Austrian defeats, particularly after Napoleon assumed power in France in 1799, France absorbed the German lands west of the River Rhine and reorganised much of the rest of the German west and south into a series of client buffer states.

The old *Reich*'s legitimacy was irrevocably shaken by these events. The larger German states, keen to protect their own interests, abandoned their smaller neighbours; the *Reich*, dependent for its military strength on the willingness of individual states to provide soldiers, had proved incapable of fulfilling its principal task of preserving the German status quo. This reality was underlined by the *Reichsdeputationshauptschluss* of 1803. This treaty, passed by the *Reichstag* and the *Kaiser*, effectively determined the territorial consequences of the *Reich*'s defeat. The large and medium-sized German states which had lost land and subjects to France were compensated by absorbing the church states and most of the *Reichsstädte* east of the Rhine.

In the following three years, with France dominant and the Habsburgs unable to resist, the remaining structures of the *Reich* collapsed. Realising that the imperial title had become worthless, the *Kaiser*, Franz II, proclaimed himself *Kaiser von Österreich* in 1804, a title which referred to his own hereditary Habsburg lands as distinct from the German *Reich*. In 1806, the western German states joined a new organisation, the *Rheinbund* ('Confederation of the Rhine'), created by Napoleon to assert his hegemony in Germany. Napoleon decreed that membership of the *Rheinbund* was incompatible with membership of the old *Reich*. For these German rulers, alliance with Napoleon in the *Rheinbund* guaranteed their political survival, and enabled them to absorb the lands of the *Reichsritter* in a process of 'mediatisation'. Additionally, the rulers of Bavaria and Württemberg (who had fought with Napoleon against Austria since 1805), freed from their duties to the *Reich*, now assumed the title *König*. The defection of the western states and the French threat to the Habsburgs' core territories finally moved Franz II to lay down the crown of the *Heiliges Römisches Reich* in 1806, bringing down the final curtain on an empire which had been created by Karl der Große (Charlemagne) more than a thousand years earlier.

With Napoleon so clearly ascendant, Prussia – neutral since 1795, and a major beneficiary of the territorial redistribution of 1803 – finally attempted to reverse French hegemony in Europe, fearful of the threat to its own position. The result was a catastrophic Prussian defeat in the Battle of Jena in 1806. Following the defeat also of her ally Russia, Prussia's western territories were transferred into French hands, and her Polish possessions were transferred to Saxony (Sachsen), a French ally, also raised to the status of kingdom by Napoleon. The *Rheinbund* expanded to include the Kingdom of Westphalia (*Königreich Westfalen*) and the *Großherzogtümer* of Berg and Frankfurt am Main, new states formed from occupied territory, the first two ruled by Napoleon's relatives. Only the Habsburg lands and the rump of Prussia remained outside direct or indirect French control.

The consequences of French victory were profound throughout the German lands. The territories west of the Rhine and in the northwest were integrated into the French Empire itself and experienced Napoleonic rule at first hand. Here, church lands were seized and ecclesiastical privileges overturned, the peasantry relieved of its duties to the aristocracy, the guilds disbanded, and the uniform Napoleonic legal code (the *Code Napoléon*, based on the principle that all men – but not women – are equal) was introduced. Similar reforms were introduced in the Kingdom of Westphalia and the *Großherzogtümer* of Berg and Frankfurt, designed to be run as French 'model states'. However, the constitutions which promised democratic parliaments were never put fully into effect; the requirement on peasants to compensate their feudal landlords for their freedom, combined with Napoleon's practice of granting estates in these territories to his French supporters, meant that equal opportunities for land ownership remained unrealised. In these areas under direct French control, there was little enthusiasm for foreign rule, not least among the poorer strata of society who found that relief from the taxes and duties paid to their former masters came at the expense of new French taxes and conscription into the French army.

In the other *Rheinbund* states, the German rulers embarked upon a process of administrative consolidation, motivated by a desire to bring their expanded realms, including the mediatised *Reichsstädte*, ecclesiastical states and knightly territories, under their central rule. This led to the expansion of the bureaucratic state and administrative reorganisations which cut across traditional borders, removing swathes of particularist rights and privileges. New central ministries were established with clearer areas of responsibility. Watered-down versions of the *Code Napoléon* were introduced in many of the states. Here, too, the churches lost their lands and properties, as well as their political powers, but the *Reichsritter*, though deprived of their political sovereignty, generally retained their lands and preserved their economic and social status by negotiating exemptions from the new supposedly uniform legal and fiscal frameworks. Though the rulers of the medium-sized German states were largely able to integrate the towns they had acquired into their administrative systems, the removal of all guild privileges could not always be achieved. The impression that remains is one of incomplete reform. The centralised states, now firmly established as *Verwaltungsstaaten* with strong administrative staffs and procedures, emerged strengthened from the Napoleonic period, but the nobility had retained important rights and the peasantry's lot was barely altered in practice.

Perhaps the most noteworthy series of changes was introduced by the rump Prussian state. A number of high-ranking bureaucrats had already been inspired by *Aufklärung* ideas to introduce sweeping reform, but Prussia's crushing defeat of 1806 emphasised the need for modernisation of the state's administrative and military systems. The reformers seized their chance to abolish serfdom, reorganised central government along more rational lines and extended self-government to the towns, expanded education, removed many of the restrictive powers of the guilds (thereby boosting economic development) and placed the army on a firmer footing. As in the *Rheinbund* states, these reforms did not entail a complete overhaul of societal structures, since the nobility were powerful enough in Prussia as well to preserve many of their own rights and even to reverse some of the changes later on. As a result, the liberated serfs and peasants often found themselves worse off than when tied to the land, and in the following decades hurried to the cities where they fed the labour demands of the coming industrial revolution. One net effect of the Prussian reforms was far greater social mobility. By contrast Austria felt no need to modernise her creaking structures. Franz II was a cautious ruler, anxious to preserve the status quo. Although his uncle, Joseph II, had already introduced reforms to liberate Austrian peasants, they remained in possession of the land. These different traditions were already indicating the relative strength of the Hohenzollern and Habsburg dynasties in the nineteenth century.

A final consequence of French occupation and German humiliation was the stirring of a greater national sentiment. The literature of Goethe and Schiller had already inspired a revival of the German literary tradition in the late eighteenth century, and rising literacy rates had already enabled the emergence of an influential German press which circulated beyond the boundaries of individual states. However, direct confrontation with the clearly different French culture (particularly in occupied and humiliated Berlin) awakened the sense of separate German national traditions. Johann Gottlieb Fichte's *Reden an die deutsche Nation* ('Addresses to the German nation') claimed a certain superiority for German culture over French, while *Turnvater* Ludwig Jahn organised patriotic gymnasts in communal exercise after 1811. Nonetheless, these stirrings did not yet constitute a nationalist patriotic movement. After the French defeat, most Germans initially contented themselves with local, dynastic loyalties.

The brief, but eventful, Napoleonic era was brought to an end by Napoleon's failed attempt to crush Russia. Finally acting in unison after 1813 against the power which threatened now to dominate all of Europe, Prussia and Austria joined Russia and Britain in the *Befreiungskriege* (Wars of Liberation), the battle to roll back the French armies, unseat Napoleon and restore the old, 'legitimate' monarchical order. Under-resourced, overextended and finally outnumbered, French armies were defeated in Russia during late 1812 and defeated again in a 'battle of the nations' (*Völkerschlacht*) outside Leipzig in October 1813. By the following spring, allied armies had taken Paris, and the *Rheinbund* had collapsed, its German members having signed treaties with the allies once Napoleon's defeat seemed assured. The French-dominated creations such as the Kingdom of Westphalia were washed away by the advancing German forces. It only remained to reorganise the German-speaking lands for the post-Napoleonic world.

Document: Ernst Moritz Arndt, 'Des Deutschen Vaterland', 1813

Was ist des Deutschen Vaterland?
Ist's Preußenland, ist's Schwabenland?
Ist's, wo am Rhein die Rebe blüht?
Ist's, wo am Rhein die Möwe zieht?
O nein! nein! nein!
Sein Vaterland muß größer sein.

Was ist des Deutschen Vaterland?
Ist's Bayernland, ist's Steierland?
Ist's, wo des Marsen Rind sich streckt?
Ist's, wo der Märker Eisen reckt?
O nein! nein! nein!
Sein Vaterland muß größer sein.

Was ist des Deutschen Vaterland?
Ist's Pommerland, Westfalenland?
Ist's, wo der Sand der Dünen weht?
Ist's, wo die Donau brausend geht?
O nein! nein! nein!
Sein Vaterland muß größer sein.

Was ist des Deutschen Vaterland?
So nenne mir das große Land!
Ist's Land der Schweizer, ist's Tirol?
Das Land und Volk gefiel mir wohl;
O nein! nein! nein!
Sein Vaterland muß größer sein.

Was ist des Deutschen Vaterland?
So nenne mir das große Land!
Gewiß, es ist das Österreich,
An Ehren und an Siegen reich?
O nein! nein! nein!
Sein Vaterland muß größer sein!

Was ist des Deutschen Vaterland?
So nenne mir das große Land!
So weit die deutsche Zunge klingt
Und Gott im Himmel Lieder singt,
Das soll es sein.
Das, wackrer Deutscher, nenne dein!

Das ist des Deutschen Vaterland,
Wo Eide schwört der Druck der Hand,
Wo Treue hell vom Auge blitzt
Und Liebe warm im Herzen sitzt –
Das soll es sein!
Das, wackrer Deutscher, nenne dein!

Das ist des Deutschen Vaterland,
Wo Zorn vertilgt den welschen Tand,
Wo jeder Franzmann heißet Feind,
Wo jeder Deutsche heißet Freund –
Das soll es sein!
Das ganze Deutschland soll es sein!

Das ganze Deutschland soll es sein!
O Gott vom Himmel sieh darein
Und gib uns rechten Deutschen Mut,
Daß wir es lieben treu und gut!
Das soll es sein!
Das ganze Deutschland soll es sein!

Source: Dr Kurt Elwenspoek (ed.), *Das Ernst Moritz Arndt Buch* (Stuttgart: Walter Hädecke Verlag, 1925), pp. 249–51.

Topics

FOR DISCUSSION / FURTHER RESEARCH

- Which criteria does Arndt deploy to define 'Deutschland' in his poem 'Des Deutschen Vaterland'?

- What are the defining features of your own nation?

- How, and to what extent, does Arndt's vision contrast with the German princes' concept of 'Deutschland' at the start of the nineteenth century?

- Which factors facilitated the French conquest of the *Heiliges Römisches Reich*?

- Discuss the view that the French Revolution altered Germany irrevocably, taking into account political, economic and social factors.

Reform postponed: 1814–1871

Throughout Europe, Napoleon's defeat consolidated the victorious monarchies, and enabled others to restore their power. However, the original French revolutionary principles encouraged more representative political systems in much of western Europe, particularly after renewed revolutionary activity during 1830. In the Habsburg Empire, Russia and many German states, meanwhile, democracy remained taboo. Economic advances, improved communications and wider access to education furthered national sentiment in many regions (notably the divided Italian peninsula, finally united in 1861), though some European nations – particularly in eastern Europe – remained locked within larger empires. While many western European states expanded their colonial empires, the great powers' 'concert of nations', forged to preserve the status quo following Napoleon's defeat, generally maintained peace in Europe. A further wave of revolutions in 1848, triggered by an economic downturn, proved a greater threat to stability. Nonetheless, the old order again triumphed, albeit with a new French Empire under Napoleon III and a partially weakened 'concert system'.

1814–1840: Restoration and change

The period following the collapse of Napoleon's *Rheinbund* in 1814 is often described as the *'Restauration'* (restoration), since many of the German princes resumed the political control they had enjoyed under the old *Reich*. However, the term *'Restauration'* is really a misnomer, since the impact of Napoleonic rule could not simply be ignored; the status quo of 1789 was not fully restored.

Germany's – and Europe's – future was determined at the *Wiener Kongress* (Congress of Vienna), where rulers and their ministers gathered from October 1814 to June 1815 to shape post-Napoleonic Europe. The larger states undertook to uphold the final settlement, with force if necessary. The only German states represented in Vienna were those which had survived Napoleon's reorganisation of the old *Reich*. They included the *Rheinbund* states, nearly all of which had abandoned Napoleon as the war turned against him. The princes, counts and knights of the *Reich* whose independent statelets Napoleon had merged into larger units were not invited; nor were the representatives of most of the *Reichsstädte* or the old independent church states which had been absorbed by their larger neighbours. None of the rulers who had retained their thrones had any interest in surrendering these newly won territories to their former petty rulers. Instead, the states which Napoleon had strengthened largely retained their status. The principal exceptions were the French-dominated creations, the Kingdom of Westphalia and the Duchy of Berg, which were quickly dismantled.

Nonetheless, much territorial reorganisation was carried out. The criterion was not the wishes of local populations, but rather an attempt to reward the principal powers which had defeated Napoleon – Russia, Prussia, Austria and Great Britain. As the British and Hanoverian thrones were still linked, the Kingdom of Hanover (*Königreich Hannover*) also expanded.

Of greatest significance were the changes to Austrian and Prussian territory, since these modified the nature of the two principal German states. Austria ceded her distant possessions in the Low Countries to the north and along the southern Rhine to the west, but was compensated with new territories in northern Italy and along the Adriatic coast. Consequently the Habsburg realms were henceforth concentrated in the south and east, with no Austrian presence elsewhere in Germany. For Prussia, the reverse was true: Russia's prize at the *Wiener Kongress* was large parts of Poland, partly gained at Prussia's expense. As compensation, Prussia was awarded the northern two-thirds of the Kingdom of Saxony, whose ruler had defiantly supported Napoleon to the end. Prussia also acquired extensive territories along the Rhine, formerly dominated by the *Reichsritter* and church possessions; this represented partial compensation for Hanover's expansion into former Prussian regions. The loss of the Polish provinces made Prussia a more coherently German state, with a heightened stake in the defence of the western German borders and considerable natural resources in the Rhineland, whose significance for the coming industrial revolution was not yet fully appreciated.

Once the negotiations were complete, thirty-nine German states remained. Though this was significantly fewer than the hundreds which had composed the old

Reich, many principalities were still tiny, and some states were divided into separate parcels of land: Prussia's western provinces were separated by Hanover from its eastern heartlands, while Bavaria's new southwestern districts were not geographically connected to the kingdom's main possessions. The map of Germany was chequered with tiny exclaves and enclaves. The principle of territorial reform had been dynastic interest; national German considerations remained secondary, and *Kleinstaaterei* continued.

The vested interests of the individual states – often referred to as 'particularism' – were to the fore when the German states debated their future relationship with one another. The outcome of the *Befreiungskriege* had confirmed an old truth: Austria and Prussia were the dominant German states. Nonetheless, the rulers of the smaller '*Mittelstaaten*', sometimes known as '*das dritte Deutschland*', were unwilling to relinquish or even dilute their newly won sovereignty by restoring the old *Reich* or creating any alternative system of central power. Consequently, the various early plans drawn up separately by the Austrian and Prussian chancellors, Prince Metternich and Karl August von Hardenberg, for federal systems led by Austria and Prussia proved unacceptable to the other rulers. Instead, a *Deutscher Bund* (German Confederation) was agreed in the *Bundesakte* of 1815. Its borders were essentially those of the old *Reich*, and, as before, did not encompass large tracts of Prussia and the Habsburg Empire. Conversely this nominally German confederation did include numerous Czechs and Poles, and smaller numbers of some other nationalities.

The *Deutscher Bund* represented neither a rebirth of the old *Reich*, nor a new state: there was no central government, no head of state, no representative parliament and no common citizenship. The *Bund* was not a national union to represent the German people: it was simply a treaty between the rulers of the thirty-nine states. Its principal organ, the *Bundestag*, had nothing in common with its modern, democratically elected namesake, but was an assembly of envoys from the different governments to discuss matters of common concern and to agree laws on important issues. As a symbol of the Habsburgs' former imperial glory, the *Bundestag* sat under permanent Austrian chairmanship. Though the *Bund*'s member states were forbidden to pursue an independent foreign policy once the *Bund* had declared war – the *Bundesakte* had made provision for federal armed forces, though the individual states jealously guarded command over their own soldiers – and could not leave the union, the internal rights of the individual sovereign states remained intact.

The dominant force in the *Bund* was the Austrian chancellor Metternich, whose principal concern after the French Revolution was to restore monarchical legitimacy, the only guarantee of peace and order in the eyes of his fellow conservatives. Consequently, the *Bund* was one of the principal organs of reaction against radical or revolutionary threats, and exerted a wholly repressive influence. It intervened to preserve monarchical authority and prohibit opposition throughout the German states. Metternich – perhaps the leading reactionary of his age – was concerned that the cancer of liberal and reformist ideas would seep across borders if they were ever established in an individual state. In Austria itself, Metternich was able to maintain a harsh authoritarian regime for more than three decades, during which he resisted all calls for

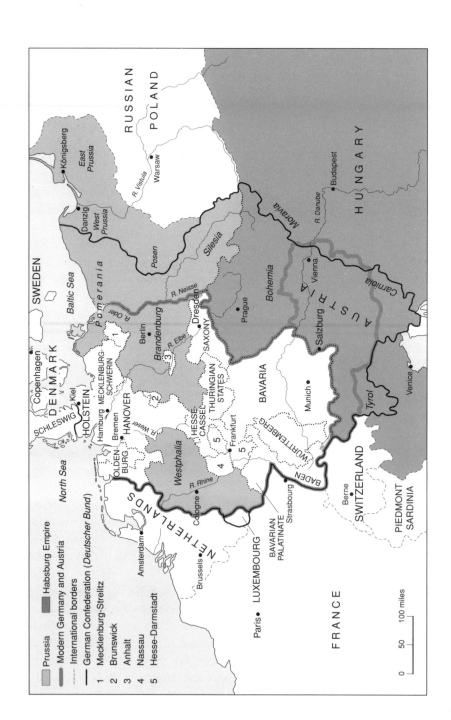

Map 1.1: The German Confederation in 1815

a national representative parliament. Similarly in Prussia, the king broke his repeated promises of a degree of power sharing enshrined in a written constitution. The preservation of royal authority in the face of potentially revolutionary opposition united Austria and Prussia politically, and was a more potent force than their competition for supremacy within the *Bund*. Consequently, Habsburg–Hohenzollern rivalry was largely adjourned, and the two powers cooperated in maintaining the status quo, an arrangement often termed 'dualism'.

Nonetheless, the states permitted some chinks to emerge in the armour of absolutist rule. One was the continuing rise of the new class of *Beamten* (state officials), who had become essential in the modernisation of increasingly bureaucratic states. The process of legal codification and administrative reform had already begun in some states, including Prussia, before the Napoleonic invasions, but was given added impetus after 1815 as many states attempted to integrate newly acquired territories under royal authority and to collect taxes efficiently. *Beamten* also limited the autonomy of the old nobility, which had hitherto often been responsible for local administration. Crucially, the *Beamten* behaved as servants of the state rather than the ruler. The standardised procedures they introduced increasingly limited the sovereigns' ability to rule at will. To an extent, these educated officials were able to introduce enlightened policies (the spread of education, the growth of the universities and the rule of law – the *Rechtsstaat* – were established at the initiative of senior royal officials in Prussia by 1820). Many came to champion the introduction of constitutions, not least as a means of enshrining their own position. Cases such as that of the **Göttinger Sieben** (see p. 17) illustrate the autonomy and reforming zeal of some members of the educated *Beamten* class.

Some of the southern German states (notably Baden, Bavaria and Württemberg) introduced constitutions based partly on liberal concepts after the *Wiener Kongress*. Here, though, the rulers' aim was not democratisation but the effective organisation of disparate, newly won territories into a single, centrally managed state, in which traditional local privileges were abolished or codified under central royal power. A further motive was to underline their independence within the *Bund*. Even in states where the constitution permitted a parliament, the vote was restricted to an elite group of propertied men, and the government remained responsible to the ruler, not the elected assembly. Meanwhile, in Austria, the northern states and the smaller duchies, even these limited constitutional reforms were generally resisted, and government remained entirely a matter for the ruler and the senior aristocracy.

Besides political repression, the German national question slowly emerged as the other key characteristic of the 1815–48 period. The ruling elites' dogged refusal to share power in most of the separate states caused the still small minority of frustrated liberals to consider that real reforms might not be possible within the existing system of *Kleinstaaterei*. One alternative might be a German national state with little or no role for the individual monarchs. This lent a political air to the concept of national identity, which had previously rested largely on linguistic and cultural community. The experience of French invasion and domination, and then the victory over French forces, had already fostered stronger national sentiment by developing a sense of common

Burschenschaften

The first *Burschenschaft*, a student society, was established at Jena University in June 1815; similar groups were quickly founded in other universities. They were inspired by a patriotic volunteer corps under Adolf Freiherr von Lützow which had fought for the German fatherland – not any individual German state – during the *Befreiungskriege*, and adopted its colours, black, red and gold, later to become Germany's national colours. Their motto was 'Ehre, Freiheit, Vaterland', clearly linking the liberal cause with the concept of national unity. After the *Wartburgfest*, a national association of *Burschenschaften* was formed in 1818, but the movement was banned in 1819, as Metternich feared the threat from republican radicals in its midst.

resistance to an external foe. Young intellectuals in particular felt that the autocratic *Bund* was frustrating the German patriotism which they had imbibed during the *Befreiungskriege*. The student **Burschenschaften** organised a patriotic festival at the Wartburg castle near Eisenach in October 1817 – the *Wartburgfest* – to commemorate both the victory at Leipzig four years earlier and the three hundredth anniversary of Martin Luther's Protestant Reformation, itself a symbol of the emergence of German religious identity as distinct from the global authority of the Roman Catholic church.

The students' celebration of a national German identity and calls for liberal reforms alarmed the hereditary rulers, whose positions depended on both the continuing division of the German lands along dynastic borders and the exclusion of the masses from political participation. When Karl Sand, an over-enthusiastic *Burschenschaftler*, murdered the reactionary playwright August von Kotzebue in 1819, Metternich seized his opportunity to launch a wave of repression in the interests of preserving 'legitimate' government from radical insurgents. At his instigation, the *Bundestag* decreed the *Karlsbader Beschlüsse* (Document 1a) later that year, banning the *Burschenschaften* and introducing press censorship, strict controls on students and teachers at the universities (the chief source of the *Burschenschaft* threat), and a special commission with powers to investigate and prosecute radical opponents throughout the *Bund*. In practice, the states implemented these decrees with varying levels of efficiency and commitment – the political diversity of *Kleinstaaterei* acted as a partial hindrance to blanket repression. Some determined reformists found it easier to circumvent the censorship authorities in certain states than in others, and moved their activities accordingly.

Nonetheless, the 'Metternich system' persisted for more than thirty years, and was reinforced following renewed revolutionary upheavals in much of Europe during 1830. The impulse for this unrest came from Paris when the French king, Charles X, was forced to flee after seeking to reimpose full monarchical authority and to ignore the French parliament. Unrest in Germany was limited, but initially prompted the granting of constitutions with limited political freedoms in several more states. The renewed interest in liberal thought is perhaps best illustrated by the emergence of a *Vaterlandsverein zur Unterstützung der freien Presse* (Patriotic Society to Support the Free Press) in southwest Germany, close to the French border, during 1832. The activities of the *Vaterlandsverein*, which called for greater freedom throughout the German states, found increasing resonance, and culminated in a popular festival at Hambach, supported by the *Burschenschaften*. Up to thirty thousand people heard speakers calling for a German rebirth. Supporters of political reform invoked the cause of national unity not merely from romantic aspirations, but because the creation of a new German national state seemed to be the only means of circumventing both the restrictive nature of the *Bund* and the autocratic rule of the individual princes. Metternich's crackdown following the *Hambacher Fest* cemented the link between liberal reforms and the national cause.

Some rulers were particularly determined to stamp out liberalism. In 1837 the new king of Hanover (no longer united with the British throne due to different succession laws) revoked the constitution only recently granted by his predecessor and attempted to rule by virtue of his monarchical authority alone. However, the opposition led by the **Göttinger Sieben** became a *cause célèbre* throughout Germany, and indicated that governments were finding it practically impossible to censor and ban the growing flood of reformist publications, made possible by increasing literacy rates and the growth of the educated middle classes.

Economic developments also contributed to a growing sense of German national identity in the early nineteenth century. Though a conservative power politically, Prussia was to the fore in economic liberalisation, having been stung by defeat in 1806 to introduce various reforms which strengthened the state. After 1815, the need to inte-grate the newly acquired western territories prompted Prussia to adopt the fashionable theories of free trade pioneered by the British economist Adam Smith. Initially this involved abolishing most of the customs duties which had been payable on goods transported across the provincial boundaries within Prussia. However, goods to be transported across Prussia from one state to another attracted higher levies. This system slowly encouraged the smaller states which bordered Prussia to merge their customs systems with the Prussian union, creating a larger free trade area under Prussian control. Prussian manufacturers benefited from the larger market for their goods. Attempts by the larger *Mittelstaaten* to form their own customs unions and thus avoid economic subordina-tion to Prussia eventually failed since their own producers required access to the Prussian market. On 1 January 1834, the *Deutscher Zollverein* ('German Customs Union') united most of the *Bund* states within a single free trading area under Prussia's economic control.

A notable absentee from the *Zollverein* then, and later, was the Habsburg Empire. Austrian merchants feared the effects of free

Göttinger Sieben

King Ernst August of Hanover's abolition of the constitution in 1837 – itself an unconstitutional act – drew sharp criticism from seven professors at Göttingen University. As state employees, they had sworn to uphold the old constitution, and now refused to accept the validity of the king's actions. All seven were sacked, and three expelled from the kingdom. The case roused liberal anger throughout Germany, as by the mid-nineteenth century better communications networks transformed events in one state into national issues.

trade on their business, while Habsburg politicians were concerned that including Austria's German provinces in the *Zollverein* would undermine the integrity of the empire. Economic historians remain unconvinced that the *Zollverein* in itself contributed greatly to Germany's economic growth in the early nineteenth century; nor did the *Zollverein* lead to a single currency throughout the *Bund*. However, what began as a Prussian attempt to unite disparate provinces proved the most potent force in advancing German unity at a time when defensive *Kleinstaaterei* precluded Germany's political unification. Crucially, as Prussia headed this movement, she was widely regarded by liberals as Germany's natural leader, while Austria appeared increasingly isolated.

Better communications also helped to draw the German states closer together, though investment in the infrastructure was principally led by economic rather than nationalist motives. The growing network of improved roads facilitated trade, as did steamboats and railways. These new technologies, coupled with the invention of telegraphy, also encouraged the exchange of news and ideas, and strengthened the sense of a national dialogue among the educated classes. Nonetheless, the multiplicity of capital cities and royal residences within the *Bund* (Berlin, Vienna, Munich, Frankfurt am Main, Dresden and many others) ensured that no one centre emerged as the focus of a national movement.

1840–1849: From *Vormärz* to revolution

By the early 1840s tensions were building which signalled the end of the Metternich system. Historians have seen the period from 1840, or even 1830, as a preparation for the revolutions which broke out in March 1848, and coined the term *Vormärz*.

The year 1840 brought a renewed threat of war with France, whose government had designs on the Rhineland. The prospect of renewed French occupation incited a broadly based German national, patriotic fervour. Though the French threat receded, the impact on German public opinion was great. The year also saw the accession to the Prussian throne of Friedrich Wilhelm IV, hailed as a bright hope by liberals. However, Friedrich Wilhelm refused to grant the constitution his father had promised thirty years earlier; only in 1847, when political pressures approached breaking point, did he summon a united meeting of the provincial *Landtage* (parliaments). Even this was not granted any real share in political decision making.

Neither liberalism nor a yearning for German national unity sparked the wave of revolutionary activity which swept across the German-speaking world in March 1848, with revolts in Vienna, Berlin, Munich and most of the princely capitals. Instead, rising food prices and food shortages following a poor harvest in 1847 were the final catalyst for revolutionary upheaval in many European countries. German revolutionaries were inspired by the news that the French had deposed another king, Louis Philippe, and declared a republic. However, the revolutions in the German states reflected a disparate variety of longer-standing grievances. Peasants, for instance, hoped for the abolition of the aristocracy's remaining feudal rights over them in many regions; the master craftsmen felt threatened by growing free trade, the new factories and the decline of the guilds which had protected their status and guaranteed their income; homeworkers (such as the Silesian weavers who had already revolted in 1844) were impoverished by the falling prices for goods caused by industrialised competition abroad (notably in England); the urban population was growing as peasants moved to the towns in search of a better living, but as the industrial revolution had barely begun many were unemployed and living in squalor; the merchant and middle classes, meanwhile, desired a stake in political power and greater freedom to trade; those from educated backgrounds had loftier aspirations to democratisation and constitutional rule (Document 1b is a good example of such aims).

In short, there was no single goal which united the 1848 revolutionaries, and this disunity enabled the ruling classes to reestablish their authority within months by making minimal concessions and playing one group off against another. The abolition of remaining feudal privileges, for instance, quickly removed the interest of most rural subjects in pursuing wider political reforms.

The national question quickly emerged as a general theme. Here, the improved communications networks quickly disseminated news throughout the German states and fostered a national discourse. There was widespread agreement that the *Deutscher Bund* was ripe for reform, since the often autocratic and arbitrary local rulers had failed to settle the various grievances. A German nation state would remedy this and also give shape to the growing national aspirations. Briefly, in March 1848, with revolutionary activity at its height, Friedrich Wilhelm IV introduced apparently democratic constitutional reforms which, his ministers hoped, would secure support for Prussian leadership of a renewed German federation with a stronger central government. (The appeal in Document 1b was issued shortly after the first, limited, royal promises of reform in Prussia.) Only a radical minority proposed a national republic which would entirely sweep away the individual monarchies. The middle classes still looked to monarchical authority to maintain order and protect their own status by keeping the lower orders in their places. These sentiments explain the moderation of their aspiration in the following months.

In the short term, the liberal, educated middle classes were the main beneficiaries of the 1848 crisis. Their representatives were appointed ministers in the so-called *Märzregierungen* in place of the conservatives who had implemented the Metternich system. Metternich himself resigned on 13 March, the clearest symbol that the old order was changing. The princely rulers – only one of whom was actually toppled by the revolutionary events – also scrapped the restrictive censorship laws and granted relatively liberal constitutions, in which parliaments elected by men from a broader social and economic background acquired wide-ranging powers. This fulfilled the key aim of many revolutionary groups and reflected the widespread belief that a written constitution would create the political prerequisites to right all wrongs.

In Heidelberg on 5 March, a self-appointed group of fifty-one educated liberals summoned leading figures from across the German states to meet as a *Vorparlament* (pre-parliament). This subsequently resolved to call the first ever directly elected *Nationalversammlung* (national assembly). In their hour of weakness, the states of the *Bund*, many of them now under the influence of liberal ministers, agreed to hold elections for this parliament, which met in the *Paulskirche* in Frankfurt am Main. However, since the vote was granted only to men of independent means, and as elections were indirect in many states, the bulk of the peasant class was disenfranchised and the *Frankfurter Parlament* was dominated by academics, liberals and state officials.

The *Frankfurter Parlament* seized the opportunity to begin creating the German nation state which liberals had idealised for decades, and appointed a national government under a *Reichsverweser* ('imperial administrator'), the liberally minded Austrian *Erzherzog* (Archduke) Johann. Though an important symbolic act, this central government lacked any practical means of implementing either its own decisions or those taken by the *Nationalversammlung*, as the *Beamten* and, crucially, the military remained under the control of the individual princely states and the free cities.

Only the most radical parliamentarians could conceive of asserting their own power, and the popular will which had created the parliament, by removing the local and dynastic structures which retained the natural loyalty of most of the population. The weakness of the *Frankfurter Parlament* and government was fully revealed when it called upon Prussia to resist by force rising Danish influence in the mainly German-speaking northern duchy of Schleswig. Prussia ignored the parliament, guided instead by her own strategic interests and having no wish to provoke conflict with other European powers by seeming to expand her power in the region.

This humiliation notwithstanding, the *Nationalversammlung* began debating a constitution for the new German nation state it envisaged. The final product was in many respects path-breaking, as it contained an extensive catalogue of human rights and basic liberties, the essence of which found its way into the democratic German constitutions of 1919 and 1949. Nonetheless, the Frankfurt liberals did not favour a full democratisation. At national level power would be shared between a *Kaiser*, with extensive residual powers, and a parliament. There was general agreement that Germany should be organised along federal lines: power would be shared between a central German government and the governments of the individual princely states, which would continue to exist as separate units within the whole.

However, the extent of Germany's future boundaries was far less clear. The liberal principles of many of the *Paulskirche* parliamentarians did not always extend to recognising the equal rights of other groups to national self-determination. It was generally expected, for instance, that the new state would include Habsburg Bohemia (now part of the Czech Republic but historically part of the *Heiliges Römisches Reich* and the *Bund*), even though working-class and peasant Czechs outnumbered its middle-class and noble German population.

The sticking point proved to be the Habsburg territories. Two principal possible solutions emerged. First, in a plan which came to be known as *Großdeutschland*, the new state might encompass the traditional area of the old *Reich/Bund*. This solution was popular with many Catholic parliamentarians who wished to avoid Protestant Prussian dominance. However, the Habsburg lands within Germany would be linked with those outside only by a common ruler, but not by a common government. The Habsburgs, once their armies had subdued the revolts which broke out across their empire during 1848, wished to cement their central power, not to redivide their territories, and consequently rejected this plan. Austria's new chancellor, Schwarzenberg, later countered with a proposal for a vast federation encompassing the German states and all the Habsburg dominions – including Hungary and the Slav and Romanian provinces. This would have placed the revived conservative Austria firmly in Germany's driving seat, to the horror of liberals, and would have diluted German national identity in an empire in which half of the inhabitants would have been Slavs or Hungarians.

Only the remaining option, a *Kleindeutschland* which excluded all the Habsburg lands, remained viable once the Habsburgs had restored central authority over their own empire. The *Nationalversammlung* finally voted for this solution, even though a Germany which excluded Vienna and its provinces was unattractive to many national-ists and traditionalists. Friedrich Wilhelm IV of Prussia, the strongest German state, was the only possible candidate as *Kaiser* of the proposed federation, and was duly elected by the *Paulskirche*. Though Prussia certainly had ambitions to lead Germany, the proud Hohenzollern monarchy had no wish to be shackled to a liberal constitution drawn up by a parliament which owed its very existence to the insurrection of March 1848. Thus Friedrich Wilhelm, himself imbued with romantic notions of Habsburg supremacy, refused the offer. It was beneath his royal dignity to accept a crown from commoners; he believed that only the other German princes had the authority to anoint him with the imperial dignity.

The king's refusal marked the beginning of the end for the *Frankfurter Parlament*, whose government was powerless and whose constitution could not be implemented. Though nearly all the smaller states urged Prussia to accept the throne and the consti-tution, Friedrich Wilhelm remained adamant. When popular unrest again broke out during spring 1849 in defence of the liberal Frankfurt constitution, the moderates left the *Paulskirche*, preferring the safety of monarchism to the rule of the revolutionary masses. The Prussian army, which remained loyal to its king, was deployed to subdue and disperse rioters in Prussia and other states. Meanwhile, troops of the king of Württemberg disbanded the radical rump of the *Frankfurter Parlament*, sitting in Stuttgart by mid-1849. Royal authority was quickly restored. The radicals were power-less, and the liberal camp was in disarray.

In any case, the impetus which had inspired the 1848 revolution had dissipated. The rural population was largely satisfied with the abolition of the remnants of the feudal system and, being inherently conservative, desired no radical break with the local dynasties. The liberals of the *Märzregierungen* had no interest in reforms which would threaten their own power. By the autumn of 1848 they were already suppressing workers' movements attempting to extend the vote to the unpropertied classes, and resisting the efforts of craftsmen and journeymen to restrict the economic freedoms upon which the prosperity of the new business and middle classes depended.

Within little more than a year, the liberal constitutional concessions of 1848 had been revoked in most of the states. In Austria, where the Habsburgs had exploited differences between the various nationalities of the empire to reassert their power (for instance, Hungarian independence was prevented by a Croat military commander), the

Franz Josef (1830–1916)

Franz Josef became *Kaiser von Österreich* in 1848 on the abdication of his mentally unfit uncle, Ferdinand, and presided over the Austrian empire for sixty-eight years. His principal aim was to preserve the Habsburgs' multinational empire and monarchical authority, despite the challenges of nationalism and democracy. His very longevity was the key force maintaining imperial unity by the late nineteenth century. The murder of his empress, Sissi, the suicide of his son, Rudolf, the execution of his brother, Maximilian (the ill-fated and short-lived emperor of Mexico), and the assassination in Sarajevo in 1914 of his nephew and heir, Franz Ferdinand, brought the ageing *Kaiser* much public sympathy.

new emperor, **Franz Josef**, embarked on a period of personal, centralist rule. In Prussia, too, Friedrich Wilhelm rediscovered his innate conservatism and severely restricted the role of elected assemblies.

Nonetheless, the upheavals of 1848–49 did have some lasting effects. State investment was forthcoming to alleviate the economic woes of the urban middle and working classes, helping to spread and deepen the industrial revolution. The ancient feudal rights of the aristocracy were not reimposed in rural areas, though (just as in the regions which had limited or abolished feudal privilege before 1848) the chief beneficiaries were the large, usually noble, estate owners who received compensation for these lost rights and prevented many of the rural poor from farming on estate lands. Increasing numbers of the landless rural poor headed for the new industrial jobs being created in the towns.

Monarchical authority had been re-imposed, yet the liberal and nationalist agendas raised to prominence in 1848–49 could not be ignored. It was widely recognised, not least by the princes, that a return to despotism was impossible; half-hearted concessions to power sharing were eventually made in nearly every state. Though the *Frankfurter Parlament* ultimately failed, it did set important precedents for democratic parliamentary procedure.

Equally, the conflict of interests between revolutionary and counter-revolutionary forces, as well as disputes and differences of emphasis within the revolutionary movement itself, helped to define the different political viewpoints within society. Several political parties emerged in the following decades (see p. 37), all shaped to some extent by the clashes of 1848–49: the conservatives, often noblemen or landowners anxious to preserve the status quo as a guarantee of their own position; the liberals, a broad church concerned with human rights, constitutional rule and personal freedom, including the freedom to prosper through unfettered commercial activity and thus champions of the right to private property; and radical socialists, enraged by the failure to achieve true economic and political reform for the masses within the monarchical framework, and hoping to achieve fuller equality within society than the liberals believed was prudent. Karl Marx and Friedrich Engels, both intellectuals from middle-class backgrounds, championed the cause of the working masses in their *Kommunistisches Manifest* ('Communist Manifesto') of 1848, later the inspiration of the international socialist and communist movements.

Finally, the national question was clearly unfinished business. The liberal parliamentarians of 1848 had finally placed the issue firmly on the public agenda, but had failed to resolve the issue satisfactorily. Instead, conservative forces would complete what the liberals had begun.

1850–1871: The road to unification

The collapse of the liberals' unification hopes did not mean that national unity was a dead letter. The Prussian government still had hopes of finally achieving full dominance over the German states and unifying them on its terms. To this end Prussia proposed a new union under its control, the 'Erfurt Union'. However, the smaller states remained cautious of overbearing Prussian power which, they feared, would remove their freedoms. By 1851 Prussia had been outmanoeuvred by Austria, and the old *Deutscher Bund* was reestablished under permanent Austrian chairmanship. This was the most that the states could agree on, though both Austria and Prussia continued to attempt supremacy in Germany during the 1850s and early 1860s.

Meanwhile, the forces which had contributed to a growing *de facto* German unity before 1848 continued unabated. The *Zollverein* remained Prussia's key to growing influence throughout non-Habsburg Germany, and the road, rail and telegraph networks continued to bind Germans in the different states more closely. The balance of power between Austria and Prussia also shifted. Austria was diplomatically weakened by her neutrality during the **Crimean War**. Russia, which had helped the Habsburgs to regain control of their eastern provinces in 1849, was aggrieved at the Austrian stance, while France forged an alliance with the principal northern Italian state, Piedmont, in its battle to unify Italy. When the Habsburgs became drawn into war over Piedmont's threat to their own Italian possessions, France intervened and Austria lost the province of Lombardy at the Battle of Solferino in 1859. This development revealed the Austrian army's weakness and prompted the relaxation of autocratic rule, which had proved unable to guarantee the preservation of the Habsburg Empire.

Meanwhile, German national feeling deepened among the liberal middle classes, encouraged by the unification of Italy in 1861. As Prussia appeared to pursue a more liberal course after 1858 when Prince Wilhelm replaced his sick brother, Friedrich Wilhelm IV, as regent, these 'national liberals' increasingly

Crimean War

When Russia occupied territories of the slowly crumbling Turkish Ottoman Empire in 1853, Britain and France came to the Turks' aid to prevent Russia emerging as too dominant a force in southeastern Europe. Austrian mediation to avoid a war proved unsuccessful; instead she threatened Russia on the countries' mutual border, tying down troops which Russia might otherwise have deployed against Britain in the Crimea. When the war was settled in 1856, the Ottoman Empire was shored up but Russia was humiliated. More significantly, good relations between the European powers were soured, while Austria's stance of supporting neither side ensured her growing isolation.

looked to Prussia for a lead on the national question. Austria's weakness seemed to invite a challenge.

However, Prussia required firm leadership to seize the opportunities which these favourable circumstances suggested. This came in 1862 with the appointment of a new Prussian *Ministerpräsident* (prime minister), Otto von Bismarck. Bismarck, drawn from the *Junker* class of landed aristocracy, was a Prussian patriot whose political ambitions centred on strengthening the Hohenzollern monarchy at the expense of both the Habsburgs and liberalism. As Prussia's representative at the *Bundestag* of the *Deutscher Bund*, Bismarck delighted in baiting the Austrian representative. Yet Bismarck was originally appointed as *Ministerpräsident* not to extend Prussian rule over Germany, but to confirm royal authority over the Prussian *Landtag*.

The liberal-dominated *Landtag* had refused to vote higher taxes to support a greatly extended Prussian army. Interference with royal authority over the army, the pride of the Prussian state, was anathema to Wilhelm, by now king in his own right. A constitutional crisis developed over the *Landtag*'s attempt to extend its power at the king's expense. Wilhelm appointed Bismarck as Prussian *Ministerpräsident* for his reputation as a political heavyweight. Bismarck faced down the *Landtag* and simply proceeded to collect the necessary taxes without parliamentary approval. Royal authority triumphed; Wilhelm's gratitude secured Bismarck's political primacy for almost thirty years.

The relationship between the king and his *Ministerpräsident* was unequal. In most matters Wilhelm demonstrated no overwhelming desire to rule personally and recognised his dependence on a strong, loyal minister; Bismarck was invariably able to steer the king to his point of view. From this strong base, Bismarck pursued his plans to extend Prussian power in Germany. He made no secret of these ambitions. Even in 1862 Bismarck boldly announced that:

> Preußens Grenzen nach den Wiener Verträgen [1815] sind zu einem gesunden Staatsleben nicht günstig; nicht durch Reden und Majoritätsbeschlüsse werden die großen Fragen der Zeit entschieden – das ist der große Fehler von 1848 und 1849 gewesen – sondern durch Eisen und Blut.[1]

It would be easy to conclude from this statement and similar quotes that Bismarck assumed office with a firm plan for achieving German unity. But he did not; the circumstances which allowed Prussia's rise in the following years were chiefly not of his own making. While Bismarck clearly had firm goals, he was an opportunist who made the most of the chances which presented themselves. It is also essential to note that Bismarck's aim was, as he told Disraeli, the British prime minister, a 'national union

---

1 'Prussia's frontiers as drawn by the Vienna Treaty do not favour a healthy political existence. The great questions of the day will be decided not by speeches and majority votes – that was the great mistake of 1848 and 1849 – but by iron and blood.' The German original is cited in Theodor Schieder, *Vom Deutschen Bund zum Deutschen Reich*, 'Gebhardt Handbuch der deutschen Geschichte', Band 15 (Munich: dtv, 1995), p. 144; the translation is in Edward Crankshaw, *Bismarck* (London: Macmillan, 1981), p. 133.

under the leadership of Prussia'. In other words, Bismarck aimed not for national unification for nationalism's sake, but rather for an extension of Prussian power. As we shall see, Bismarck did not unify all the German lands, but only those where this was politically possible in the circumstances of the time. Bismarck was also not fussy about the partners he chose to advance his cause. Though a *Junker*, and a staunch advocate of the monarchical principle, Bismarck was prepared to utilise and exploit liberalism, democracy and German nationalist (as distinct from pro-Prussian) fervour if he could harness them to the Prussian cause.

Bismarck's first opportunity presented itself in 1863 when the king of Denmark died, reopening the highly complex question of succession in the north German provinces of Schleswig and Holstein, in part a legacy of the entangled dynastic structures of the old *Heiliges Römisches Reich*. Briefly summarised, the problem was that the duchies of Schleswig and Holstein had both been ruled by the Danish crown for centuries, but were not integral parts of the Danish state. The more southerly of the two duchies, Holstein, was German-speaking and also a part of the *Deutscher Bund*, while Schleswig to the north, which adjoined Denmark proper, contained both Danish and German speakers and had never been a part of the *Reich* or the *Bund*. Nonetheless, the two duchies were considered to form an indissoluble whole. To complicate matters still further, only the male line of succession was deemed legitimate in the two duchies, while females could inherit the throne in Denmark itself. The death of the Danish king in 1863 brought long-standing tensions to the boil, as the Danish succession now passed through the female line. German nationalists in the two duchies, supported by the rising tide of German nationalist opinion in much of the *Bund*, now argued that both duchies should pass to the German prince who represented a junior male line, even though his father had renounced the family's rights years earlier.

Bismarck hoped from the outset that this complicated set of circumstances would enable him simply to annex both duchies to the Prussian state, and in the process gain the important port of Kiel. Yet Bismarck was careful to avoid angering the other European powers by expanding Prussian territory by force. He also saw an opportunity to involve Austria in the crisis and thereby to weaken her.

As Holstein at least belonged to the *Bund*, federal troops were able to intervene there to prevent the new Danish king's attempts to claim sovereignty over both duchies. A war ensued in 1864, in which Denmark was soundly beaten by Austrian and Prussian forces. Schleswig and Holstein were both occupied until agreement could be reached about the rights of the German claimant to the duchies, the Duke of Augustenburg.

Bismarck was unable to persuade the Duke of Augustenburg to agree to turn Schleswig and Holstein into a satellite state of Prussia; having contributed to the Danish defeat, the Austrians were also unwilling simply to leave both duchies to Prussia. As a compromise, Prussia and Austria agreed to share the region's occupation, and also to determine the duchies' future without reference to the other *Bund* states, most of which supported the Duke of Augustenburg.

Bismarck had effectively locked Austria into a situation which he could escalate into conflict at any time. Yet the time was not yet right. Bismarck recognised that the

Prussian army would require strengthening before he turned it against Austria in the battle for Germany. Consequently, Bismarck avoided hostilities when Austria attempted to support the duke against Prussian aspirations in 1865.

By 1866, Bismarck was more confident of the Prussian army, and held back no longer when Austria again attempted to back the duke. By this time Bismarck had assured himself that foreign powers would not intervene against Prussia in a war with Austria. Furthermore, he had concluded a secret treaty with Italy. If Prussia engaged in war with Austria, Italy would follow suit, forcing Austria to fight on two fronts. Italy's reward would be the region around Venice, still held by the Habsburgs. Meanwhile, Napoleon III of France was pacified by Bismarck's vague promises of extra territory to maintain the European balance of power if Prussia expanded.

With the most important prerequisites in place, Bismarck stoked tensions by proposing an apparently democratic reform of the *Deutscher Bund* which he knew would be entirely unacceptable to the conservative forces in Austria. When, finally, in June 1866 Austria referred the two duchies' future to the *Bundestag*, in breach of the earlier agreement with Prussia, Prussia invaded Holstein, still in Austrian hands. The *Bundestag* adopted an Austrian motion calling for Prussian forces to withdraw, whereupon Prussia declared the *Bund* dissolved and called upon the other states to form a new confederation without Austria and effectively under Prussian control.

The long-simmering tensions between the two leading German powers now finally boiled over. The smaller states had to decide whether to support the multinational Austrian Habsburg Empire or the economically stronger and mainly German Prussia in what was clearly the decisive battle for supremacy in Germany. Several northern states did support Austria, but Prussian forces made short work of them. To the surprise of most observers, the better-equipped Prussian army soundly defeated the Habsburgs at the Battle of Königgrätz (Sadowa) in Bohemia on 3 July 1866.

With Austria defeated, Bismarck could now extend Prussian power into the rest of Germany. Austria's north German supporters, including the Kingdom of Hanover, were simply annexed to become an integral part of Prussia. The same fate befell the duchies of Schleswig and Holstein: the dynastic struggles and considerations of local autonomy which had sparked the initial crisis were now entirely overlooked.

Rather than reviving the old *Bund* without Austria, Bismarck established a new, more centralised *Norddeutscher Bund* (North German Confederation). This included all the German states north of the River Main and was led by the Prussian king. None of the smaller states was in a position to resist Prussia's military dominance, but with the exception of the states already annexed to Prussia proper, Bismarck's new *Bund* allowed the individual rulers to retain their thrones and local administrations. (The structures of the new *Bund* served as a model for the *Reich* of 1871, and will be considered in Chapter 2.)

Despite Prussia's triumph, Bismarck was not yet ready to force the southern German states into the *Norddeutscher Bund*. He recognised that proud Bavaria, Baden and Württemberg would not relinquish their independence so easily, and understood the difficulty of incorporating the south's mainly Roman Catholic populations into a predominantly Protestant confederation against their will. Instead, Bismarck waited for

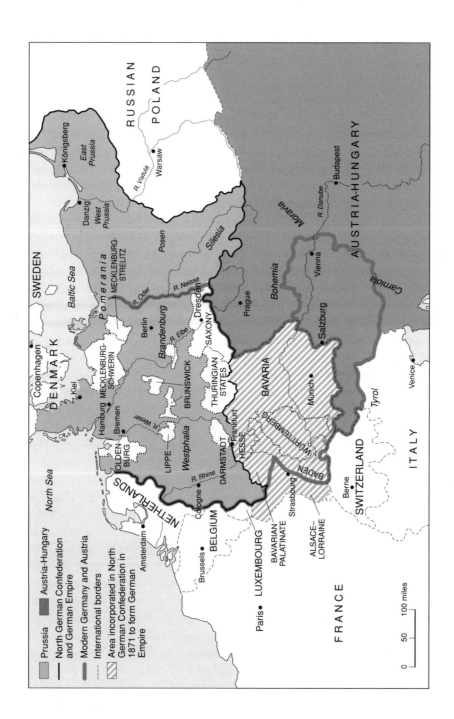

Map 1.2: The creation of Kleindeutschland, 1867–1871

German national sentiment to grow in the south. In the meantime, the southern states were included in the Prussian *Zollverein*, helping to break their economic attachment to the Habsburg Empire. Bismarck also secured promises from the southern states that their armies would be placed under Prussian control in the event of future conflicts.

Bismarck resisted the temptation to punish and perhaps dismember the Habsburg Empire after Königgrätz, anticipating Prussia's likely need of a German ally in the future. Nonetheless, the Habsburgs were now excluded from German affairs for the first time in centuries. This is the clearest proof that Bismarck's aim was the extension of Prussian power rather than the ideal of German unification, for it is impossible to speak of a German 'nation state' which excludes Vienna, Salzburg and many other historic German cities. The Habsburgs' dynastic ambitions to retain a multinational empire had clearly exacerbated this situation. Henceforth, the Habsburgs looked southwards and eastwards to consolidate their power (a development explored in Chapter 2).

As Bismarck consolidated Prussian authority over the *Norddeutscher Bund*, he remained alert to opportunities to bring the southern states under Prussian control. Though normally anxious to avoid politics being determined by the public, Bismarck recognised that German nationalism in the south could best be encouraged (as in 1840) by a foreign threat. Conflict with the old rival, France, would be the most potent stimulus. Again, Bismarck was cautious not to act before satisfying himself that the German armies under Prussian command could withstand a French challenge. Thus, Bismarck initially restricted himself to creating French mistrust of Prussia, suggesting to Napoleon in 1866 that he should acquire Luxembourg from the Netherlands, before resisting the move in the following year.

Bismarck did not create, and could not have foreseen, the event which finally sparked a decisive conflict between Prussia and France. In 1868 Queen Isabella of Spain was deposed in a revolution. The Spanish offered their vacant throne to a distant Catholic relative of the Prussian king, Leopold Hohenzollern-Sigmaringen. This incensed the French government, which feared the prospect of Hohenzollern-ruled countries on both its eastern and southern borders. The French prevailed upon Spain to allow the Hohenzollern prince to withdraw. Bismarck was angered that Prussia had lost a chance of greater influence. There the matter might have rested had the French not overplayed their hand. The French ambassador sought out King Wilhelm in the spa town of Ems and asked him not only to confirm that his nephew's candidacy had been withdrawn, but also to guarantee that the Hohenzollern would never again seek the Spanish throne. The king firmly but politely refused to give any such permanent undertaking, considering it unworthy of his status, and telegraphed Bismarck with an account of the meeting. Bismarck saw his chance: he edited the king's telegram to make it sound as though the French ambassador and the French Empire itself had received a humiliating rebuttal. This altered version, the *Emser Depesche* (Ems telegram), was published, reaching the French papers on the morning of Bastille Day, 14 July 1870.

Napoleon III, convinced of France's military superiority and desperate for a foreign success to shore up his diminishing domestic authority, declared war on Prussia. Supported by a great tide of German patriotism throughout the *Norddeutscher Bund* and, crucially, the south German states, the Germans defeated France by the autumn.

The anniversary of the decisive Battle of Sedan – 2 September 1870 – was celebrated as a national holiday until 1918. In the wake of this great German victory, the southern Germans were enthusiastic for a union with the north and negotiations began. Bismarck conceded several mainly symbolic rights to pacify the proud south German kings, who retained the outer vestiges of sovereignty, but on 1 January 1871 the new *Deutsches Reich* came into being, solemnly proclaimed in a ceremony in the Hall of Mirrors at the Palace of Versailles on 18 January 1871.

Bismarck's prediction of 1862 was confirmed. The popular will for German unity had grown through the nineteenth century, but unification was achieved not by democratic assent and political consensus, but by the force of arms controlled by antidemocratic monarchs. This development was fundamental to the character of the new German *Kaiserreich*.

Document 1a: Extract from the *Karlsbader Beschlüsse*, 1819

The *Karlsbader Beschlüsse* of 1819 comprised measures to control the universities and to restrict press freedom, and also established a central authority to investigate and prevent revolutionary activity. The extract below gives a flavour of the repressive nature of these laws.

Bundes-Universitätsgesetz vom 20. September 1819

1   Es soll bei jeder Universität ein mit zweckmäßigen Instructionen und ausgedehnten Befugnissen versehener, am Orte der Universität residirender, außerordentlicher landesherrlicher Bevollmächtigter, entweder in der Person des bisherigen Curators oder eines andern, von der Regierung dazu tüchtig befundnen Mannes angestellt werden.

    Das Amt dieses Bevollmächtigten soll sein, über die strengste Vollziehung der bestehenden Gesetze- und Disciplinar-Vorschriften zu wachen, den Geist, in welchem die akademischen Lehrer bei ihren öffentlichen und Privat-Vorträgen verfahren, sorgfältig zu beobachten, und demselben, jedoch ohne unmittelbare Einmischung in das Wissenschaftliche und die Lehrmethoden eine heilsame, auf die künftige Bestimmung der studierenden Jugend berechnete Richtung zu geben, endlich Allem, was zur Beförderung der Sittlichkeit, der guten Ordnung und des äußern Anstandes unter den Studierenden dienen kann, seine unausgesetzte Aufmerksamkeit zu widmen. . . .

2   Die Bundesregierungen verpflichten sich gegeneinander, Universitäts- und andere öffentliche Lehrer, die durch erweisliche Abweichung ihrer Pflicht oder Ueberschreitung der Grenzen ihres Berufes, durch Mißbrauch ihres rechtmäßigen Einflusses auf die Gemüther der Jugend, durch Verbreitung verderblicher, der öffentlichen Ordnung und Ruhe feindseliger oder die Grundlagen der bestehenden Staatseinrichtungen untergrabender Lehren, ihre Unfähigkeit zu Verwaltung des ihnen anvertrauten wichtigen Amtes unverkennbar an den Tag gelegt zu haben, von den Universitäten und sonstigen Lehranstalten zu entfernen, ohne daß ihnen hierbei . . . irgend ein Hinderniß im Wege stehen könne. . . .

Ein auf solche Weise ausgeschlossener Lehrer darf in keinem andern Bundesstaate bei irgend einem öffentlichen Lehr-Institute wieder angestellt werden.

3   Die seit langer Zeit bestehenden Gesetze gegen geheime oder nicht autorisirte Verbindungen auf den Universitäten sollen in ihrer ganzen Kraft und Strenge aufrechterhalten, und insbesondere auf den seit einigen Jahren gestifteten, unter dem Namen der allgemeinen Burschenschaft bekannten Verein um so bestimmter ausgedehnt werden, als diesem Verein die schlechterdings unzulässige Voraussetzung einer fortdauernden Gemeinschaft und Correspondenz zwischen den verschiedenen Universitäten zum Grunde liegt. . . .

Die Regierungen vereinigen sich darüber, daß Individuen, die nach Bekanntmachung des gegenwärtigen Beschlusses einweislich in geheimen oder nicht autorisirten Verbindungen geblieben oder in solche getreten sind, bei keinem öffentlichen Amte zugelassen werden sollen.

4   Kein Studirender, der durch einen von dem Regierungs-Bevollmächtigten bestätigten oder auf dessen Antrag erfolgten Beschluß eines akademischen Senats von einer Universität verwiesen worden ist, oder der, um einem solchen Beschlusse zu entgehen, sich von der Universität entfernt hat, soll auf einer andern Universität zugelassen, auch überhaupt kein Studirender ohne ein befriedigendes Zeugniß seines Wohlverhaltens auf der von ihm verlassenen Universität von irgend einer andern Universität aufgenommen werden.

Source: Protokolle der Bundesversammlung 1819, 35. Sitzung, §220, cited in documentArchiv.de (ed.), http://www.documentArchiv.de/nzjh/bduniges.html, Stand: 2 May 2001.

Document 1b: An untitled leaflet from the early days of the 1848 revolution

Majestät!

Heute hat in Köln eine Versammlung der untenbenannten Städte der Rheinprovinz stattgefunden. . . . Diese Versammlung hat das Königliche Wort, durch welches Preußen in die Reihe der konstitutionellen Staaten eingerückt ist, mit Freude begrüßt. . . .

Noch aber herrscht Mißtrauen in allen Gemütern darüber, in welcher Weise die Zukunft die wesentlichen Rechte der Verfassung festsetzen, welcher Inhalt dem von Ewr. Königl. Majestät proklamierten Ausdrucke des Systems gegeben werde. Dieses Mißtrauen ist es, welches die herrschende Spannung in allen Verhältnissen aufrechterhält. . . .

Nach ernster Beratung sehen sich daher die unterzeichneten Städte genötigt, Ewr. Königl. Majestät zu erklären, daß die alsbaldige Zusicherung der nachfolgenden wesentlichen Bestandteile einer zeitgemäßen Verfassung schon vor dem Zusammentreten des vereinigten Landtages dringend notwendig ist:

1. Umänderung der bisherigen ständischen Verfassung in eine Volksvertretung, frei gewählt vom Volke aus dem Volke, ohne Rücksicht auf die bisherige oder eine andere Einteilung in Stände oder Klassen, mit möglichst niedrigem Zensus für die aktive Wahlfähigkeit, ohne Zensus für die passive Wahlfähigkeit.
2. Der Volksvertretung muß beschließende Mitwirkung in der gesamten Gesetzgebung und im Staatshaushalte ohne Ausnahme mit einfacher Majorität zustehen.
3. Die Minister sind der Volksvertretung verantwortlich.
4. Die Gleichheit aller Staatsbürger vor dem Gesetze, Schutz der persönlichen Freiheit, sowie Unverletzlichkeit der Wohnung: die persönliche Freiheit, die Freiheit der Wohnung dürfen nur auf richterlichem Wege und mit Angabe von Gründen beschränkt werden.
5. Freiheit der Gottesverehrung, gleiche politische Berechtigung aller Staatsbürger ohne Unterschied des religiösen Bekenntnisses und gänzliche Trennung der Kirche vom Staate.
6. Unterrichts- und Lehrfreiheit.
7. Unbedingte Freiheit der Presse, ohne Konzession, ohne Kaution, ohne alle Präventivmaßregeln und Aburteilung aller Preßvergehen durch die Geschworen.
8. Unbeschränktes Petitionsrecht.
9. Das Recht zu Versammlungen sowie zur Vereinigung in Gesellschaften.
10. Öffentliches und mündliches Gerichtsverfahren; Geschworenengericht und Aburteilung aller politischen Vergehen durch Geschworene.
11. Volksbewaffnung mit freier Wahl der Führer.
12. Absetzbarkeit und Versetzbarkeit der Richter nur durch richterlichen Spruch.

. . .

Ewr. Königl. Majestät getreue

(folgen die Unterschriften)

Köln, den 24. März 1848

Source: Karl Obermann (ed.), *Flugblätter der Revolution. Eine Flugblattsammlung zur Geschichte der Revolution von 1848/49 in Deutschland* (Munich: dtv, 1972), pp. 72–4.

Topics

■ How does the language/spelling used in Document 1a (which has not been altered from the original) differ from the conventions of modern German?

■ How does Metternich's conception of university education (see Document 1a) differ from the modern role of universities in democratic states?

■ To what extent was the Metternich system counterproductive?

■ How greatly would the implementation of the demands in Document 1b have undermined royal authority in 1848?

■ To what extent did Bismarck's policies in the 1862–70 period accord with popular sentiment?

CHAPTER 2

Imperial adventure: 1871–1918

Timeline

18 January 1871
Kaiserriech proclaimed at Versailles

1878
Bismarck's change of course

18 October 1878
Sozialistengesetz

15 June 1888
Accession of Wilhelm II

20 March 1890
Bismarck resigns

28 June 1914
The Austrian crown prince, Franz Ferdinand, is assassinated by Serb terrorists in Sarajevo

1 August 1914
The First World War begins

9 November 1918
Wilhelm II's abdication announced; republic declared

The late nineteenth and early twentieth centuries saw the European states expand their colonial empires to their greatest extent, with most of Africa, Asia and Australasia under European rule. At home, liberals secured the expansion of education and public health and, in some countries, greater democratisation. The rapid scientific and medical advances of this era enabled rising living standards for many, but the continuing industrial revolution condemned the growing urban working classes to impoverished conditions and fuelled the growth of socialist movements based on the teachings of Karl Marx and Friedrich Engels. The mutual suspicion of the principal European powers, and the new force of populist nationalism, encouraged an arms race and competition for political dominance in Europe; when the delicately poised system of mutually opposed diplomatic alliances collapsed in 1914, the First World War ensued, revealing the inherent weaknesses of the Turkish, Russian, German and Austrian empires, none of which survived this challenge.

For many historians seeking to explain the origins and strength of Hitler's national socialism, the age of Germany's 'second empire' has seemed to hold many of the long-term causes. This chapter demonstrates how Germany retained the political hallmarks of the old monarchical structures, despite developing a strong industrial economy in which the working class rapidly expanded. These trends caused economic power to shift to the new capitalist classes, who had benefited from the industrial revolution but remained largely excluded from political power, which remained with the landed aristocracy. Germany's failure to democratise at a time when liberalism was reforming many of the western European states has given rise to the theory of a German *Sonderweg* ('special path'). It has been argued – but also disputed – that the dislocation caused by the concentration of political power in the hands of the *Kaiser* and his ministers on the one hand, and the growth of popular but powerless political movements on the other, prevented Germany from making the transition to a modern democracy. In studying the *Kaiserreich*, it is worth bearing in mind these ideas; they will be explored more fully in Chapter 4, which discusses these questions of continuities across disparate chronological periods of German history.

Structures of the *Kaiserreich*

The new *Kaiserreich* was officially proclaimed in the Hall of Mirrors at the Palace of Versailles, just outside occupied Paris, on 18 January 1871 (see Document 2a). Bismarck understood that the formal ceremony could not in itself create a truly united country. In the following years he worked to achieve a sense of cohesion among the disparate German states which made up the *Reich*, determined that Germany should stake its claim to be a major European power. However, Bismarck also aimed to ensure that the *Reich* was effectively a Greater Prussia and that the powers of the old aristocratic elites, on which his own authority also depended, were preserved.

The principal political structures of the *Kaiserreich* had been created for the *Norddeutscher Bund* of 1867, and were designed to guarantee Prussian supremacy over the other states. In 1871 the *Norddeutscher Bund* was extended to include the southern *Länder* with very little alteration. The new *Reich* was structured along federal lines, a system which allowed power sharing between the central government and the twenty-five constituent states. Apart from three *freie Städte* (the 'free cities' Hamburg, Bremen and Lübeck), all were monarchies whose ruling kings, grand-dukes and dukes retained their titles. In theory, the *Reich* represented no more than a contract between these sovereigns, whose individual governments continued to exercise authority over local matters such as education, policing and public hygiene. Apart from avoiding opposition which might have followed any attempt to dethrone the regional dynasties, this arrangement also allowed the Prussian state itself to continue as a distinct unit. The larger southern states such as Bavaria and Baden were additionally permitted largely symbolic rights over postal services, railways and army regiments, which underlined their remaining autonomies.

National, or 'imperial', sovereign power was formally vested jointly in the twenty-five states, and not the German people – a clear repudiation of the principles of

1848–49, emphasising that national unity had been achieved from above by the old order. The *Reichsverfassung* (imperial constitution) stipulated that questions of key importance, such as foreign and military policy and control over the currency, should be decided at the national level. The twenty-five governments were each represented in the *Bundesrat*, chaired in perpetuity by the king of Prussia. As such, the Prussian king held the title *Deutscher Kaiser*. Each state had at least one vote in the *Bundesrat*, the larger states more. Prussia's dominance was not immediately visible: although Prussia comprised two-thirds of the *Reich* following its annexation of territory in the war of 1866, it held only seventeen of the *Bundesrat's* fifty-eight seats. However, only fourteen votes were required to veto proposed constitutional changes, so nothing of far-reaching significance could be done against Prussian opposition. In practice, the smallest states knew better than to oppose mighty Prussia.

As the *Bundesrat* was not equipped with the administrative staff to govern Germany on a day-to-day basis, real power lay with the *Reichskanzler* (imperial chancellor), appointed by, and responsible only to, the *Kaiser*. The *Kaiser* normally appointed his Prussian *Ministerpräsident* to this post. Under Wilhelm I, who reigned until 1888, Bismarck himself filled this central role and enjoyed almost unlimited power, as the *Kaiser* did not seek to direct the everyday affairs of government. Within this system, the Prussian ministries took the lead in governing Germany as a whole. Increasingly, the separate identity of the Prussian government intermingled with the national ministries of the *Reich*.

The *Reichsverfassung* also provided for a parliament, the *Reichstag*, elected by all men (but no women), regardless of wealth. Though apparently a progressive, democratic institution, the *Reichstag* was in fact conceived only as a figleaf of democracy in the autocratic system. As the *Reichskanzler* and his ministers were accountable to the *Kaiser*, not the *Reichstag*, the elected parliament could not remove a government which lacked its support. The government's proposed legislation and taxation required the approval of the *Reichstag*, but the *Reichstag* could be dissolved and new elections called if approval were not forthcoming. The threat of fresh elections was often enough to secure the agreement of sufficient *Reichstag* members for government bills to pass.

Though the *Reichstag* had only limited powers, and could not legally challenge the crown's authority, parliament clearly had some potential to disrupt government action. Bismarck accepted that the *Reichskanzler* would need the support of a parliamentary majority to govern comfortably. However, he believed that the risks inherent in creating a democratic – if largely powerless – institution were worth taking as they would secure popular support for the new *Reich*. Furthermore, with the bulk of the working population still not organised in party political structures in 1871, Bismarck believed that ordinary men could be relied upon to do their patriotic duty and support the *Kaiser* and his government at elections. As we shall see, while Bismarck remained as *Reichskanzler* before 1890, his political skills were often – though not always – sufficient to dominate the *Reichstag* and to ensure election outcomes which favoured the government. Nonetheless central government found it far harder to achieve its goals as the political parties developed, particularly the socialist movement which was strengthened by a sharp increase in the size of the industrial working class as the industrial revolution progressed. The succession of politically less talented chancellors after Bismarck's resignation in 1890 was often unable to dominate the elected *Reichstag* or to swing the electorate behind the *Kaiser*'s government. This exposed the flaws and conflicts in a system which had been designed to give the German people only the semblance but not the substance of power over their country's development.

Democracy was further hindered by two other factors. In Prussia itself the composition of the *Landtag* was determined by a *Dreiklassenwahlrecht* ('three class suffrage'), in which a small noble and wealthy elite elected one-third of the members, a somewhat larger group of the wealthy middle classes elected a further third, while the mass of the population, the poor industrial working class and the peasantry, were restricted to electing the remaining third of the *Landtag* members. This ensured that the Prussian *Landtag* was dominated by conservatives and aristocrats. As the *Reichskanzler* was also Prussian *Ministerpräsident*, he had always to ensure that his national policies did not alienate the basis of his majority in Prussia. Second, the army, also a bastion of Prussian conservatives who feared the rise of mass political influence, remained firmly under the *Kaiser*'s control. The *Reichstag*'s influence extended only to the size of the military budget, for which taxes had to be agreed (as we saw in Chapter 1, it was the controversy over this issue which brought Bismarck to power in 1862). The liberal parties in particular sometimes attempted to secure more frequent scrutiny of the military budget, or to make their agreement dependent on greater ministerial accountability to parliament. However, if the military budget appeared endangered, Bismarck and his successors were often able to engineer electoral victories for the more loyal conservative parties by conjuring up the spectre of foreign military threats which seemed to legitimise greater military expenditure. Once the budget had been agreed, the army command and the *Kaiser* remained paramount in the conduct of military policy, sometimes even to the exclusion of the *Reichskanzler*'s influence after Bismarck's resignation in 1890.

1871–1890: Bismarck and the *Reich*

As we have already noted, Bismarck's priority after 1871 was to consolidate the internal cohesion of the *Reich* under Prussian control, and to ensure that the *Reichstag* did not block government policies. This meant that Bismarck, and his successors as *Reichskanzler*, needed to find support among the various parties and groupings in the *Reichstag* (see p. 37).

However, Bismarck faced opposition in the first *Reichstag*, elected in 1871. The *Konservativen* were men in Bismarck's mould, but highly suspicious of the *Reichskanzler*'s tactics in creating a *Reich* with a popularly elected parliament. The Roman Catholic *Zentrum* was also suspicious of the new Protestant-dominated state which excluded Catholic Austria. To secure parliamentary support for the government, Bismarck turned to the *Freikonservativen* and the *Nationalliberalen*, both enthused by

Political parties in the *Kaiserreich*

Germany's political parties emerged as fixed organisations with membership structures in the mid-nineteenth century, inspired by the conflicts of 1848–49, and alongside the development of the first parliaments elected by the general public, particularly the Prussian *Landtag* and Bismarck's *Reichstag*. Many of the political parties which dominated twentieth-century German history and which are represented in the modern *Bundesrepublik* can trace a direct line of succession from these early parties.

Deutsch-Konservative Partei: Formed in 1876, the party principally represented Prussian agrarian interests, but also antisemites who feared Jewish infiltration of Germany. Initially suspicious that the *Kaiserreich* would dilute traditional Prussian interests, it vigorously opposed democratisation and economic reform, while supporting an expansionist foreign policy and the acquisition of German colonies.

Freikonservative Partei / Reichs- und freikonservative Partei (RFKP): Top drawer industrialists, businessmen and aristocrats with a more liberal outlook than those in the *Konservative Partei* created their own *Freikonservative Partei* in 1867. Unlike the *Konservativen*, who feared for the future of an independent Prussia, the *Freikonservativen* supported Bismarck's national unification. As the *Deutsche Reichspartei* after 1871, the party drifted to the right, remaining more determined to uphold the natural order and to build a colonial empire than the *Nationalliberalen*, but more moderate than the *Konservativen*.

Nationalliberalen: The heirs to the liberals of 1848–49 divided into two principal groups. The *Nationalliberalen*, firmly established in 1867, called for further democratisation and social reforms, but essentially supported the *Kaiserreich*'s strong central government, clear divisions between church and state, Germany's increasingly expansionist foreign policy and Bismarck's attempt to destroy the political working-class movement, perceived as a threat to order. Business interests within the party supported customs taxes to protect German products against cheaper foreign imports.

Deutsche Fortschrittspartei / Fortschrittliche Volkspartei: The home of more radical liberals, drawn mainly from the educated and economically independent middle classes, the *Fortschrittspartei* was founded in 1861. Despite internal disputes which led to the emergence of breakaway groups and changes of name (the principal group formed the *Deutsche Freisinnige Partei* in 1884), the left-wing liberals were reunited within the *Fortschrittliche Volkspartei* in 1910. During the *Kaiserreich* they remained broadly committed to democratisation (including government based on parliamentary control and freedom for the political working-class movement), the clear division of church and state, and free trade.

Sozialdemokratische Partei Deutschlands (SPD): Parties for the industrial working class were formed in 1863 and 1869, but united as the *Sozialistische Arbeiterpartei Deutschlands* in 1875, adopting the title SPD in 1890. The party aimed for comprehensive democratisation and fair wealth distribution, enabling workers to profit fully from their labours. However, the party was divided between those who believed that change would come naturally as the working class increased in size and won more votes, and those who followed the Marxist line that only revolution could bring true liberation. These theoretical differences began to split the party during the First World War.

Zentrum: A party to represent Roman Catholics of all classes, originally founded in mainly Protestant Prussia in 1858; the *Zentrum* grew once the Catholic southern states joined the *Reich* in 1871. Its policies were neither systematically of the left nor the right, but principally designed to protect religious rights.

TABLE 2.1: *REICHSTAG* ELECTION RESULTS (SEATS WON), 1871–1912

	1871	1874	1877	1878	1881	1884	1887	1890	1893	1898	1903	1907	1912
Konservativen	57	22	40	59	50	78	80	73	72	56	54	60	43
RFKP	37	33	38	57	28	28	41	20	28	23	21	24	14
Nationalliberalen	125	155	128	99	47	51	99	42	53	46	51	54	45
Fortschrittspartei	76	52	48	36	106	67	32	66	37	41	30	42	42
Zentrum	63	91	93	94	100	99	98	106	96	102	100	105	91
SPD	2	9	12	9	12	24	11	35	44	56	81	43	110
Other parties	22	35	38	43	54	50	36	55	67	73	60	81	52

Source: Manfred Görtemaker, *Deutschland im 19. Jahrhundert. Entwicklungslinien* (Bonn: Bundeszentrale für politische Bildung, 1989), pp. 266–7.

the military successes which had secured national unification, the liberal goal of 1848–49.

The liberal parties' support for the government was bolstered in the early 1870s by Bismarck's decision to turn against Roman Catholicism. Bismarck was concerned that the internal opponents of Prussian rule (not only the suspicious German Catholics, but also Prussia's sizeable Polish population and the inhabitants of Alsace-Lorraine, seized from France after the war of 1870) tended to cluster around the *Zentrum*. He also feared that the Catholic population would show greater loyalty to the Vatican, the seat of the pope, than to the new national German state. The papacy's claims to greater authority over Catholics in particular and world affairs in general, set out in declarations of 1864 and 1870, also appeared to challenge the *Kaiserreich*'s authority. Further, the *Zentrum*'s insistence on the federal nature of the *Kaiserreich*, which it hoped would preserve the special place of Catholicism in the southern states, seemed calculated to prevent Bismarck's aim of the *Reich*'s full integration under Prussian rule.

Thus, having created the framework for the *Kaiserreich* by uniting the population against external threats to Germany's national unity, Bismarck attempted to consolidate the empire's cohesion by calling on Germans to unite against the supposed Catholic enemy within. Given the liberals' traditional determination to weaken the churches, which they regarded as a hindrance to the free development of the individual, fighting Roman Catholicism also strengthened Bismarck's support base in the *Reichstag*.

These considerations culminated in the *Kulturkampf*, portrayed as a fight for Germany's own cultural identity against the Vatican's foreign influences. The *Kulturkampf* principally amounted to an extension of state authority at the expense of the Roman Catholic church's autonomy, though the new restrictions affected the Protestant churches as much as the Catholic. The measures, some introduced throughout Germany, some just in Prussia, ended church jurisdiction over schools, required registration of births, marriages and deaths with the state rather than the churches, imposed minimum education requirements for new priests, banned the work of the proselytising Roman Catholic Jesuit Order in Germany, and enabled the states to restrict the clergy's freedom of movement.

Although the *Nationalliberalen* and even the *Fortschrittlichen* applauded these developments, the *Konservativen* were further alienated from the *Reichskanzler*, given their strong connections with the Protestant churches whose status was also affected. Furthermore, the *Kulturkampf* demonstrated Bismarck's failure to understand fully either the contours of German public opinion or the consequences of the democratic elections he himself had introduced. Unsurprisingly, the many Catholics of the *Reich* felt aggrieved at being designated the enemies of the *Vaterland* and reacted by voting for the *Zentrum* in far greater numbers at the elections of 1874. Rather than uniting the country behind him, Bismarck was opening up new rifts along Germany's well-established denominational faultlines.

Bismarck reconsidered the composition of his political alliances in the mid-1870s. The election of a new pope in 1878 enabled him to renegotiate church–state relations and secure the support of the strengthened *Zentrum* for at least some government measures in the following years, while alienating the liberals. At the same time Bismarck reacted to an economic downturn which followed the ***Gründerjahre*** with a shift towards higher import taxes to protect German goods, particularly in the agricultural sector. This endeared Bismarck to the two conservative parties, which principally represented business interests and landowners. The *Nationalliberalen* still supported the principle of free trade (the party later split on the issue), but were prepared to accept some restrictions in return for ministerial posts. This was an option Bismarck could not countenance, as it would have weakened monarchical government in favour of government on the basis of electoral support. Bismarck dropped the liberals in 1878 as opportunistically as he had exploited their support earlier in the decade.

Bismarck found other supporters to achieve a majority for his change of course. The *Zentrum*, still concerned to maintain regional autonomies and to avoid overbearing centralism, was persuaded to accept the new economic legislation in return for concessions which secured a continued role for the *Länder* in the *Reich*'s central finances. Accepting the *Zentrum*'s support underlined Bismarck's refusal to make political concessions to the *Nationalliberalen*.

More significantly still, in 1878 the *Reichskanzler* found a new internal enemy against whom most of the political spectrum could unite. This time the socialists became

Gründerjahre

The *Gründerjahre* (sometimes *Gründerzeit*) is the term applied to the first years following the creation of the *Kaiserreich*. This period saw an enormous boost in economic activity, financed by the five billion francs paid by France to Germany as the price of defeat in the war of 1870, and given further impetus by the acquisition of Alsace-Lorraine, a centre of iron and steel production. Ambitious building projects were undertaken in Germany and new businesses flourished, leading to a speculative boom. When the market crashed in 1873, an economic depression followed. German producers increasingly demanded new taxes to curb imports as a means of protecting their position.

the scapegoat for Bismarck's political manoeuvrings. Though still a relatively small party without any seats in the unrepresentative Prussian *Landtag*, the social democrats were presented as a criminal band which threatened the end of all natural order. Initially, the two liberal parties and the *Zentrum* refused to support a new law to outlaw the *Sozialistische Arbeiterpartei* (SAP), regarding the measure as an infringement of basic political rights. However, following a serious assassination attempt on the *Kaiser* in 1878, Bismarck (falsely) cast the blame on the socialist 'anarchists', dissolved the *Reichstag* and called early elections. In the hysterical public reaction which followed, the inherently antisocialist conservative parties increased their share of the vote, and the *Nationalliberalen* felt they had little option but to support the *Sozialistengesetz*. This introduced wide-ranging restrictions on the socialists' political activity, though the SAP was permitted to contest elections, a concession which enabled the party to grow consistently through the 1880s. As with the *Kulturkampf*, the *Sozialistengesetz* achieved the opposite of what had been intended, casting the socialists in the role of an oppressed minority which fought all the harder for its rights.

Bismarck's election tactics of 1878 and the *Sozialistengesetz* were not merely a cynical attempt to engineer a supportive majority for the government in the *Reichstag*. Bismarck sincerely believed that the socialists presented a serious long-term threat to the monarchical order and hoped instead to persuade the industrial working class that there was no need to support the potentially revolutionary socialist party, since the monarchical state would itself provide for them. Consequently, he introduced a range of social security measures during the 1880s which provided workers with insurance against sickness, accidents and funeral costs, and which by 1889 included a basic pension for the disabled and the over-seventies. This legislation, far ahead of the other European states, has sometimes been dubbed *Staatssozialismus* (state socialism), and represented an extension into the modern state of the old landed aristocracy's traditionally paternalist role towards the peasants who worked their land. To some extent, Bismarck's policies achieved their goal: even though the *Sozialistengesetz* alienated radical socialists from the state, moderates held the balance of power within the social democratic party, arguing that reform was clearly possible within the existing order and that socialism would eventually be achieved without revolution. Nonetheless, the *Sozialdemokratische Partei Deutschlands* (SPD) continued to grow, becoming the largest *Reichstag* party by 1912. This achievement was all the greater given that the constituency boundaries for *Reichstag* seats had not been altered since 1871. Consequently the rural areas, whose population had declined as the industrial revolution continued, had retained all their seats, while the vastly expanded industrial areas where the SPD's voters were concentrated were limited to an increasingly dispro-portionate share of *Reichstag* seats.

During the 1880s, Bismarck found that even he could not control the *Reichstag* as he had hoped, and that the government was regularly held to ransom by shifting parliamentary majorities. Bismarck generally relied on the alliance of *Roggen und Eisen* (rye and iron), effectively the conservative landowners and industrialists who favoured protective taxes. When frustrated in his aims, though, Bismarck considered simply ridding himself of the inconvenient figleaf of parliamentary accountability he had created. Only in the late 1880s did Bismarck's control of the *Reichstag* briefly seem complete when he secured a majority for the *Nationalliberalen* and the two conservative parties (a coalition known as the *Kartell*) by whipping up the spectre of a war threat and insisting on the importance of adequate funding for the armed forces.

Bismarck handled foreign policy in a comparable way to domestic policy, building whichever alliances were most likely to secure his principal goal of consolidating the new *Reich*. The countries of late-nineteenth-century Europe had still not recognised that their common interests (peace and prosperity) were best served by an all-embracing alliance system. It would take two world wars to integrate western Europe in this fashion, while a security system which included Russia was never achieved during the twentieth century. Instead, European relations rested on a precarious balance of power between the five principal states: the established actors were Britain, France, Russia and Austria-Hungary; united Germany was a new player. The Turkish Ottoman Empire was, as we saw in the last chapter, already in terminal decline, while the nations of the Balkan region were emerging as entities in their own right. The system was further complicated by the scramble for colonial empires, a competition in which Britain and France had emerged dominant.

Bismarck's guiding principle, in a system which for him resembled a complex chess game, was to preserve the balance of power in Europe. He had no wish to extend the *Kaiserreich*, and made clear that Germany was 'saturated' with no further territorial aspirations, but also wished to avoid any territorial losses. Consequently, it was essential to avoid Germany becoming embroiled in wars in which she might sustain losses.

Bismarck recognised that success depended on preventing any anti-German alliance of two or more powers. In particular, French anger towards Germany over the loss of Alsace-Lorraine made it imperative to remain on good terms with Russia, since a Franco-Russian alliance (Bismarck used the French term '*cauchemar des coalitions*', a nightmare scenario) would leave Germany open to attack on two fronts simultaneously (a *Zweifrontenkrieg*). Similarly, it was in Germany's interests to encourage antipathy between Britain and France. Meanwhile, a balance had to be preserved between Austria-Hungary and Russia to prevent either power becoming too dominant in the east; Bismarck's attitude to the Habsburg Empire thus changed after the 1866 Battle of Königgrätz from hostility towards a power which threatened Prussian hegemony in Germany to friendship towards a multinational empire which served a useful strategic purpose in southern and central Europe. However, while an alliance of the three autocratic monarchies (Germany, Habsburg Austria-Hungary and tsarist Russia) seemed advantageous to the German aim of preserving the status quo, both from strategic considerations and as a bulwark against revolution and republicanism, the situation was complicated by the rivalry between Austria and Russia to assume leadership of the Slav nations in the crumbling Ottoman Empire.

Against this complex background, further complicated by successive crises in the Balkans and shifting attitudes in other countries, Bismarck cobbled together a pragmatic foreign policy which succeeded in preserving European peace and protecting the *Kaiserreich*. The first step was the *Dreikaiserabkommen* ('Three Emperors' League') of 1873. This represented merely a loose agreement between Germany, Austria-Hungary and Russia to consult in the event of threats to European peace. Within five years, however, competition between Austria and Russia for greater influence in the Balkans had undermined the League. Despite Bismarck's success in achieving a compromise between the great powers to defuse the Balkan crisis at the *Berliner Kongress* which he chaired in 1878, Russia felt cheated by the outcome, since she had failed to bring all the Bulgarians by then released from Ottoman rule under her own control. Russian–German relations cooled, particularly as the new customs duties on imports into Germany hit hard at Russian wheat exporters.

Recognising the breakdown of the *Dreikaiserabkommen*, Bismarck concluded a new alliance with Austria-Hungary, the *Zweibund* of 1879. In this treaty, Germany and Austria-Hungary agreed to fight jointly if Russia attacked either country. Each country would remain neutral if the other were involved in another war, unless Russia intervened. This ensured that if Russia intervened to assist France in any future war against Germany, Austria-Hungary would be bound to intervene on Germany's side. Germany remained tied to this Habsburg guarantee until almost the end of the First World War, with the disadvantage that Germany could easily be drawn into Balkan disputes on Austria's side.

By 1881 Russia's own precarious international situation and a perceived English naval threat led her to renew the alliance with Germany and Austria. By the terms of the *Dreikaiserbündnis* ('Three Emperors' Alliance'), if any of the three partners were involved in a war with another country, the other two would remain neutral. For Bismarck, this further secured Germany against the dreaded *Zweifrontenkrieg*, since Russia would be unable to assist France if she went to war with Germany. Bismarck hoped that the treaty's provision for the three powers to agree in advance any change to borders in the Balkans would reduce tensions between Russia and Austria-Hungary, both in competition for additional territory as the break-up of the Ottoman Empire progressed.

The early 1880s were the highpoint of Bismarck's diplomatic achievements, since Italy also concluded an agreement (the *Dreibund*, 'Triple Alliance') with Germany and Austria-Hungary in 1882, designed to protect her interests in northern Africa from French expansion. For a short while, growing Anglo-French tensions over colonial interests enabled Bismarck also to cultivate France's friendship. However, this precarious balance could not be preserved, since the different powers' interests remained far too disparate. A further crisis over Bulgaria destroyed the basis for agreement between St Petersburg (seat of the Russian government) and Vienna, and with it any hopes of extending the *Dreikaiserbündnis*. Instead, Bismarck was only able to maintain separate alliances with the two countries: the *Dreibund* with Austria-Hungary and Italy was renewed on terms more favourable to Italy, while a new treaty with Russia, the *Rückversicherungsvertrag* ('Reinsurance Treaty'), was signed for three years in 1887. Although the *Rückversicherungsvertrag* preserved the wedge between Russia and France, and again ensured that Russia would not intervene if France attacked Germany, the relationship between St Petersburg and Berlin was far from secure, and further strained by economic considerations. Bismarck himself was partly responsible for this, since he had prevented the Berlin banks from extending loan Russia. Consequently, the Russians transferred their business to Paris and forged closer links with the French. The *Mittelmeerentente* ('Mediterranean Entente') of 1887 between England, Italy and Austria-Hungary, which Bismarck had encouraged as a means of hindering Russian expansion in the Balkans, further prompted the tsarist court to contemplate an alliance with France.

By the time Bismarck resigned in 1890, the rickety alliance system he had constructed appeared close to collapse. Its principal weakness was, perhaps, that Bismarck was the cornerstone of the entire edifice. Once he had gone, no replacement emerged who was capable of forging the complex alliances which had enabled Germany to pick a peaceful path (really a tightrope walk) between the European powers. Two further factors militated against the preservation of Bismarck's alliance system: the conflicting aspirations of Austria-Hungary and Russia over the Balkans grew increasingly incompatible on any terms; and the new German government consciously abandoned Bismarck's policy of cautious peace in favour of imperial glory.

When Bismarck fell from power in 1890, it was the *Kaiser*, not the *Reichstag*, who toppled him. Wilhelm I had been content for Bismarck to control government, but Wilhelm's death in 1888 brought his son Friedrich to the throne. Friedrich had married the eldest daughter of Britain's Queen Victoria, and openly favoured a monarchy on the British model with a government constitutionally accountable to a democratically elected parliament. Bismarck had long feared Friedrich's accession to the throne. However, by the time this occurred Friedrich was already terminally ill with throat cancer and died barely three months after his father, having had no opportunity to introduce reforms. In any case, some historians have doubted whether Friedrich would have engineered a comprehensive liberal revolution.

The throne then passed to Friedrich's headstrong son, who became Wilhelm II, later known to generations of English-speakers as 'Kaiser Bill'. The new *Kaiser* was markedly different in character from his grandfather. This young Wilhelm believed in his divine right to rule, and had ambitions to exert power in his own right rather than relying on his *Reichskanzler*. Wilhelm's aspirations to personify the whole German people set him firmly against Bismarck's plans to extend the *Sozialistengesetz* indefinitely in 1890. Angered also by the *Reichskanzler*'s habit of excluding him from government business, Wilhelm refused to accept Bismarck's exclusive hold on the reins of power. The Hohenzollern monarchy, in whose interests Bismarck had loyally governed and built an empire over the previous twenty-eight years, was the one authority before which even the *Reichskanzler* had to bow. Bismarck resigned his office in March 1890, and spent some of his remaining years compiling memoirs which glorified his own political prowess.

1890–1914: Wilhelmine Germany – a downward spiral

The young *Kaiser*, Wilhelm II, dispensed with Bismarck's services because he wished to rule in his own right. Sadly, the extent of Wilhelm's political determination was not matched by the level of his political ability. Wilhelm was an impetuous ruler whose unpredictable changes of course baffled and infuriated his ministers inherited a fragile foreign policy, the renewal of which would require omatic skill, and a set of political structures within Germany which d been unable to master. Some historians have argued that Germany's ...., ... enturous foreign policy in the Wilhelmine era (a term mainly applied only to the reign of the second Wilhelm) was an attempt to compensate for, and even to mask, the shortcomings of a constitutional settlement which denied political participation to all but an unaccountable elite, an anachronism in an era characterised by a large literate and politically well-organised industrial working class.

On the home front, the *Reichstag* generally remained difficult to manage. Initially, Bismarck's successor as *Reichskanzler*, the politically inexperienced General Leo Graf von Caprivi, a man whom the *Kaiser* expected to dominate, raised hopes by attempting a more inclusive domestic policy. This included not only the abolition of the *Sozialistengesetz*, but also extending the social security measures which Bismarck had introduced. Also, customs duties on imports were reduced, stimulating Germany's export trade for industrial goods and lowering the price of bread made from imported grain, a development which particularly improved the working classes' living standards. However, this threat to their incomes angered the rural conservatives, already suspicious of Caprivi's tolerance of the social democrats. Having lost their support and the *Kaiser*'s, who feared social revolution following socialist electoral gains in Germany and upheaval abroad, Caprivi resigned in 1894.

He was succeeded by the elderly Prince Chlodwig zu Hohenlohe-Schillingsfürst, who generally proved unable to rein in the headstrong *Kaiser*. Wilhelm's advisers, who played a greater role than the *Reichskanzler* in this period, supported firm antisocialist measures and attempted to gather the middle classes around royal authority against the prospect of revolution in a policy of 'concentration' (*Sammlungspolitik*). Though conservatives and National Liberals supported these views, the middle classes generally rejected this attempted retrenchment of authoritarian rule; there were no *Reichstag* majorities to be had for a new *Sozialistengesetz* in the 1890s. Exhausted, the *Reichskanzler* retired in 1900.

For Caprivi, Hohenlohe and their two peacetime successors as *Reichskanzler*, Graf Bernhard von Bülow (1900–9) and Theobald von Bethmann Hollweg (1909–17), politics were complicated by the new *Kaiser*'s extremely costly military ambitions, and by the enthusiasm of industrialists and a new generation of German nationalists for foreign expansion. Wilhelm II dreamed of leading a Germany which could rival Great Britain internationally, and saw the expansion of the German navy to rival the British fleet (then still dominant on the world's seas and the factor which underpinned Britain's super-power status) as the key to progress. Meanwhile, industrialists and commercial interests recognised that the steady and impressive growth of Germany's industrial economy was outstripping the requirements of the domestic market; expansion into foreign markets and the provision of reliable and cheap sources of raw materials could best be served by securing spheres of German economic dominance abroad. This might be achieved through advantageous trading alliances, Germany's territorial expansion, the acquisition of German colonies, or any combination of all three. The *Kaiser* imagined a German overseas empire alongside the British and French empires as prestigious in its own right and shared the desire of many Germans for their own *Platz in der Sonne* (place in the sun). Indeed, Bismarck – otherwise sceptical about the value to Germany of an empire, the construction of which would antagonise Britain and France – had already consented in 1884 to extend colonial protection over German traders in Africa, mainly to secure nationalist conservatives' political support in the *Reichstag*.

Other considerations also encouraged Wilhelm's desire to increase German glory. First, the conservative industrialists encouraged the naval build-up since it would raise their own profits. Second, some German nationalists became convinced by views of Charles Darwin's work on natural selection in evolution which extended the principle to human societies: it seemed legitimate to demonstrate and underpin the Germans' supposed racial supremacy by expanding Germany's *Lebensraum* ('living space'), allowing Germans to colonise other territories, even if this was at the expense of other nations. Finally, some scholars have concluded that such grandiose projects as a new national fleet and a colonial empire were designed to increase the patriotism of middle- and working-class Germans and cement their loyalty to the *Kaiserreich*, partly by distracting them from the increasingly apparent democratic deficit. Ultimately, it seems likely that both foreign policy ambitions and domestic power considerations were instrumental in Germany's determination to mount a new, if somewhat ill-defined, *Weltpolitik* by the late 1890s.

As noted, building the navy was a costly exercise and not without its political consequences. The scheme was masterminded by *Konteradmiral* Alfred von Tirpitz, who recognised the importance of presenting his grandiose plans to the *Reichstag* and the public in small stages to avoid fears of German naval competition in Britain. Though Tirpitz and *Reichskanzler* Bülow were able to beat the nationalist drum strongly enough to secure funding for the first steps in the naval programme in 1898 and 1900, Bülow's attempts to secure *Reichstag* support for increased taxation in 1905 and 1909 were firmly resisted, eventually leading to Bülow's resignation. Both he and his successor, Bethmann Hollweg, increasingly had to construct *Reichstag* majorities from vote to vote. The situation was exacerbated after 1912 when the SPD significantly increased its share of the vote and thus its ability to block government plans. Though German *Weltpolitik* encouraged patriotism in the masses, this did not translate into a more manageable *Reichstag*. Yet despite the conservative forces' fear of revolution and their resistance to any relaxation of Germany's authoritarian political structures, the SPD wished principally only to extend workers' material well-being, not to overturn the existing order.

The German government not only found itself ever less able to control domestic politics, but also increasingly boxed in diplomatically. In 1890, Caprivi had not attempted to renew the *Rückversicherungsvertrag* with Russia, regarding the Austrian link as more important and also incompatible with commitments to Russia. St Petersburg reacted by 1892–93, predictably, by instead securing the alliance with France which Bismarck had striven so long to avoid. Instead, Germany aspired to an alliance with Great Britain. The *Kaiser*, Queen Victoria's grandson and a committed Anglophile, believed that dynastic ties would strengthen the two countries' relationship.

Schlieffenplan

Schlieffen reasoned that Russia's vast territorial expanse meant that the Russian army would take longer to mobilise than the French in a *Zweifrontenkrieg*. Therefore, at the first sign of Russian mobilisation in an international crisis, Germany must immediately strike a decisive blow to knock out France before Russia could fight. The German armies would advance west on a broad front, entailing the invasion of neutral Belgium on the way. With France quickly defeated, the bulk of the German army could be diverted to the eastern front to meet the Russian threat.

However, his government's foreign policy in the first decade of the twentieth century involved ill-considered attempts to demonstrate German strength by staking claims to colonies in North Africa. Antagonised by this and the naval programme, Britain resolved her traditional differences with both Russia and France. The three powers formed a 'Triple Entente' in 1907, leading to the *Einkreisung* ('encirclement') of Germany which Bismarck had always feared.

European peace was gravely undermined by these developments. Germany's only allies were Austria-Hungary, frequently on the brink of conflict with Russia over Balkan issues, and Italy, which had meanwhile concluded a secret neutrality pact with France. The prospect of a *Zweifrontenkrieg* after the breach with Russia focused minds in the German army command. The military strategy devised to meet this challenge, known as the **Schlieffenplan** after its creator, Alfred Graf von Schlieffen, further heightened the risk of war, since it implied a German preemptive strike against France. The *Schlieffenplan* also increased domestic tensions since it presupposed more soldiers and a correspondingly higher military budget.

1914–1918: War and its consequences

The short-term causes of the First World War stemmed from ongoing instability in the Balkans. On 28 June 1914 the heir to the Austrian throne, *Erzherzog* Franz Ferdinand, and his wife were assassinated by Serbian nationalists attempting to wrest control of Bosnia-Herzegovina from Habsburg rule (for the background to this crisis, see pp. 51–2). Austria-Hungary sent an ultimatum to Serbia on 23 July which was deliberately worded to ensure a Serbian rejection, including as it did a demand that Austrian investigators should be allowed to pursue the assassins on Serbian soil. Austria-Hungary had first obtained reassurances from Germany that she could expect military assistance. Once the Serbian refusal had been received, Austria-Hungary attacked Serbia. Russia, anxious to protect fellow Slavs, responded with a partial mobilisation. Despite the *Kaiser*'s last-minute vacillation, the logic of the *Schlieffenplan* now came into play. Believing, despite evidence to the contrary, that Britain would not intervene, Germany immediately mobilised against France and invaded on 1 August. On 3 August a further wave of German troops swept into neutral Belgium. On 4 August, mindful of their guarantees to protect Belgium, the British declared war on Germany and Austria-Hungary. The Balkan pawn had set all the other pieces on the European chessboard in motion.

Some historians have postulated that Germany's involvement in the long-term origins of the First World War was considerably greater than her role as an individual player in a series of interconnected events. The German historian Fritz Fischer argued in his 1961 book, *Griff nach der Weltmacht*, that Germany had deliberately provoked a general European war as a means of clearly establishing German dominance on the European continent, and that at a meeting in December 1912 the German military command had maintained that a war must start within around eighteen months if Germany were not to lose her military advantage over competing powers. Since then, other historians have cast doubt upon the significance of the December 1912 meeting, noting that no firm planning for 1914 resulted from the meeting of the *Kaiser* with his chiefs of staff, and that the civilian government of *Reichskanzler* Bethmann Hollweg had not been represented. Some perspective is required in this debate. While Germany had expanded her armed capacity and global aspirations under Wilhelm II, and had also destabilised European relations by an ill-conceived foreign policy, Germany had nonetheless aimed to achieve no more than Britain and France had already acquired. The only significant difference was that these two leading imperial powers (in common with much smaller European countries like Belgium, Holland and Denmark) had principally expanded in Africa and Asia, while Germany's territorial ambitions were partially centred on Europe itself.

Whether or not war was intended to unite the German nation behind the government as a distraction from the domestic political stalemate, initially this was the effect. The SPD might have been expected to oppose the war – it had strong traditions of international solidarity with the working-class organisations in other countries and argued that workers of different nationalities should not fight one another in a war which could only profit the aristocratic elites and the industrialists who owned the munitions factories. Nonetheless, in common with the socialist parties in all European countries in late July and early August 1914, patriotism exerted a far greater force over the SPD and the German working class than abstract notions of international class solidarity. The government claimed that the war was defensive, and the *Kaiser* heroically declared that he no longer acknowledged different parties, only Germans. In a surge of patriotic fervour, the *Reichstag* parties united to vote in favour of the necessary finance for the war effort, and a political truce (the *Burgfriede*) was declared for the duration which, all expected, would be short.

These expectations were disappointed. The *Schlieffenplan* failed to pin down the French in a quick war; British involvement, which Schlieffen had not anticipated, bogged down the German army in a lethal war of attrition on the western front for four years. Following losses in initial skirmishes with the British navy, the *Kaiser*'s fleet was not fully deployed until 1916 and then, at the Battle of Jutland, proved unequal to the challenge. Furthermore, Italy left the *Dreibund* in 1915 to join the British and French, placing significant strain on Germany's badly organised Austro-Hungarian allies. However, the Germans enjoyed greater success on the eastern front, where *Feldmarschall* Paul von Hindenburg and General Erich Ludendorff won significant territory from the Russians. Turkey's intervention on the German side also provided some relief.

Despite these advances, the German war effort might easily have collapsed since the supplies required for a lengthy war had not been secured. Only in the autumn of 1914 were systems to prioritise raw materials for munitions production and to retain essential factory workers, instead of sending them to the front, hurriedly established. Industrialists, though normally resistant to state control of their businesses, accepted this framework since they would profit from large government war contracts. This financial advantage was supplemented by a lax tax regime: the government did not wish to alienate business interests by imposing heavy taxes, and also hoped to encourage private initiative and therefore economic growth. The price was insufficient state income to finance the war. The government instead relied on loans, running up a huge debt burden in the process, and on printing paper money. As it was assumed that victory would enable Germany to annex huge economic resources and impose a punitive reparations burden on the defeated countries, there seemed to be no great danger in mortgaging the future to this extent.

Although these mechanisms allowed Germany to fight the war in the short term, they did not adequately provide for food and fuel supplies on the home front, particularly once the war interrupted the flow of essential imports. Severe shortages and falling living standards increasingly alienated the civilian population from the regime, and led to strikes and unrest by 1917. (In the Second World War, Hitler ensured that supplies to the home front were maintained.)

During the war command over the utilisation of economic resources and manpower progressively passed from the civilian to the military authorities. In central government, a similar process occurred. Despite his penchant for elaborate military uniforms and reviewing troops, the army command realised that the *Kaiser* had little understanding of military tactics and consequently sidelined him. *Reichskanzler* Bethmann Hollweg was also viewed with suspicion, since he wished to curb the wilder war aims of the generals and to limit Germany's military risks. Nonetheless, in the first two years of the war, Bethmann Hollweg retained the upper hand. In 1916 he was still strong enough to respond to the disastrously bloody campaign on the western front at Verdun by replacing the chief of the general staff, Erich von Falkenhayn, with Hindenburg and Ludendorff, hailed as popular heroes following their eastern victories. However, their very popularity enabled the new military commanders to insist on full support for their strategy in the realms of politics and diplomacy, as well as on the battlefields. Their threats of resignation forced the *Kaiser* to accept their will. Bethmann Hollweg finally lost his post in July 1917, partly over his willingness to consider democratic constitutional reforms in the postwar era as a means of retaining popular support for the war effort, and partly because he was unable to retain the *Reichstag*'s support for the government. His successors, first the minor Prussian bureaucrat Georg Michaelis and then, in October 1917, the elderly Graf Georg von Hertling, were both incapable of reasserting civilian control over the military.

Hindenburg and particularly Ludendorff represented an influential stream of conservative opinion which called for significant German gains from the war. The demands were modified and extended during the conflict, but centred on territorial annexation in both the east and west, the creation of a series of satellite states (including a nominally independent Poland, removed from Russian control, and German control over much of Belgium and Holland), and German domination of French industrial assets. Ludendorff in particular began to dream of German domination of Europe – a prospect which only encouraged greater British determination to fight for the balance of power on the continent – and he founded a popular new political party (the *Vaterlandspartei*, 'Fatherland Party') to support these aims.

The extent of Germany's aims was demonstrated after the collapse of tsarist Russia during the revolution of 1917. In the Treaty of Brest-Litovsk the following year, Germany insisted that Russia retreat from vast areas of the former tsarist empire and attempted to mould this region into a series of German client states. This outcome rekindled a certain amount of German public support for the war, but discouraged Germany's other enemies from entering peace negotiations. The recklessness of German war aims was further underlined by the decision – against Bethmann Hollweg's recommendations – to pursue unlimited submarine (*U-Boot*) warfare, even though this would entail attacks on neutral and passenger ships. The result was the United States' decision to enter the war against Germany and Austria-Hungary in April 1917.

Despite the conservatives' hopes of enthusing the masses for the war with the promise of fantastic conquests once victory was secure, and thereby of rallying the workers and the middle classes behind the existing autocratic political system and distancing them from hopes of democratic renewal, Germany and her allies lacked the resources to sustain their war effort. This truth was reinforced when the United States also pitched her formidable potential against Germany. Belatedly, realisation of the hopelessness of the situation grew on the home front, along with anger that Germany was in fact pursuing an aggressive war rather than the defensive war of which the government had spoken in 1914. In July 1917 the *Zentrum* politician Matthias Erzberger, once an enthusiastic supporter of the annexationist war aims, demonstrated the Germans' material shortcomings to the *Reichstag*. The *Zentrum*, *Fortschrittlichen* and SPD combined to pass a resolution calling for peace. The SPD had already split over differences about the correct policy towards the war. While the majority, with increasing reluctance, still considered it their patriotic duty to support the government in time of war, a growing minority of the party's *Reichstag* members voted against new war credits during 1915. In 1916 the group was expelled from the party, and formed a breakaway *Unabhängige Sozialdemokratische Partei Deutschlands* (USPD) in 1917.

During 1918 the lack of German manpower and resources led to a series of military defeats in the west, coinciding with the slow collapse of Turkey and Austria-Hungary in the east. By September even Ludendorff was persuaded that defeat was inevitable, and he recommended that the government open peace negotiations. President Woodrow Wilson of America had already made it clear in his 'Fourteen Points' of January 1918 that he would only conclude a peace with democratic states. This, combined with high levels of popular opposition to the imperial government, finally led to extensive constitutional changes in late October, as the old elites desperately attempted to preserve at least part of their position by transforming both the *Kaiserreich* and Prussia into constitutional monarchies. New laws stipulated that the *Reichskanzler* and his ministers would henceforth be responsible to the *Reichstag*, not the *Kaiser*, and that the military should be subordinated to the civilian government. In Prussia, the *Dreiklassenwahlrecht* was abolished in favour of the *Reichstag* voting system. Representatives of the *Reichstag* parties – including the SPD – were included in government for the first time. Nonetheless, the *Kaiser* retained important prerogatives and the new *Reichskanzler*, Prince Max von Baden, was not an elected politician but Wilhelm's choice of aristocrat.

Woodrow Wilson was unconvinced that Germany's political system had really been transformed, and it appeared increasingly unlikely that peace could be concluded while Wilhelm remained on the throne. Such was the public demand for peace by late October, with the defeat clear to all and living standards falling rapidly, that a revolutionary atmosphere emerged. The old order's final collapse was heralded by the naval command's decision to mount one last offensive against the British fleet. The sailors in Wilhelmshaven realised that they were being dispatched on a pointless suicide mission and mutinied, forming *Räte* (councils) as the Russian revolutionaries had done to seize power from the officers. The example spread to ships in the other ports of northern Germany, then to the soldiers in nearby barracks and finally into factories and local administrations throughout Germany. While the central government dithered over the conclusion of an armistice, real power shifted in the first days of November from the *Kaiser*'s government to the *Arbeiter- und Soldatenräte*. Though committed radical socialist revolutionaries were but a vocal and forceful minority in this movement, which on the whole sought simply to break the political and diplomatic deadlock and end the war, they succeeded in overthrowing the Bavarian monarchy on 8 November. With tensions rising in Berlin, the SPD leadership warned Prince Max that it would have to withdraw its ministers from government and declare a general strike if the *Kaiser* did not abdicate.

Wilhelm characteristically vacillated, hoping to save at least his Prussian crown even if the imperial dignity were lost. Ultimately, the *Kaiser* was pushed before he had quite resolved to jump. Prince Max announced Wilhelm's abdication on 9 November and on his own authority transferred power to the SPD leader Friedrich Ebert. Before the day was out, rather to Ebert's annoyance, a republic had been declared.

The Wilhelmine era and the *Kaiserreich* itself were swept away on a swell of political, military and economic bankruptcy in November 1918. The conservatives' grandiose schemes for expansion had collapsed, yet the conservatives themselves survived to fight another day, and the national ambitions they had encouraged in millions of ordinary Germans remained, albeit temporarily dormant, while the *Reich*, now *Kaiser*-less, was left to face the burdens it had itself planned to inflict on other nations.

Österreich-Ungarn, 1867–1918

The Habsburg monarchy was severely weakened by its defeat at German hands in 1866 and its exclusion from German affairs. Though Bismarck persuaded Wilhelm I to preserve the Habsburg Empire, recognising that Germany would need a strong ally in the future, the rising tide of nationalism within the multinational empire began to unpick the bonds which united the Habsburg lands. The determination of the Hungarian aristocracy in the eastern half of Franz Josef's empire to assert their traditional independence and freedoms, and the *Kaiser*'s recognition that his empire could not recover its strength while internal Hungarian opposition persisted, forced the empire's division into two halves in the *Ausgleich* (Compromise) of 1867. The Hungarians recognised Franz Josef as their king (*König*), while he retained the title *Kaiser* in his 'Austrian' provinces. The two halves of the empire, now restyled *Österreich-Ungarn*, were linked by loyalty to the crown but were governed separately, from Vienna and Budapest respectively. The new dual monarchy had only a few institutions common to both halves, notably the army and the navy, to which were appended the abbreviation *k. und k.* (*kaiserlich und königlich*).

While the 1867 settlement reconfirmed the Habsburgs' rule throughout their dominions, it ignored the national aspirations of the peoples within the empire. These aspirations were intensified by the examples of German and Italian unification. Quite contrary to this general European shift towards national unity and autonomy, in the Habsburg Empire's eastern half Serbs, Croats, Slovaks, Romanians and others remained under Hungarian rule, while in the 'Austrian' half Czechs, Slovenes, Italians, Poles and more besides were mainly subordinate to German control. (Poles, Italians, Romanians and Serbs in particular were also inclined to unite with their respective fellow nationals in neighbouring states.) A federal solution appeared impossible, as in most of the empire there was a complex intermingling of the different nations. Furthermore, the Hungarians resisted Czech aspirations for autonomy in the 'Austrian' half, fearing that this would create a precedent for other nations in the eastern half to claim autonomy at the expense of Hungarian dominance.

The 'Austrian' crown lands themselves had no natural coherence, being merely a collection of provinces accumulated by dynastic expansion over centuries. Their central parliament, the *Reichsrat*, was so riven by national divisions that the degree of government accountability permitted by the *Kaiser* could not be utilised by the squabbling parties. Consequently the Viennese authorities were forced to revert to autocratic rule after the 1890s. The problem of the *Vielvölkerkäfig*, the 'prison of the nations' in its critics' eyes, proved insoluble and repeatedly flared up during the late nineteenth century in bitter disputes over the linguistic rights of the Slav communities.

The international situation further weakened the Habsburg Empire. The age of nationalisms was also destabilising the Turkish Ottoman Empire, which had for centuries dominated the Balkan region and its predominantly Slav population. As Turkish rule slowly disintegrated, Austria-Hungary and Russia, the leading Slav nation, became rivals in the struggle to exert most influence in the Balkan power vacuum, a factor which in the long term prevented peaceful relations between the two empires. The new independent states which emerged in the former Ottoman provinces of Romania and Serbia exerted a magnetic attraction over Romanians and Slav groups respectively within the Austrian empire. Conversely the Habsburgs could not extend their empire to include Ottoman territory without provoking both international opposition and conflict at home, since the inclusion of yet more Slavs in the empire would alter the ethnic balance between Germans and Hungarians and fuel demands for Slav political autonomy alongside these two dominant ethnic groups.

An internationally agreed compromise of 1878 allowed Austria-Hungary to rule the predominantly Slav province of Bosnia-Herzegovina on the Ottoman Empire's behalf, and a treaty regularised relations between the Habsburgs and the Serbian monarchy. However, when Austria-Hungary arbitrarily annexed Bosnia-Herzegovina completely in 1908 to prevent it returning to Turkish rule, Serbia, by now under a new, nationally minded king, feared this marked the start of a Habsburg crusade to occupy the remaining south Slav lands. Anti-Austrian feeling prompted Serb terrorists to assassinate the Habsburg crown prince, Franz Ferdinand, and his wife on their visit to the Bosnian capital, Sarajevo, on 28 June 1914, finally setting in train the events which sparked the First World War (see above, p. 46).

Austria-Hungary was not well prepared for war, and depended greatly on her only major ally, Germany. Despite the national tensions of the previous decades, initially the different peoples rallied to the Habsburg cause. However, three developments undermined this unity. First, the death of Franz Josef in 1916 after a reign of sixty-eight years removed the only strong bond holding the empire together. His young successor, Karl, proved incapable of imposing a new federal system based on equality between the disparate national groups in the empire. Second, the collapse of tsarist Russia in the revolution of 1917 removed a principal motive for the Slav peoples to remain under Habsburg rule, which had protected them from falling into the hands of the far more oppressive Russian Empire. The collapse of the multinational Russian and Turkish empires demonstrated the possibility of national self-determination for the peoples of Austria-Hungary too. Third, the economic hardships which the Habsburgs' subjects endured as the war continued encouraged support for a radical break.

At the outbreak of the war, only a minority of committed activists had supported full independence for their respective nations, but the Americans' recognition in mid-1918 of the self-proclaimed Czech and Slovak National Committee, based in Paris, helped to convince many that full independence offered the quickest escape from the war.

With the war clearly lost by late 1918, *Kaiser* Karl made a last-ditch attempt to salvage his empire by ending the war and decreeing national autonomies within a federally structured empire. But it was too late: the various national committees were already declaring their independence. The Austrian Poles joined with the Poles of defeated Prussia and Russia to form a new national state; the south Slavs (the Serbs, Croats, Bosnians and Slovenians) allied with independent Serbia to create a new Yugoslav (southern Slav) kingdom under the Serbian crown; the Czechs and Slovaks created their own state, as did the Hungarians, who speedily annulled the *Ausgleich* of 1867. It remained only for Karl to declare that he would no longer participate in government and to leave for exile; his attempts to reestablish his rule in Hungary and beyond were thwarted in the following years and, removed finally to remote Madeira under British supervision, he died in 1922, aged just 39. In any case, the Austrian Germans were not prepared to contemplate a Habsburg restoration after 1918; rather they looked forward to unification with the rest of Germany which only the now obsolete dynastic arrangements had prevented.

Document 2a: *Kaiserproklamation*, 1871

Wir Wilhelm, von Gottes Gnaden König von Preußen, nachdem die deutschen Fürsten und freien Städte den einmütigen Ruf an Uns gerichtet haben, mit Herstellung des Deutschen Reichs die seit mehr denn sechzig Jahren ruhende deutsche Kaiserwürde zu erneuern und zu übernehmen, und nachdem in der Verfassung des Deutschen Bundes die entsprechenden Bestimmungen vorgesehen sind, bekunden hiermit, daß Wir es als eine Pflicht gegen das gemeinsame Vaterland betrachtet haben, diesem Ruf der verbündeten deutschen Fürsten und Städte Folge zu leisten und die deutsche Kaiserwürde anzunehmen. Demgemäß werden Wir und Unsere Nachfolger an der Krone Preußens fortan den kaiserlichen Titel in allen Unseren Beziehungen und Angelegenheiten des Deutschen Reiches führen, und hoffen zu Gott, daß es der deutschen Nation gegeben sein werde, unter dem Wahrzeichen ihrer alten Herrlichkeit das Vaterland einer segensreichen Zukunft entgegenzuführen. Wir übernehmen die kaiserliche Würde in dem Bewußtsein der Pflicht, in deutscher Treue die Rechte des Reiches und seiner Glieder zu schützen, den Frieden zu wahren, die Unabhängigkeit Deutschlands, gestützt auf die geeinte Kraft seines Volkes, zu verteidigen. Wir nehmen sie an in der Hoffnung, daß dem deutschen Volke vergönnt sein wird, den Lohn seiner heißen und opfermutigen Kämpfe in dauerndem Frieden und innerhalb der Grenzen zu genießen, welche dem Vaterlande die seit Jahrhunderten entbehrte Sicherung gegen erneute Angriffe Frankreichs gewähren. Uns aber und Unseren Nachfolgern an der Kaiserkrone wolle Gott verleihen, allezeit Mehrer des Deutschen Reiches zu sein, nicht an siegreichen Eroberungen, sondern an den Gütern und Gaben des Friedens auf dem Gebiete nationaler Wohlfahrt, Freiheit und Gesittung.

Gegeben Hauptquartier Versailles, den 17. Januar 1871.

Wilhelm

Source: Manfred Görtemaker, *Deutschland im 19. Jahrhundert. Entwicklungslinien* (Leverkusen: Verlag Leske & Budrich, 1989), p. 253.

Document 2b: Bismarck's foreign policy briefing, 10 November 1887

In der Politik haben wir ebensosehr mit den Parteien wie mit den Nationen zu rechnen. Der Kampf geht heute nicht so sehr zwischen Russen, Deutschen, Italienern, Franzosen wie zwischen der Revolution und der Monarchie. Die Revolution hat Frankreich erobert, England berührt; sie ist stark in Italien und Spanien. Nur noch die drei Kaiserreiche vermögen ihr Widerstand zu leisten. Das republikanische Frankreich bedroht in erster Linie Deutschland. Wenn es siegreich wäre, würde sein Sieg die demokratische und republikanische Partei in Deutschland stärken. Darf ein russischer Kaiser das republikanische Frankreich ermutigen, sein Vorschreiten gegen den Osten Europas vorbereiten und die deutschen Monarchien mit der französisch-russischen Allianz bedrohen?

Der Kaiser Alexander will den Frieden. Er hat recht. Der Krieg, sei er nun siegreich oder nicht, wird die Revolution in mehr als einem Lande entfesseln. Trotz dieser friedlichen Anlage des Kaisers tut man in Rußland alles, was man kann, um Frankreich dazu zu ermutigen, und um die öffentliche Meinung in Rußland in kriegerischem Sinne aufzuregen; durch öffentliche Verleumdung häuft man in der russischen Nation ein Kapitel von Haß gegen uns an, dessen Gewicht früh oder spät zu groß werden wird, als daß es sich nicht der Leitung der Regierung entziehen sollte . . .

In der Zeit, in der wir leben, mehr noch als zu irgendeiner anderen geschichtlichen Epoche, fordert es das Interesse der großen Monarchien, den Krieg zu vermeiden, weil heute die Nationen stets geeignet sind, ihre Regierungen für etwa erlittene militärische Rückschläge verantwortlich zu machen. . . . Im ganzen würde der etwaige nächste Krieg viel weniger den Charakter eines Krieges von Regierung gegen Regierung, als den eines Krieges der roten Fahne gegen die Elemente der Ordnung und der Erhaltung haben.

Source: Manfred Görtemaker, *Deutschland im 19. Jahrhundert. Entwicklungslinien* (Leverkusen: Verlag Leske & Budrich, 1989), pp. 317–18.

Topics
FOR DISCUSSION / FURTHER RESEARCH

■ What does the *Kaiserproklamation* of 1871 (Document 2a) reveal about the nature of the *Kaiserreich*?

■ What does Document 2b reveal of Bismarck's policy objectives?

■ Were domestic or foreign policy considerations paramount during the reign of Wilhelm II?

■ To what extent was the imperial government able to retain absolute power in the *Kaiserreich*?

■ Were the political structures of the *Kaiserreich* or the personalities of Bismarck and Wilhelm II more significant in determining the course of German history between 1871 and 1918?

Weimar – a scapegoat republic: 1918–1933

The shock of the First World War transformed politics and society in the defeated countries. The fall of ancient dynasties left a vacuum, enabling the new ideologies which had developed in the preceding decades to strive for power. Following the Russian Revolution of 1917, Lenin's Bolsheviks began building a new Russia on the basis of Marxist socialism: the experiment inspired the left throughout Europe, but initially failed to put down roots outside the old tsarist empire. Conversely, 'anti-modern' and nationalist, anti-Marxist visions of community brought fascists to power in Italy under Benito Mussolini by 1922 and inspired similar movements throughout the continent, some (as in Germany) with expansionist aims and strong overtones of racial superiority. Political radicalism was encouraged by democracy's failure to master the difficult postwar economic conditions, particularly after the collapse of the American Wall Street markets sparked a general recession in October 1929.

In 1918, Germany's defeat in the First World War gave the country its first opportunity since 1848 to devise a democratic system for a national state unencumbered by Prussian dominance and the *Kleinstaaterei* of the old monarchical system. This vision proved unattractive to the many Germans who resented what appeared to be the imposition of democracy as the price of peace by a victorious foe (America), and particularly to the many who had prospered under the *Kaiserreich* and feared the challenges of the republic. For their part, the republic's supporters were not robust in their defence of democracy. In short, there is much truth in the old adage that post-1918 Germany was a democracy without democrats. However, Germany was not simply incapable of establishing a stable democracy, as the success of West Germany after the far greater defeat of 1945 demonstrates. Rather, the punitive peace settlement imposed upon Germany by the allies after 1918, coupled with the harsh economic climate, compounded the young republic's difficulties and encouraged Germans to seek radical alternatives which would have disastrous consequences for themselves and the wider world.

1918–1920: The battle for new structures

Having declared the *Kaiser*'s abdication on 9 November 1918, *Reichskanzler* Prince Max von Baden transferred the chancellorship to the SPD leader, Friedrich Ebert. While there was no legal basis for this action, Ebert was the only possible candidate to lead Germany given the revolutionary situation.

One pressing problem facing Ebert – the future form of the state – was quickly resolved. The moderate Ebert favoured a constitutional monarchy, initially under the *Kaiser*'s young and guiltless grandson, but rumours spread within hours of the abdication that the radical Karl Liebknecht would proclaim a socialist republic, inspired by the Russian Bolshevik revolutionaries who had already murdered the tsar and his family. To avert this danger, the SPD's Philipp Scheidemann spontaneously proclaimed a 'Deutsche Republik'. By mid-November the monarchies of all the individual *Länder* within Germany had fallen. On 11 November Germany signed an armistice with the entente powers.

Nonetheless, Ebert faced a bewildering array of difficulties: the new republic required a constitution; the imperial army had to be brought home, demobilised and the soldiers reintegrated into a peacetime economy; a peace settlement remained to be agreed; furthermore, Germany could expect a large reparations bill to cover the victors' wartime losses, and also had enormous debts run up by the *Kaiserreich* to finance the war.

To master the ongoing revolutionary situation, Ebert initially formed a new central government, the *Rat der Volksbeauftragten* ('Council of People's Commissars'), with three SPD and three USPD representatives. Though no elections had legitimised this government, it probably reflected the majority sentiment during this time of upheaval, particularly as the political right, discredited by Germany's defeat and the monarchy's collapse, preferred to abdicate responsibility for solving the crisis.

The government's first challenge was to clarify its relationship to the *Arbeiter- und Soldatenräte* which controlled real power in much of Germany. Three principal options crystallised among the left-wing groups. Radicals and revolutionaries (notably the communist 'Spartacist' group within the USPD) favoured continuing direct rule by workers' councils (*Räte*) on the Russian Soviet model. By contrast, Ebert and the moderate SPD considered proclaiming a republic revolutionary enough and proposed an elected *Nationalversammlung* to establish a parliamentary democracy on the western model. Between these two poles, most USPD members favoured continuing the rule of the *Räte* until the revolution had been consolidated by removing political and economic power from the old elites of the *Kaiserreich*, and placing it under the people's control. Only once solid republican and socialist foundations had been laid, the USPD believed, could an indirect, parliamentary democracy be introduced.

Initially, an uneasy compromise was adopted: a national council of the *Arbeiter- und Soldatenräte* nominally oversaw the *Rat der Volksbeauftragten*. Meanwhile, Ebert accepted an offer from the imperial army under General Groener to protect the government against revolutionary force. This symbolised both the survival of the old imperial and military elites into the new era, and the extent to which the SPD was unwilling to countenance a clean break with the past.

The following months witnessed political violence and the breakdown of SPD–USPD relations over the extent of radical change. Tensions grew when the army fired on revolutionary workers in Berlin in early December 1918 and intervened again against revolutionary sailors later that month. However, the revolutionary outbursts chiefly succeeded in confirming the frightened majority in its rejection of the Russian model. The moderates can certainly be criticised for not seizing their chance to remove the *Beamten* (civil servants) who had supported the old regime and to expropriate the right-wing industrialists and financiers who controlled the economy, but it was quickly clear that even on the left there was no majority for such upheaval. Most of the *Arbeiter- und Soldatenräte* representatives who met in Berlin in mid-December were SPD men who backed Ebert's proposal to hold elections for a *Nationalversammlung* on 19 January 1919.

The revolutionary left rightly feared that this development would end any hopes of radical socialist reforms. On 31 December 1918 the Spartacist movement within the USPD formed an independent party, the *Kommunistische Partei Deutschlands* (Communist Party of Germany, KPD). Though small, the KPD attempted a revolutionary putsch in early January 1919, determined to overthrow the Ebert government which, it believed, was betraying the revolution. The SPD defence minister, Gustav Noske, asked the army to defeat the coup; General Groener responded by deploying right-wing armed volunteers, known as the *Freikorps*. The communists' revolt was easily crushed; on 15 January *Freikorps* members acting on their own initiative murdered the KPD's principal leaders, Karl Liebknecht and Rosa Luxemburg, a loss which severely weakened the new party.

These events further divided the left-wing factions, permanently alienating the communist radicals from the SPD moderates who had relied on the *Freikorps* with its monarchist sympathies. Liebknecht and Luxemburg became Germany's communist martyrs, seemingly (though not actually) murdered on social democratic orders, and revered on the far left for the rest of the twentieth century. Similar bad blood was created by the central government's successful military action against the chaotic and short-lived Bavarian *Räterepublik* (Soviet republic) during spring 1919. In the long term, the left's divisions precluded cooperation against right-wing threats to the republic. In the short term, the USPD (the product of by now obsolete divisions over the correct socialist response to the *Kaiser*'s war) was rent asunder. By 1922, two-thirds of its members had joined the KPD, while the remainder returned to the SPD.

Despite dominating the political agenda since November 1918, the left did not secure a majority in the *Nationalversammlung*, elected in January 1919. The SPD was the largest party, while the USPD trailed far behind; the KPD did not compete, regarding these elections to a 'bourgeois' parliament as a further betrayal of the revolution. The remaining votes went to the Catholic *Zentrum*, at this point associated with neither the left nor the right; a new centre-left liberal party, the *Deutsche Demokratische Partei* (DDP); a new centre-right liberal party, the *Deutsche Volkspartei* (DVP); and the reformed conservative, monarchist *Deutschnationale Volkspartei* (DNVP).

The SPD, estranged from the USPD but without a majority unable to rule alone, formed an alliance with the *Zentrum* and the DDP. The *Nationalversammlung* elected Ebert president, much to the chagrin of monarchist sympathisers who could not imagine a mere former leatherworker as the heir to the Hohenzollern throne. Philipp Scheidemann (SPD) became *Reichskanzler*. The *Nationalversammlung* acted as a 'constituent assembly', its principal purpose to devise a new constitution. Given the continuing unrest in Berlin, the delegates retreated to the relative calm of Weimar, once the home of Goethe and Schiller, and met in the *Nationaltheater*. The town gave its name to the new state, the *Weimarer Republik*, though the capital remained Berlin. Similarly the government coalition of moderate parties, together representing three-quarters of German voters and the backbone of the democratic republic, became known as the *Weimarer Koalition*.

TABLE 3.1: *REICHSTAG* ELECTIONS IN THE WEIMAR REPUBLIC (SEATS WON), 1919–1933

	1919	1920	1924 (May)	1924 (Dec)	1928	1930	1932 (July)	1932 (Nov)	1933
KPD	—	4	62	45	54	77	89	100	81
USPD	22	84	—	—	—	—	—	—	—
SPD	165	102	100	131	153	143	133	121	120
DDP*	75	39	28	32	25	20	4	2	5
Zentrum**	91	85	81	88	78	87	97	90	92
DVP	19	65	45	51	45	30	7	11	2
DNVP	44	71	95	103	73	41	37	52	52
NSDAP	—	—	32	14	12	107	230	196	288
Other parties	7	9	29	29	51	72	11	12	7

Notes: * renamed *Deutsche Staatspartei* in 1930; ** including *Bayerische Volkspartei*.

Source: Eberhard Kolb, *The Weimar Republic* (London and New York: Routledge, 1988), pp. 194–5.

The Weimar constitution was hailed as the most democratic yet seen anywhere, and included an extensive catalogue of human rights, largely influenced by the 1849 constitution of the *Frankfurter Parlament*. The constitution also stipulated various social aims, including full employment and adequate housing.

In place of the *Kaiser*'s sovereign rights, Article 1 proclaimed that: 'Die Staatsgewalt geht vom Volke aus' ('State authority emanates from the people'). This principle was reflected in the position of the *Reichstag*, now elected by men and women on the basis of proportional representation: each vote counted equally, a clear rebuttal of the old Prussian *Dreiklassenwahlrecht*. Whereas the government had previously been responsible only to the *Kaiser*, now the *Reichskanzler* and his ministers required the confidence of the *Reichstag*, which could vote to dismiss them. The federal system was retained, but the *Reichsrat*, the chamber of parliament representing the *Länder* governments, had limited powers and the dominance of the Prussian central government was diluted by permitting separate voting rights for the individual Prussian provinces.

A *Reichspräsident* replaced the *Kaiser* as head of state. In normal times, the president's powers were extremely limited; his principal role was to appoint the *Reichskanzler* and the government ministers, though the *Reichstag* could reject his choice. However, Article 48 provided for the *Reichspräsident* to exercise emergency powers if law and order were threatened, and to authorise military intervention if any of the *Länder* disobeyed the constitution. The precise circumstances in which these powers might apply were not clarified. While the inclusion of such potentially wide-ranging powers may seem incongruous within a democratic constitution, the continuing revolutionary unrest which threatened the new state made these measures imperative from the perspective of 1919.

The constitution's weaknesses became clear in later years. Chief among them was Article 48. Under an autocratically minded *Reichspräsident*, the reserve powers could

Principal parties of the *Weimarer Republik*

Kommunistische Partei Deutschlands (KPD): revolutionary left-wing party which split from the USPD in 1918; generally loyal to the Communist Party of Russia/the Soviet Union.

Unabhängige Sozialdemokratische Partei Deutschlands (USPD): radical left-wing party which split from the SPD in 1917 over support for the war; most members joined the KPD or rejoined the SPD by 1922.

Sozialdemokratische Partei Deutschlands (SPD): mainstream socialist party.

Deutsche Demokratische Partei (DDP): left-leaning liberal party, with a middle-class basis; supporter of liberal freedoms.

Zentrum: Roman Catholic party which moved from the political centre to the right in the late 1920s.

Deutsche Volkspartei (DVP): right-leaning liberals, principally representing business interests favouring a free economy.

Deutschnationale Volkspartei (DNVP): successor to the pre-1918 *Konservativen*, representing industrialists and large landowners.

Nationalsozialistische Deutsche Arbeiterpartei (NSDAP): fascist party led by Adolf Hitler (see pp. 85–8).

undermine the entire fabric of the republic. As the *Reichspräsident* was directly elected after 1925, he could also claim a popular mandate for his actions. Though there was no intention in 1919 for the *Reichspräsident* ever to become an '*Ersatzkaiser*' (substitute emperor), this was precisely what occurred after 1930. However, unlimited proportional representation also proved problematic, as it enabled a multiplicity of fairly small parties to enter the *Reichstag*. Small extremist parties could also acquire a national platform with a very small share of the vote. These factors complicated the formation of stable government coalitions. The focus of decision making shifted from the *Reichstag* to the party executives who negotiated deals to make or break coalitions. The modern *Bundesrepublik* avoids some of these dangers by requiring parties to achieve at least 5 per cent of the vote in order to enter parliament. Parliamentary democracy was greatly weakened in the *Weimarer Republik* both by the absence of this provision and by the parties' inexperience in taking government responsibility. Previously, the *Kaiser* and his ministers had governed, giving the parties the luxury of opposition. After 1918 these parties were slow to learn that political compromise is usually necessary to achieve majorities. Instead, they mainly represented focused interest groups (industrial workers, landowners, industrialists, small businessmen, etc.) and were often principally concerned to avoid responsibility for difficult decisions which might alienate their respective voters.

Unfortunately for this embryonic democracy, difficult decisions were pressing from the outset. The terms of the peace settlement imposed by the victorious countries presented the first challenge. The **Versailler Vertrag** (Treaty of Versailles) made Germany and her allies responsible for the outbreak of the war. This war guilt clause, which vastly oversimplified a far more complex chain of events, served to justify the punitive settlement imposed on Germany without negotiation.

Versailler Vertrag

The victorious powers (principally the USA, Great Britain and France) met at the Palace of Versailles near Paris from January to June 1919 to determine the terms of the peace. The treaty included the following terms:

- Germany was stripped of all her colonies.
- Some 13 per cent of her territory was assigned to neighbouring countries: Alsace-Lorraine to France; Posen, West Prussia and parts of Upper Silesia, Pomerania and East Prussia to Poland; the Memelland to Lithuania; and further small areas to Denmark and Belgium. Danzig became a 'free city' under international control; East Prussia remained German but was cut off from the rest of Germany by the 'Danzig corridor', which gave Poland access to the Baltic Sea.
- The coal-rich Saarland was placed under the supervision of the League of Nations (forerunner to the modern United Nations).
- The *Reichswehr* (army) was restricted to 100,000 men, and the area left of the River Rhine was demilitarised to protect France; submarines, an airforce and a military general staff were forbidden.
- Union with Austria was banned.
- A commission was established to determine the level of reparations payments.

While the treaty seemed to secure the allies against future German threats and provided for some reparation of their war costs, in Germany it created outrage and resentment among all parties and destabilised politics. The Scheidemann government resigned rather than sign the treaty. However, the alternative was a resumption of the war; even the army high command under Hindenburg and Groener acknowledged that Germany could not withstand renewed allied attacks. On 28 June 1919 the *Reichstag* reluctantly voted to accept the treaty. The DNVP, DVP and various other members voted against, but formally accepted the patriotic motives of the other parties who acknowledged the treaty.

Despite these assurances, the harsh treaty emboldened the political right to attack the basis of the republic. The ministers who signed the treaty were labelled *Verräter* (traitors) for agreeing the *Schanddiktat* (shameful dictate). This period also saw the emergence of the *Dolchstoßlegende* ('stab in the back legend'), a myth initiated by conservatives such as Hindenburg (see Document 3a) that the German army had been defeated not by the enemy on the battlefield but by the revolutionary machinations of treacherous socialist leaders on the home front. Hindenburg knew better than most that this was a gross distortion of the truth: the *Reichswehr* had actually succumbed to superior forces. Nonetheless, the left-wing government and its new republic represented convenient scapegoats for a public angered by the humiliation of Versailles. At the next elections in June 1920, the parties of the *Weimarer Koalition* could muster only 43.6 per cent of the vote, a fall of 33 per cent since 1919; the SPD lost almost half its support, mainly to the more radical USPD. Between them, the right-wing DVP and DNVP almost doubled their share of the vote. Anxious to avoid further losses, the SPD withdrew from the responsibility of government, making way for a centre-right coalition which lacked a parliamentary majority and depended on toleration in the *Reichstag* by the SPD.

Further humiliation came in 1921 when the allies imposed a reparations bill of 132 billion (132,000,000,000) marks to be paid in annual instalments of three billion marks. As the allies linked the sum to the mark's value in gold at 1914 rates, the government could not simply pay the bill in paper money. The reparations bill hung over Germany throughout the *Weimarer Republik*, causing far more psychological than financial harm, since Germany's poor finances prevented the repayment of much of the sum, and because foreign loans offset much of the money paid out. The allies' demands were designed to be humiliating and punitive, but were also motivated by the need of some countries – France in particular – to repay the enormous debts they had themselves incurred in financing the war. Within Germany, the main effect was on the political stability of·the republic. In 1921, the government resigned rather than accept the allies' ultimatum on the reparations bill. The *Weimarer Koalition* regrouped (albeit also without a parliamentary majority) under a *Zentrum* politician, Joseph Wirth, as *Reichskanzler*. Reluctantly the *Reichstag* accepted the reparations bill.

1920–1923: Descent into chaos

To many Germans after 1918, particularly those who believed the *Dolchstoßlegende*, it was easy to associate the republic itself, and the socialists in particular, with Germany's

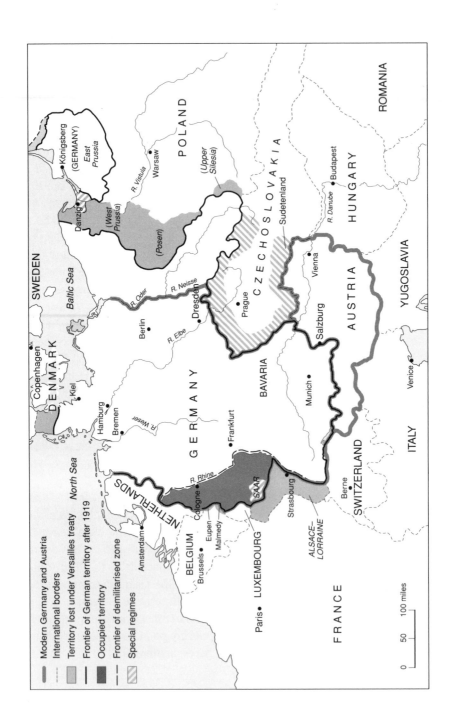

Map 3.1: *Germany and Austria in 1919*

Modern Germany and Austria
International borders
Territory lost under Versailles treaty
Frontier of German territory after 1919
Occupied territory
Frontier of demilitarised zone
Special regimes

SWEDEN

DENMARK

Copenhagen

Baltic Sea

North Sea

Kiel

Königsberg
(GERMANY)
East
Prussia

Danzig

(West
Prussia)

R. Vistula

Warsaw

POLAND

(Posen)

(Upper
Silesia)

NETHERLANDS

Amsterdam

Hamburg

Bremen

R. Weser

Berlin

R. Oder

R. Neisse

Dresden

R. Elbe

Prague

CZECHOSLOVAKIA

Sudetenland

R. Danube

Budapest

HUNGARY

Vienna

GERMANY

Frankfurt

BAVARIA

AUSTRIA

Salzburg

BELGIUM

Brussels

Eupen

Malmedy

Cologne

R. Rhine

SAAR

Munich

Venice

YUGOSLAVIA

LUXEMBOURG

Strasbourg

ALSACE-
LORRAINE

Berne

SWITZERLAND

ITALY

Paris

FRANCE

ROMANIA

0   50   100 miles

defeats and humiliations. The republic faced attacks from both the radical left and the right, the latter often led by *Freikorps* soldiers and officers still loyal to the *Kaiserreich*. One such group, led by the *Freikorps* stalwart General von Lüttwitz and Wolfgang Kapp, an East Prussian officer, attempted to overthrow the republic in March 1920 in protest at the enforced reduction of the *Reichswehr*'s size and the government's attempts to disband certain *Freikorps* regiments. The army failed to intervene to defend the government; General von Seeckt told Noske, still armed forces minister: 'Truppe schießt nicht auf Truppe' ('Troops do not fire on troops'). Nonetheless, the 'Kapp Putsch' was defeated by a general strike and the *Beamten* who defied the self-proclaimed new government. The *Reichswehr* was quicker, however, to put down communist uprisings in the *Ruhrgebiet* during 1920, and in Saxony the following year, clearly demonstrating its true allegiances.

Political assassinations also dominated the period, reflecting the anger at Germany's reduced status. Two prominent victims, in 1921 and 1922 respectively, were Matthias Erzberger, who had signed the *Versailler Vertrag* and attempted to salvage Germany's finances with tax increases which penalised the rich; and Walter Rathenau, the foreign minister and architect of the **Vertrag von Rapallo** (Treaty of Rapallo) who had embarked on an *Erfüllungspolitik* ('policy of fulfilment') in 1921, attempting to appease Germany's creditors by paying the reparations bill, chiefly to demonstrate the impossibility of Germany's burden and gain concessions. Though neither man was a socialist, both were gunned down by nationalists with *Freikorps* connections who mistakenly saw in Erzberger and Rathenau traitors to Germany's national interest. Rathenau's Jewish origins were also suspicious to these antisemitic forces.

The assassins were either acquitted or given lenient sentences, demonstrating that the judiciary, like the army, still fostered antirepublican sympathies. As *Reichskanzler* Wirth noted following Rathenau's death, 'Der Feind steht rechts' ('The enemy is on the right'), yet beyond new penalties for political crimes, no practical measures were taken to strengthen the republican order by reforming the civil service, the judiciary, the armed forces or the economy.

Against this unsettled political background, Germany's economic situation was deteriorating rapidly. Besides the enormous reparations bill, the territorial losses had robbed Germany of much of her iron and steel production, and the *Kaiser*'s excessive war loans also had to be repaid. The printing presses had already provided much additional paper currency during the war, sparking an inflation far higher than in the other belligerent countries. Foreign loans continued beyond the war, partly to finance the *Erfüllungspolitik*. By late 1921 Germany was unable to repay either these or the next instalment of the reparations bill.

> ### *Vertrag von Rapallo*
>
> In April 1922 Germany and Soviet Russia agreed to waive all mutual reparations claims deriving from the war and the nationalisation of German interests in Russia following the Bolshevik revolution. Germany gained protection from further financial demands and demonstrated her independence; Soviet Russia benefited from international recognition. Improved relations later allowed the *Reichswehr* to rearm and train in secrecy on Russian soil.

Unwilling in late 1922 to accept Germany's pleas for a further moratorium on the various repayments, and angered by her failure to deliver a consignment of telegraph poles in lieu of reparations, France occupied the industrial *Ruhrgebiet* in early 1923, intending to operate the region's mines and other industrial centres for her own profit. This was the catalyst for a disastrous economic and political meltdown. The German government, by now a centre-right coalition under *Reichskanzler* Wilhelm Cuno, decided on a policy of passive resistance to the French occupiers. With Berlin's approval, workers in the *Ruhrgebiet* downed tools in the French-occupied enterprises, and drew strike money from the central government. To finance the operation, and to compensate for lost revenues and tax income, the government printed ever more paper money, further fuelling the inflation spiral: as money flooded the market, its value weakened since there were no additional goods to be bought. Equally, the value of the mark plummeted on world markets.

The crisis affected some groups more than others. The working classes had few savings and their wages generally kept pace with inflation, while wealthy capitalists paid off their debts with the increasingly worthless currency and snapped up new properties at bargain prices, shored up by the value of their fixed assets. Meanwhile, the middle classes saw the value of their savings, already diminished by the inflation of the 1914–22 period, finally wiped out. Pensioners and those who depended on investment income were quickly impoverished. The shock of this crisis created deep disillusionment with the republic and caused many to consider supporting a radical party.

By July 1923, 353,412 marks were necessary to buy a single American dollar; in August the rate was 4,620,455 marks to the dollar; the printing presses found it hard to keep up with demand. The Cuno government finally resigned that month, ushering in a *große Koalition* ('grand coalition') of all the parties which were prepared to support the republic: the SPD, DDP, DVP and *Zentrum*. Significantly, the *Reichstag* abrogated responsibility for the crisis and granted the government full powers to control the situation.

The new *Reichskanzler*, the DVP's Gustav Stresemann, was no natural republican. He was, however, a pragmatist, and prepared (unlike many Weimar politicians) to place the national interest first. For the following six years, until his death, Stresemann was the focal point of Germany's political stability.

Stresemann acted quickly to resolve the financial crisis. He ended passive resistance and declared Germany's willingness to recommence reparations payments – a promise which cost little in practice as Germany still had insufficient resources actually to pay any money, but which underlined the new government's goodwill towards the allied powers. In September Stresemann presided over a comprehensive currency reform. The worthless mark was replaced by a new currency, the *Rentenmark*, backed by the country's agricultural and industrial assets as there was insufficient gold in the *Reichsbank*. Only a fixed amount of the new currency was issued to prevent renewed inflation, while the government cut its costs and increased taxation. To the surprise of most, the new currency was a success and the economy began to recover, buoyed up by foreign loans made possible by the Stresemann government's conciliatory attitude.

However, political crisis also loomed. The right-wing Bavarian government (wrongly) believed that unpatriotic Marxists controlled the German central government and were undermining the German nation, particularly after passive resistance was abandoned. Inspired by Mussolini's march on Rome, which brought the Italian fascist party to power in 1922, the Bavarian right began considering a similar march on Berlin. They were further provoked by an autonomy movement in the Rhineland which threatened to reduce Germany's size still further, and the existence of SPD–KPD coalition governments in Saxony and Thuringia. With Soviet encouragement communists in these regions and elsewhere began planning their own putsches to avert the danger of a fascist takeover on the Italian model.

Anxious to appease the right, the Stresemann government used the *Reichswehr* to overturn the legal governments of Saxony and Thuringia. A bungled communist putsch attempt in Hamburg was easily doused. The KPD was enraged that its regional ministers had been ousted on the orders of an SPD *Reichspräsident* (Ebert), and the gulf between the two parties widened; they did not cooperate again during the Weimar years. The communists later dubbed the social democrats *Sozialfaschisten* (social fascists), and regarded them as a worse threat to the working class than the extreme right fascists.

The government, unable to count on the *Reichswehr* to disarm renegade Bavarian army units, acted less decisively against the right-wing threat than against the left. However, the crushing of the left defused much of the Bavarian right's anger. Anxious that the opportunity to bring Germany under firm authoritarian rule was slipping away, Adolf Hitler, leader of one of Bavaria's various far-right movements, attempted a putsch against the Bavarian and German governments on 8 November 1923. Despite temporarily involving the Bavarian head of government and the regional *Reichswehr* commander by launching the attempt in a *Bierkeller* where both were attending a meeting, Hitler was unable to secure their active support and the putsch fizzled out the following morning when a police detachment fired on Hitler's inadequate forces. The courts again displayed their right-wing sympathies the following year: despite having tried to overturn the state, Hitler received a light sentence and was permitted to use the courtroom for a much-publicised denunciation of republican democracy.

Stresemann received little gratitude for ending Germany's political, economic and diplomatic crisis. Instead, his government fell in November 1923 when the SPD withdrew its support, angered over Stresemann's actions in Saxony and Thuringia and his failure to treat the Bavarian right equally. Nonetheless, he remained as foreign minister in the succession of short-lived governments which followed.

1924–1929: 'Golden years'?

The middle years of the *Weimarer Republik*, from 1924 to 1929, are often seen as a golden era. They witnessed Germany's reemergence as a significant player on the world stage, and the decadent lifestyle enjoyed by café society in Berlin, celebrated in the musical *Cabaret* and documented in the stories of Christopher Isherwood. The economy recovered and there were no political crises to compare with those of the first postwar years.

Nonetheless, pressing problems remained, not least the reparations settlement. The 1923 crisis had at least convinced the creditor nations that Germany could only pay her debts if she were allowed to recover economically. The prosperity of Germany's trading partners – and France in particular – also depended partly on German economic strength. The American-inspired Dawes Plan of 1924 recognised these imperatives and for the first time linked Germany's reparations payments to the country's ability to pay. The Dawes Plan was, however, a temporary measure: once Germany's economy had sufficiently recovered, a final payments plan would be agreed. Meanwhile, foreign loans and investment began entering Germany, stimulating economic recovery and out-stripping the amount spent on reparations payments.

Germany's willingness to cooperate on the reparations issue enabled her diplomatic rehabilitation and encouraged the wartime allies to withdraw their occupation powers from Germany. In 1925 Stresemann signed the **Locarno-Verträge** (Locarno Treaties) with the western powers and the *Berliner Vertrag* (Berlin Treaty) with the Soviet Union the following year, further strengthening German–Soviet military co-operation. Locarno enabled Germany to enter the League of Nations ('*Völkerbund*') in 1926, the final sign that Germany had resumed her status as a nation of equal status with the powers which had defeated her in 1918.

Economic recovery and diplomatic settle-ments distracted attention from continuing structural problems. Politically the general recovery weakened the radical parties and strengthened the SPD at the *Reichstag* elections of 1924 and 1928 (see Table 3.1, p. 60). Nonetheless, the centrist parties (*Zentrum*, DVP and DDP) all began their slow decline, and the *Reichstag* remained divided between too many rival interest groups to secure a lasting majority for any government coalition. The parties remained unwilling or unable to compromise – one government fell over the colours of the naval flag – and failed to distinguish between support or opposition for a particular government and loyalty to the state itself. Such petty, yet embittered disputes severely damaged the *Reichstag*'s reputation.

Strong government was clearly impossible on this basis. Seven governments came and went in the relatively stable period between November 1923 (after Stresemann was ousted) and March 1930 (before parliamentary

---

Locarno-Verträge, 1925

Stresemann's treaties with the western powers signified Germany's acknowledgement of the post-1918 frontiers in western Europe, and thus tacit acceptance of the loss of Alsace-Lorraine and other territories. Though criticised by nationalists, Stresemann was merely conceding what had already been lost and could not be regained. He hoped to strengthen Germany by good relations with her western neighbours, a policy strikingly similar to that of Konrad Adenauer, the West German *Bundeskanzler*, after the Second World War (see Chapter 6). However, Stresemann pointedly refused to agree a similar treaty covering Germany's eastern frontier: neither the Rapallo nor the Berlin treaties mentioned territorial issues.

government was finally abandoned). A few had narrow majorities, providing the *Reichstag* members of all the coalition parties voted with the government – which they did not always. Other governments represented less than a third of the electorate. The SPD, the greatest proponent of parliamentary republicanism, chose to remain outside government until 1928, further weakening the basis of the various cabinets and rendering itself unable to act decisively to strengthen the republic. Having succeeded in its chief objective of reforming the *Kaiserreich* and now devoid of clear objectives for the republic, the SPD fell into a relative lethargy. Its uncharismatic leaders failed to inspire younger voters. Meanwhile, leadership changes in the DNVP and the *Zentrum* pushed both parties towards the right. By the late 1920s the DNVP was confirmed in its rejection of the republican form of government. From different motives, the KPD shared this view, seeing in Weimar a betrayal of the working class and aspiring to the wholesale restructuring which had occurred in the communist Soviet Union.

Changes in Germany's economic structures also undermined the centrist parties which had depended on the middle-class vote. New technologies and more effective business strategies were making white-collar workers redundant, while the 'rationalisation' programme which led large companies to merge and cut costs exacerbated this tendency. Underlying unemployment rose steadily after 1927, peaking in the winter months. More than three million were unemployed in early 1929. While the industrial unemployed tended to support the KPD, and Roman Catholicism was motivation enough to protect the *Zentrum*'s share of the vote, the white-collar workers and small business owners who had voted for the DVP or DDP were increasingly drawn to more radical parties which, they hoped, would secure them greater protection. Often these white-collar workers were not yet unemployed themselves, but feared that economic insecurity would drive them out of business or into the dole queues, robbing them of the social status which placed them slightly above the blue-collar working classes. For the middle classes, proletarianisation was the ultimate dread.

There were two further bad omens for the republic in the 'stable' years. First, following Friedrich Ebert's death in 1925, *Feldmarschall* Paul von Hindenburg, the hero of the First World War and foremost representative of the old imperial order, was elected *Reichspräsident*. Significantly, the SPD – theoretically the republic's greatest champion – did not even contest the second round of voting, preferring to back the *Zentrum*'s Wilhelm Marx. In the event, Hindenburg respected the republican constitution throughout the 1920s, but his natural antipathy to democratic rule prevented him from defending the republic when parliamentary government finally collapsed in 1930. His very presence as head of state represented a safety valve of authoritarian order should the new system prove unworkable.

Second, the psychologically destabilising reparations issue reemerged in 1929. By this point, the German economy appeared strong enough to the allies (despite underlying weaknesses) for a definitive settlement of Germany's obligations, codified in the **Young Plan**. Angered by this continuing national humiliation, the DNVP launched a referendum, calling on voters to reject the latest settlement. The party's leader, Alfred Hugenberg, was a press magnate who used his extensive network of newspapers and magazines to campaign against the Young Plan. Astutely, the radical Adolf Hitler lent

Young Plan, 1929

An international commission headed by the American banker Owen Young drew up a plan envisaged as the final settlement of Germany's outstanding reparations. The total sum – 37,000 million marks – was only 28 per cent of the original 1921 demand, to be paid over fifty-nine years. In negotiating the deal, Stresemann perhaps expected that further amendments might be possible before 1988. The deal was linked to the withdrawal of allied troops from the Rhineland and the end of international supervision of Germany's finances, both important steps towards restoring full German sovereignty.

the support of his own nationalist party, the *Nationalsozialistische Deutsche Arbeiterpartei* (National Socialist German Workers' Party, NSDAP) to the campaign. Though the referendum failed to secure popular backing to reject the Young Plan, Hitler and the NSDAP – a splinter party with just 2.6 per cent of the vote in the 1928 *Reichstag* elections – received valuable nationwide publicity.

The *Weimarer Republik* had limped through the late 1920s, intact on the surface but deeply holed beneath the waterline. Its parlous state of health was fully revealed by a new economic crisis following the **Wall Street Crash** of October 1929. Just ten days earlier, Gustav Stresemann, the principal figure of stability, had died, prematurely aged by the burden of maintaining the republic over the previous six years.

1929–1933: National socialism and the collapse of republican democracy

The Wall Street Crash gradually revealed the underlying instability of the German economy, particularly once foreign investors withdrew their funds. Rising un-employment meant a greater burden on the state budget for social security pay-ments, and a dilemma for the coalition government led by the SPD's Hermann Müller. A deadlock emerged within the *Reichstag* as the different parties attempted to defend the interest groups they represented: the SPD was unwilling to reduce unemployment benefit for fear of alienating the working class, while the right-wing parties opposed tax rises to finance the higher bill. Unable to secure a compromise, Müller resigned at the end of March 1930. Parliamentary government had failed to resolve the crisis.

Hindenburg's role as *Reichspräsident* now assumed greater importance. Rather than call new elections or attempt to cobble together a new coalition government based on a *Reichstag* majority, he appointed Heinrich von Brüning (a politician on the right of the *Zentrum*, impatient with ineffectual democracy) as *Reichskanzler*. He headed a right-wing cabinet which reflected Hindenburg's own political instincts, and was partly independent of political party machinations. Should the *Reichstag* fail to support Brüning, the president would enable the new government to rule by emergency decrees under Article 48 of the constitution. Hindenburg's decision was greatly influenced by his friends in the *Reichswehr* command, particularly General Kurt von Schleicher, who desired a strong, nationalist government.

Brüning preferred a cautious approach to deal with the mounting economic disaster. Rather than intervening to stimulate the economy into recovery by borrowing to finance public projects, he attempted to balance the budget at the cost of spending cuts, lower wages and higher taxation. Brüning hoped to demonstrate Germany's inability to meet the Young Plan's requirements, and thus to secure the allies' willingness to cancel reparations altogether – if it could be achieved, this foreign policy triumph might appease the nationalist groups. In the short term, the working and middle classes paid the price, as production dropped and unemployment steadily rose. When the *Reichstag* rejected the emergency decree which had introduced Brüning's budget proposals in July 1930, he dissolved parliament and ruled by emergency decree until new elections on 14 September, the latest legal date on which they could be held. Brüning and Schleicher had hoped to rally centrist and national forces behind the government's recovery programme. However, the *Reichskanzler* lacked the charisma to secure a popular majority for his painful course. Instead the liberal and traditional right-wing parties on whom he had pinned his hopes (notably the DVP, the DNVP and the DDP – by now renamed as the *Staatspartei*) lost heavily to the extremist parties of the right and left. Brüning's own *Zentrum* party could only maintain its share of the vote. No matter: Brüning continued in power for almost two more years, covered by presidential decrees which the SPD, fearful of further losses to the extremists, preferred not to overturn.

Though the 1930 elections had no immediate effect on the government, their longer-term significance was immense. Besides the KPD's gains (the party became the third largest in the *Reichstag*), Hitler's NSDAP also achieved an electoral breakthrough, securing 18.3 per cent of the vote and 107 seats. Throughout the 1920s, the NSDAP (whose origins are explored more fully in Chapter 4) had denounced the republic and parliamentary democracy, regarding competition between parties as a splintering and thus a weakening of the nation. Building on the *Dolchstoßlegende*, and playing on the ingrained antisemitism of many Germans, the party had also consistently castigated the *Novemberverbrecher* of 1918, claiming that their acceptance of defeat and subjugation before the victors at Versailles and the international reparations commissions had brought shame on Germany. During the years of apparent stability, the attacks on the very substance of the Weimar system by both the NSDAP and KPD had

Wall Street Crash, October 1929

The 1920s saw economic growth and rising affluence in the United States. This, and the availability of cheap credit, encouraged increased investment in the stock markets, causing shares to rise far in excess of companies' real earnings. When credit ran out and confidence flagged, the boom collapsed. The Stock Exchange in New York's Wall Street lost around half its highest (paper) value. While this represented a return to more realistic share prices, the psychological effect was immense, sparking a prolonged depression characterised by mass unemployment. The depression spread as American investors withdrew their money from Europe to remain solvent at home. With less money in America for imports, the European exporters suffered and the recession deepened.

gone largely unheeded; in 1930, with the country again in turmoil and parliament unable to cope, both parties were well positioned to benefit.

The NSDAP had several advantages over the KPD. Whereas the communists had a fixed ideology (Marxism), were clearly in the sway of a foreign power (the Soviet Union) and appealed to a particular section of the population (the working and unemployed classes), the NSDAP had none of these constraints. Its ideology was fluid, largely based on rejection of the failing Weimar system rather than the promotion of any particular alternative, and thus quickly adaptable to the various disgruntled sections of society. In particular, the *Mittelstand* – the craftsmen, traders, small business owners and officials who had suffered economic reversals and feared worse – felt betrayed by their traditional parties and were attracted by the NSDAP's call to rebel. The NSDAP's only consistent themes in its electoral appeals – nationalism and a repudiation of the Versailles humiliation – were low common denominators with wide appeal. (The more hateful aspects of antisemitic bigotry were present, but not emphasised.) Furthermore, the NSDAP benefited from perhaps the most persuasive and dynamic politician of the era – Adolf Hitler – and an intensive exploitation of the most innovative publicity methods.

The vote for both extremist parties grew in the early 1930s and this polarisation of politics away from the discredited centre parties was repeated at *Land* level. As neither party would support the government, parliamentary politics faced a stalemate. Meanwhile, the focus of political life increasingly shifted to the streets where the Nazis' paramilitary groups, the *Schutzstaffeln* (SS) and the *Sturmabteilungen* (SA), did battle with their communist equivalent, the *Roter Frontkämpferbund* (RFB), though the two occasionally joined forces if this might undermine the democratic order further. Political violence grew in the early 1930s as the Nazis in particular attempted to intimidate their opponents.

As the economic climate worsened, Brüning at least demonstrated the need to relieve Germany of further reparations payments, not least in the interests of a global economic recovery which the USA and Great Britain urgently required. However, by the time agreements to end German reparations were reached, Brüning himself had been ousted. He had lost the confidence of Schleicher, who now recognised Brüning's inability to achieve a popular majority for firm right-wing rule, and of Hindenburg. The *Reichspräsident*, having been persuaded that his duty in the fraught political climate was to accept a second term of office, was angered by Brüning's failure to achieve a simple extension of the presidential term in the *Reichstag*, forcing him to endure the indignity of a democratic election in 1932. Hindenburg was further dismayed not to achieve an absolute majority in the first round of voting. Nonetheless, he beat Hitler convincingly in the run-offs: almost two-thirds voted against the would-be *Führer* less than a year before he achieved power.

Brüning finally fell when he proposed breaking up the unviable large landed estates in the east, and banned the Nazis' paramilitary organisations. Both moves angered the right: the landed *Junker* feared the erosion of their power and status, while the military elites viewed the paramilitaries as a potential source of expansion for the German armed forces. Hindenburg had links with both camps. At Schleicher's suggestion, and without new elections, he responded by installing a new presidential cabinet under *Reichskanzler* Franz von Papen.

Papen's 'barons' cabinet' (most of the ministers were aristocrats, despite the 1919 constitution's ban on titles) had almost no basis in the *Reichstag*. The new government almost immediately lost a parliamentary confidence vote, sparking new elections in July 1932. In the hope of securing Nazi support, the new government lifted the ban on the SA and SS, effectively permitting a renewed wave of violence throughout the election campaign. In an attempt to reassure the nationalist right, Papen also deposed the SPD-led Prussian government by declaring a state of emergency and appointing himself *Reichskommissar* (Reich commissioner) in Prussia. In fact, the unrest in Prussia had resulted principally from the freedom Papen had allowed the NSDAP para-militaries. It was significant that the SPD did not deploy its own paramilitaries, the *Reichsbanner Schwarz-Rot-Gold*, to defend the legitimate Prussian government against this so-called *Preußenschlag*. Yet nothing could restore power to the traditional parties of the right and centre-right. Instead, the NSDAP more than doubled its support, achieving 37.3 per cent of the vote in the July elections. Still Hitler refused to consider participation in government unless he became *Reichskanzler*, a step *Feldmarschall* Hindenburg refused to contemplate: the upstart Hitler had only achieved the rank of corporal.

With the *Reichstag* deadlocked, new elections were called for November 1932. The NSDAP, by now short of money and a disappointment to the millions of voters who had hoped since 1930 to see Hitler take radical action, lost some two million votes but still dominated the *Reichstag*. Papen proposed abolishing the still unworkable *Reichstag*, banning the KPD and NSDAP, and establishing a new, authoritarian regime. Hindenburg refused to countenance such a sharp breach of the constitution, and even Schleicher recognised that civil war would ensue. Papen had to go.

Hindenburg, still reluctant to appoint Hitler *Reichskanzler*, since his radical nationalism represented an assault on the traditional conservative order, turned to Schleicher himself. Now in the spotlight as *Reichskanzler* rather than pulling strings behind the scenes, Schleicher attempted to secure the support of at least some of the NSDAP *Reichstag* members by driving a wedge between Hitler and Georg Strasser, who represented the apparently milder section of the party's membership. As Hitler was able to assert his authority within the NSDAP these plans collapsed. Schleicher quickly concluded that Papen's scheme for an authoritarian *coup d'état* was the only alternative to the political stalemate. Hindenburg proved no more receptive to this idea in January 1933 than he had the previous month.

Papen had by now himself won the ear of the *Reichspräsident*, suggesting to Hindenburg that Hitler be allowed to lead a government in which a majority of the ministers would represent the old conservative elites. Neither Papen nor Hindenburg fully appreciated Hitler's political skills, and believed he would be their puppet, while also delivering the substantial parliamentary support of the NSDAP and putting govern-ment back on a majority footing. On 30 January 1933 Hindenburg finally appointed Hitler *Reichskanzler*, heading an NSDAP–DNVP coalition government with only two Nazi ministers.

Conclusion

In January 1933 few anticipated the speed, tenacity and skill with which Hitler would outmanoeuvre his political opponents to secure full power for the NSDAP and finally demolish the battered structures of the *Weimarer Republik*. Only the jubilant celebrations of Hitler's supporters in Berlin's government district on that first night suggested that this would not be yet another in the long line of here today, gone tomorrow governments which had characterised the Weimar years. As we shall see in Chapter 4, Hitler secured an effective power monopoly within months of his appointment.

Yet in reality the republic had already passed away in 1930 after a troubled infancy and prolonged illness. Thereafter only the empty shell of the republic remained; the principles of the 1919 constitution had long since been undermined by the political parties' unwillingness to compromise for the national good in times of crisis. On the left, the SPD displayed a critical lack of imagination, while the KPD decided its only choice was to pursue all or nothing and had chosen the latter, unable to persuade the German people (not even the working class) that the example of Leninist/Stalinist Russia was the only way forward. The two parties' failure to unite against the right compounded their failure to protect the republic, the prize for which previous generations had striven. On the right, the increasing levels of nationalist rhetoric did the greatest disservice of all to the German nation itself, since they often ignored the reality of Germany's international obligations after the lost war. For all their tub thumping, the traditional and business elites of the DNVP and DVP were not the nation, merely one privileged part of it, largely discredited for their support of the *Kaiser*'s war. Many Germans recognised this, and instead decamped to the NSDAP, which appeared to represent the whole nation. By 1932, no democratic system could ignore the Nazis' strong showing at the ballot box. By this point also, German voters could be excused for desiring a radical break with the shortcomings of Weimar democracy, under which they had suffered hyperinflation, mass unemployment, economic uncertainty, national humiliation and political farce. The Nazis were careful not to spell out too clearly what the alternative would look like; it was enough that there would be an alternative.

The *Weimarer Republik* was not, however, doomed from the outset. Indeed, it survived the crisis years of the early 1920s and recovered sufficiently to prosper quietly in the latter half of the decade as Stresemann negotiated Germany's international rehabilitation. The political structures of Weimar did not in themselves preclude a stable democracy. To be effective, however, these structures depended on people who believed in them. Germany had not evolved a tradition of democratic political participation under the *Kaiserreich*; nor had the imperial system been so repressive as to spawn a strongly democratic resistance. The victorious allies had insisted merely on the removal of the *Kaiser* and the downsizing of the military, but had not stipulated safeguards for a new democratic system. In short, there were simply too few politicians, and voters, who placed democracy first and personal or party political advantage second. There is a striking contrast between Germany's descent into dictatorship in the 1930s, on the one hand, and on the other the survival of democratic government in the longer-established democracies of Britain and America following the Wall Street Crash, despite the severe economic crises which also affected these countries and were addressed within the existing political framework. For many, the Weimar years seemed to prove that democracy was not right for Germany. Even for many of those (the majority) who had not voted for the NSDAP, the end of weak government and political uncertainty was greeted with great relief.

Republik Österreich, 1918–1933

After the defeat of 1918, Austria shared many of Germany's difficulties; however, while Germany remained essentially intact, the German speakers of the Habsburg Empire found themselves abandoned by the other nationalities which formed independent states (Hungary, Czechoslovakia, etc.). Despite Woodrow Wilson's vision of 'national self-determination', border changes after the war meant that some four million German Austrians in South Tyrol and the Bohemian Sudetenland were included in Italy and Czechoslovakia respectively. Further territory was lost to Hungary. The remaining German-speaking provinces had no common traditions other than the historical ties of the Habsburg dynasty; consequently there was little sense of a specifically Austrian nationhood. After the last *Kaiser*'s departure, the hastily formed Vienna government proclaimed that the new republic of *Deutschösterreich* would be united with Germany.

The allies, however, believed that defeated Germany should not emerge from the war enlarged. In the 1919 Treaty of Saint-Germain, the Austrian government was forced to abandon the name *Deutschösterreich* (in favour of *Republik Österreich*) and accept a ban on the proposed *Anschluss* with Germany. Even so, unofficial referenda held in several *Länder* between 1919 and 1921 revealed huge support for union with Germany or Switzerland; without allied vetoes on these secessionist movements, the Vienna government might well have been unable to maintain unity. But, cut off from its natural trading lands and sources of natural resources in the east, Austria appeared to many of its citizens to be economically unviable, a conclusion strengthened by the unemployment and famine which gripped the country in the first postwar years, and exacerbated by the war debt inherited from the empire.

The Austrian Republic's first constitution, agreed in 1920, bore strong resemblances to that of the Weimar Republic: a federal system gave the various provinces significant autonomies, the indirectly elected *Bundespräsident* had only symbolic powers, and the main house of parliament – the *Nationalrat* – was elected by proportional representation. The upper house of parliament, the *Bundesrat*, represented the governments of the *Länder*, albeit with somewhat more restricted powers than the German *Reichsrat*.

Unlike Germany, the electoral system did not produce the same multiplicity of political parties. The *Sozialdemokratische Arbeiterpartei* (SDAP) recognised the importance of working-class unity and embraced a much broader ideological spectrum than the German SPD, leaving the *Kommunistische Partei Österreichs* (KPÖ) as an ineffectual splinter group. To the SDAP's right stood the *Christlichsoziale Partei* (CSP), representing rural and Roman Catholic interests, and the *Großdeutsche Volkspartei* (GDVP), traditionally opposed to the Habsburgs' multinational empire and emphasising German national aspirations.

Despite having so few political parties, Austria was nonetheless riven by a deep political rift. The SDAP was strongest in Vienna, Austria's major industrial heartland, where the federal system enabled it to embark on an ambitious programme of public housing and social services, financed by high taxes on the rich. Such apparently revolutionary developments caused anxiety in the rest of Austria, traditionally rural and conservative, and strongly influenced by the Roman Catholic church. Both sides feared that the other would attempt to nullify its cause.

At national level, social democrats led the first postwar government, but were soon ousted amid recriminations over the peace treaty, strikes, food and fuel shortages, and the resultant deaths from disease and starvation, all directly or indirectly related to the dislocation which accompanied the collapse of the empire and the erection of borders across a formerly integrated economic unit. After 1920 a small majority for the right kept the socialists permanently outside national government. However, the implacable opposition between left and right, and the normally small government majorities, produced increasingly untenable and farcical scenes in the *Nationalrat*, which quickly undermined optimism in parliamentary government.

Though *Bundeskanzler* came and went during the 1920s, the constant powerbroker was the CSP leader, Ignaz Seipel, a senior Catholic clergyman whose rise to political authority underlined the strong clerical influence on Austrian government in this period. Though he did nothing to resolve Austria's internal political tensions, he did ease the dire economic difficulties by securing significant foreign loans and, in 1924, replacing the Austrian *Krone* – rendered worthless by the same hyperinflation which damaged the German mark – with a stronger currency, the *Schilling*. There was a heavy political price for both measures. Foreign loans were offered in return for Austria's agreement not to pursue the forbidden *Anschluss* for at least ten years, and provoked sharp opposition from both the GDVP and the socialists (the latter hoped for a united German republic under socialist rule). The stable currency required a sharp cut in public expenditure, financed by higher taxes and forcibly retiring some 85,000 civil servants.

The tensions between the two principal political camps (*Lager*) were underlined by the growth of paramilitary groupings. The socialists, when in government, had close links with the national armed forces (*Volkswehr*), forged during the 1918 revolution; once a regular army was formed under CSP rule in 1922, they instead created their own *Republikanischer Schutzbund*. Meanwhile, the German nationalists and other anti-socialist forces had formed their own local militias in 1918 to secure law and order. Inspired by the fascist movements growing in neighbouring countries (notably Italy, where Mussolini took power in 1922), they formed their own armed *Heimwehren* (the name varied in different *Länder*). Together with their political wing, the *Heimatblock*, these later supplanted the GDVP as the focus of nationalist activity.

For much of the 1920s, these two *Lager* faced each other off, accumulated weapons and trained their members. As political tensions grew amid ongoing economic hardships, and fuelled by the radical rhetoric of the left (in fact the SDAP was a fairly moderate party with no intention of sparking a revolution to seize power), so the gulf between the two sides grew. An incident in the village of Schattendorf brought matters to a head in early 1927: shots were fired when the *Schutzbund* and right-wing *Frontkämpfer* met, killing a boy and a war veteran. When the accused *Frontkämpfer* were fully acquitted in July 1927, tensions boiled over into a minor but spontaneous civil war in the streets of Vienna on 15 July, despite calls for restraint by the SDAP's moderate leadership. The *Justizpalast* was burned to the ground; eighty-five demonstrators and four police lay dead. The riots demonstrated the deep rifts within Austria and further undermined the republic.

Seipel refused to consider a policy of reconciliation and compromise between left and right, and continued as before. In the following years, political life became still further radicalised, particularly following the economic upheaval caused by the Wall Street Crash. The growing frustration for many Austrians with their unworkable parliamentary democracy was reflected in the growing popularity and radicalisation of the *Heimwehren*. Their political creed, itself a threat of war against the left, was formulated in the oath sworn at a mass meeting in Korneuburg in 1930 (see Document 3b). Meanwhile, the Austrian Nazi party, though still small and divided between revolutionaries and those who favoured a legal road to power, also made inroads into Austria's political system.

The increasingly polarised and radicalised political parties, and a continuing widespread belief that Austria could not survive alone, made government practically impossible by the early 1930s. One possible solution – a customs union with Germany and general cooperation between the two governments – was blocked by the allied powers in 1931, still anxious to prevent an *Anschluss*, yet the loans they offered were insufficient to resolve the economic slump or to achieve political harmony. By 1930, no government could maintain parliamentary support for long. In desperation, the *Bundespräsident* appointed the relatively unknown CSP agriculture minister, Engelbert Dollfuß, as *Bundeskanzler* in May 1932. When a dispute erupted in the finely balanced *Nationalrat* the following March, the parliament's chairman and his two deputies all resigned their posts to vote with their respective parties, leaving no one to chair proceedings. Seeing an opportunity finally to remove the unworkable democratic system, Dollfuß declared that the *Nationalrat* had dissolved itself. Thus March 1933 saw the removal of parliamentary democracy in both Germany and Austria.

Document 3a: *Generalfeldmarschall* von Hindenburg before the Commission of Enquiry into the German Collapse, 18 November 1919

. . . trotz der ungeheuren Ansprüche an Truppen und Führung, trotz der zahlenmäßigen Überlegenheit des Feindes konnten wir den ungleichen Kampf zu einem günstigen Ende führen, wenn die geschlossene und einheitliche Zusammenwirkung von Heer und Heimat eingetreten wäre. . . .

Doch was geschah nun? Während sich beim Feinde trotz seiner Überlegenheit an lebendem und totem Material alle Parteien, alle Schichten der Bevölkerung in dem Willen zum Siege immer fester zusammenschlossen, und zwar um so mehr, je schwieriger ihre Lage wurde, machten sich bei uns, wo dieser Zusammenschluß bei unserer Unterlegenheit viel notwendiger war, Parteiinteressen breit, und diese Umstände führten sehr bald zu einer Spaltung und Lockerung des Siegeswillens. . . .

Als wir unser Amt übernahmen, stellten wir bei der Reichsleitung eine Reihe von Anträgen, die den Zweck hatten, alle nationalen Kräfte zur schnellen und günstigen Kriegsentscheidung zusammenzufassen; sie zeigten der Reichsleitung zugleich ihre riesengroßen Aufgaben. Was aber schließlich, zum Teil wieder durch Einwirkung der Parteien, aus unserern Anträgen geworden ist, ist bekannt: Ich wollte kraftvolle und freudige Mitarbeit, und bekam Versagen und Schwäche. Die Sorge, ob die Heimat fest genug bliebe, bis der Krieg gewonnen sei, hat uns von diesem Augenblicke an nie mehr verlassen. Wir erhoben noch oft unsere warnende Stimme bei der Reichsregierung. In dieser Zeit setzte die heimliche planmäßige Zersetzung von Flotte und Heer als Fortsetzung ähnlicher Erscheinungen im Frieden ein. . . . Die braven Truppen, die sich von der revolutionären Zermürbung freihielten, hatten unter dem pflichtwidrigen Verhalten der revolutionären Kameraden schwer zu leiden; sie mußten die ganze Last des Kampfes tragen. Die Absichten der Führung konnten nicht mehr zur Ausführung gebracht werden. Unsere wiederholten Anträge auf strenge Zucht und strenge Gesetzgebung wurden nicht erfüllt. So mußten unsere Operationen mißlingen, es mußte der Zusammenbruch kommen; die Revolution bildete nur den Schlußstein. Ein englischer General sagte mit Recht: »Die deutsche Armee ist von hinten erdolcht worden.« Den guten Kern des Heeres trifft keine Schuld. Seine Leistung ist ebenso bewunderungswürdig wie die des Offizierkorps. Wo die Schuld liegt, ist klar erwiesen. Bedurfte es noch eines Beweises, so liegt er in dem angeführten Ausspruche des englischen Generals und in dem maßlosen Erstaunen unserer Feinde über ihren Sieg.

Das ist die große Linie der tragischen Entwicklung des Krieges für Deutschland nach einer Reihe so glänzender, nie dagewesener Erfolge an zahlreichen Fronten, nach einer Leistung von Heer und Volk, für die kein Lob groß genug ist.

Source: 'Stenographischer Bericht über die öffentlichen Verhandlungen des Untersuchungsausschusses', Berlin 1919, pp. 729 ff., reprinted in Peter Longerich (ed.), *Die Erste Republik* (Munich: Piper, 1992), pp. 134–5.

Document 3b: *Der Korneuburger Eid*, 18 May 1930

Wir wollen Österreich von Grund aus erneuern. Wir wollen den Volksstaat der Heimwehren.

Wir fordern von jedem Kameraden: den unverzagten Glauben ans Vaterland, den restlosen Eifer der Mitarbeit und die leidenschaftliche Liebe zur Heimat. Wir wollen nach der Macht im Staate greifen und zum Wohle des gesamten Volkes Staat und Wirtschaft neu ordnen.

Wir müssen eigenen Vorteil vergessen, müssen alle Bindungen und Forderungen der Parteien unserem Kampfziel unterordnen, da wir der Gemeinschaft des ganzen deutschen Volkes dienen wollen.

Wir verwerfen den westlich-demokratischen Parlamentarismus und den Parteienstaat. Wir wollen an seine Stelle die Selbstverwaltung der Stände setzen und eine starke Staatsführung, die nicht aus Parteivertretern, sondern aus den führenden Personen der großen Stände und den fähigsten und bewährtesten Männern unserer Volksbewegung gebildet wird.

Wir kämpfen gegen die Zersetzung unseres Volkes durch den marxistischen Klassenkampf und durch die liberal-kapitalistische Wirtschaftsgestaltung. Wir wollen auf berufsständischer Grundlage die Selbstverwaltung der Wirtschaft verwirklichen. Wir werden den Klassenkampf überwinden, die soziale Würde und Gerechtigkeit herstellen.

Wir wollen durch eine bodenständige und gemeinnützige Wirtschaft den Wohlstand unseres Volkes heben. Der Staat ist die Verkörperung des Volksganzen; seine Macht und Führung wacht darüber, daß die Stände den Notwendigkeiten der Volksgemeinschaft eingeordnet bleiben.

Jeder Kamerad fühle und bekenne sich als Träger der neuen deutschen Staatsgesinnung; er sei bereit Gut und Blut einzusetzen, er kenne die drei Gewalten: den Gottesglauben, seinen eigenen harten Willen, das Wort seiner Führer.

Source: Klaus Berchtold (ed.), *Österreichische Parteiprogramme 1868–1966* (Vienna: Verlag für Geschichte und Politik, 1967), pp. 402–3.

Topics

■ How justified were the accusations made by Hindenburg in Document 3a?

■ Discuss how the *Korneuburger Eid* (Document 3b) reflects the tensions in Austrian politics and society after 1918.

■ To what extent were the Weimar and Austrian First Republics weakened by the same factors?

■ Are political or economic factors more important in explaining the collapse of the Weimar and/or Austrian First Republics?

■ Discuss the view that the *Weimarer Republik* suffered from too much democracy.

■ To what extent must the international community bear responsibility for Germany and Austria's crises in the 1919–33 period?

Chaotic dictatorship and genocidal war: 1933–1945

Even during the mid-1930s, many Europeans feared renewed war. The communist Soviet Union proclaimed a global revolutionary mission, while nationalist states (notably Germany and Italy) dreamed of empire. In Spain, civil war broke out in 1936 between republicans and fascists, a conflict which the latter won by 1939. Anxious to preserve peace, and more fearful of communism than Nazism, Britain attempted to appease Hitler, allowing Germany to swallow Austria and Czecho-slovakia in 1938–39. Besides emboldening Hitler, this dissuaded the Soviet leader, Joseph Stalin, from allying with the west when conflict came in 1939 over Germany's invasion of Poland. The war which followed encompassed much of the globe, as Germany's Japanese allies sought a new empire in Asia, and the USA defended the European democracies. The cost in human sacrifice was unparalleled, not least because of Hitler's systematic attempt to exterminate the Jewish people. By 1945 millions had lost their lives, and millions more were destitute and homeless.

Less than twelve and a half years separate Hitler's triumphal entry into the *Reichskanzlei* on 30 January 1933 and his squalid suicide in a bunker beneath the ruins of the *Reichshauptstadt* on 30 April 1945. Yet this brief chronological period has generated more historical writing and controversy than any other era in German history. The legacy of Hitler's *Drittes Reich* (the *Heiliges Römisches Reich* and the *Kaiserreich* having been the first and second empires respectively) resounds in Germany and beyond to this day.

Historians, political scientists and others have often disagreed in their attempts to define what Nazi Germany represented. For some it was a totalitarian dictatorship, suggesting a system in which the totality of life was totally controlled by the *Führer* and his party, while others have noted that in many ways Nazi Germany was chaotically run and retained niches where Germans could ignore party and state. Some scholars locate Nazism firmly in the broader context of European **fascism**, highlighting the extremely authoritarian and nationalist agenda Nazism shared with systems such as Mussolini's Italy and Franco's Spain. Others have (controversially) attempted to equate Nazism and communism as equally criminal, destructive ideologies, comparing Hitler's Germany with Stalin's Soviet Union. For others again, the very specific characteristics of German Nazism – notably its rabid hatred of the Jews, generally termed antisemitism – mark it out as a unique system, perhaps ultimately reducible to the person of Adolf Hitler himself. Certain observers highlight the central importance of the Jewish Holocaust and believe that it must be sufficient to denounce Nazism without needing to explain it. At the other extreme, renegades have even attempted to deny the historical truth of the Holocaust.

The following introduction can only begin to address these important debates about the national socialist period in German history. Some questions are more easily tackled than others. For instance, the structures of the Nazi government machine can be more readily described than the extent of ordinary Germans' complicity in – or even awareness of – the crimes of the Third Reich.

> ### Fascism
>
> The term has been applied to movements which attempt to overcome societal divisions by focusing all national energies on patriotic causes, led by a single, paramount leader. Individuals and interest groups are subordinated to the whole, resulting in political and judicial repression, particularly of minorities or foreigners within the state. The nation's strength is symbolised by an emphasis on military force, and often directed into territorial aggrandisement, frequently at the expense of supposedly inferior nations. In practice, the states and movements termed 'fascist' (most frequently Mussolini's Italy, Franco's Spain and Hitler's Germany, but also political parties in Britain, France and elsewhere) have displayed significant differences in content and emphasis. Unlike Marxist communism, there is no single, codified 'fascist' ideology.

The long-term causes of national socialism – a German *Sonderweg*?

For many historians, politicians and everyday citizens of the postwar world, the enormity of the Second World War meant that the Nazi era could not simply be written off as another bygone era of German history. The fact that Germany had launched two world wars within a quarter of a century suggested that there was something unusual about the Germans which predisposed them towards aggressive politics. Historians were naturally influenced by the horrors of the war and the barbarity exposed when the Nazis' *Konzentrationslager* (concentration camps) were liberated to reveal mass graves and skeletal figures clinging to life. A. J. P. Taylor, in the 1961 preface to his *Course of German History*, believed that 'it was no more a mistake for the German people to end up with Hitler than it is an accident when a river flows into the sea'. Other historians, conversely, have argued that the emergence of Hitler was merely a *Betriebsstörung*, a spanner in the works, in other words a historical accident.

Neither explanation is entirely satisfactory, since the first suggests some grand trajectory of German history – indeed of history generally – according to which Hitler and national socialism were Germany's preordained fate, while the other could suggest that Hitler came from nowhere.

Those who see well-established roots which gave rise to Hitler look back far further than the period covered by this book to at least the Reformation of the early sixteenth century, when Martin Luther, a dissident monk, established a Protestant church in Germany in opposition to the previously dominant Roman Catholic order. Luther's Reformation was enthusiastically embraced by the princes and dukes of the *Heiliges Römisches Reich*, since it gave them far greater independence from the Catholic *Kaiser* and removed the rights of Rome to tax revenues and interference in the legal system. Crucially for the argument here, Luther resisted the wider political revolt of the peasantry and other classes against the ruling nobility which the Reformation inspired. Rather, Luther emphasised the Bible teachings that Christians owed loyalty to the secular authorities in worldly matters. Arguably this began a strong German tradition of obedience to the state.

State authority in Germany was given greater force by the development (particularly in the eighteenth century) of the strong Prussian state, built on the principles of firm military authority. Control of the Prussian army remained a strictly royal prerogative until 1918. The army command, free of responsibility to parliament, considered itself the principal pillar of state authority and was able to preserve its position, as we have seen, throughout the *Weimarer Republik*. In the early 1930s the *Reichspräsident* was a retired *Feldmarschall*, and his principal advisers (notably von Schleicher) were drawn from the upper echelons of the military. The traditional army commanders retained much of their authority well into the *Drittes Reich* and, despite the caution of many senior generals about the feasibility of Hitler's war plans and their half-hearted support for national socialism, the army fought with commitment in the Second World War. The allies who defeated Germany in 1945 were so concerned about the Prussian-German militarist tradition that the German armed forces were entirely dismantled after the war, and Prussia, regarded as the cradle of these expansionist traditions, was itself disbanded and divided into smaller *Länder* in 1947.

The principal strand of the arguments about the continuities which arguably led to Hitler concerns developments in the nineteenth century. The failure of the 1848 revolution to establish a liberal democracy and national unity is regarded as a key turning point, or rather a turning point where German history failed to turn. Despite the growth of an industrial economy and the emergence of a new *Bildungsbürgertum* (educated middle class) whose wealth derived from commerce or their involvement as *Beamten* in the expanded public service, real power essentially remained in the hands of the landed aristocracy and ultimately with the established monarchies. In the *Kaiserreich*, it has been argued, the retention of power by these old elites under a single strong leader (Bismarck and then Wilhelm II) prevented the emergence of liberal democracy and encouraged support for strong leaders as the cornerstone of German political life. The bourgeoisie (the *Bürgertum*, that is the richer, professional middle classes) arguably aligned themselves with this seemingly natural order to underpin their own place in society.

Bismarck's political balancing act to preserve the exclusive power of the old order also necessitated, it is argued, two key trends which outlived the *Kaiserreich*. First was the political isolation and demonisation of the socialist working classes, quickly reinforced after 1918 by the *Dolchstoßlegende*, initiated by conservative figures such as Hindenburg. Second, arguably as a distraction from domestic tensions, the *Kaiserreich* deliberately pursued expansionist goals. This thesis was encouraged particularly by the publication in 1961 of Fritz Fischer's book *Griff nach der Weltmacht*, which, as we have seen, produced evidence of the German government's supposedly clear intention in 1912 to launch a war by 1914. It is easy to see Stresemann's policies in the 1920s (regaining Germany's rights as an equal partner in international affairs while simultaneously and surreptitiously rebuilding Germany's armed forces) and Hitler's broad foreign policy goals as forming a continuity with the objectives of *Kaiserreich* politicians.

The form taken by German nationalism is also seen as crucial in explaining long-term historical continuities. Taking the emergence of unified political states based largely on a single nation as the expected norm, many historians saw Germany as a 'belated nation' whose emergence as a single state in 1871 came significantly later than the creation of, for example, England, France and Spain, having been prevented for centuries by the dynastic resistance inherent in *Kleinstaaterei*. Arguably, this belated unity made German national aspirations all the more intense when it was achieved, particularly since the Prussian military tradition was the dominant factor in the creation of the united state. Nineteenth-century German historians glorified Prussian Germany's political model and contributed to a sense that the supposed glories represented by the *Kaiserreich* were superior to the state forms in countries such as Britain and France, where parliamentary democracy seemed to encourage national weakness. Such sentiments stimulated many Germans' enthusiasm for the First World War, seen as an opportunity to extend these strengths to the rest of Europe, much as the French revolutionaries had tried to export their forms of liberty and progress to the rest of Europe in the wars of the 1790s. Nationalist enthusiasm also encouraged suspicion of foreign elements within German society during the *Kaiserreich*. In particular, long-established antisemitic prejudice was given new impetus in this environment, particularly as it coincided with the theories of social Darwinism, the extension to the subdivisions within the human race of Charles Darwin's notions of the survival of the fittest in biological evolutionary development.

The theory of the peculiarity, indeed singularity, of Germany's long-term development into the *Drittes Reich* and the Holocaust was principally consolidated by Hans-Ulrich Wehler, who spoke of a German *Sonderweg* ('special path') in his work on the *Kaiserreich* in the 1970s. However, the theory was challenged in later years, not least because it presupposed a standard model of historical development in other countries which, on closer examination, proved hard to demonstrate. Further research revealed that the German *Bürgertum* had not, in fact, rushed to embrace the trappings of the aristocratic system which dominated the *Kaiserreich*; nor was Germany unique in its nationalism (and certainly not in its enthusiasm for acquiring a colonial empire). Some historians have also felt that the model did not pay enough attention to the alternative trends which continued to exist in German society, not least the development of a very strong body of opinion which favoured democratisation and which, in the shape of the SPD and the left-leaning liberals, made it much harder to operate the political system of the *Kaiserreich* than Bismarck had intended. In particular the social democrats' social networks created a largely self-contained industrial working-class community or milieu.

These considerations do not nullify the recognition of continuities across different periods of German history. It is clear, for instance, that Hitler drew heavily on both the widespread antisemitism of the *Kaiserreich* and the long-standing goal of extending territory in the east. Nonetheless, many historians have come to see the roots of Nazism's political success in 1933 as lying principally in the shortcomings of the Weimar years. In this analysis, the Germans were not inherently incapable of establishing a functioning democracy, and the collapse into Nazism was precipitated by the external pressures on the republic as much as by its internal weaknesses. Furthermore, even though the republic's early opponents in particular were inspired by the prospect of reestablishing the 'natural' order of the *Kaiserreich*, the national socialist order which ultimately buried the republic represented anything but a return to conservative values.

The short-term origins and nature of national socialism

The NSDAP had its origins in the *Deutsche Arbeiterpartei* (DAP), launched in Munich just after Germany's defeat in the First World War. The founders (Anton Drexler, a railway worker, and Karl Harrer, a journalist, neither destined for political greatness) hoped to alienate workers from the Marxist left-wing parties, which propounded the class struggle (nationally divisive) and the international solidarity of workers (at the expense of national strength and independence).

The DAP might have remained one of the many such insignificant splinter groups in southern Germany had it not been for its discovery by Adolf Hitler. Born in Austria in 1889, close to the border with Germany, Hitler had grown up detesting the multi-racial Habsburg Empire and, like many Austrian German nationalists, dreaming of a true German nation state. A loner whose parents died while he was still young, Hitler drifted to Vienna in 1907. Having failed to enter the prestigious Viennese

Kunsthochschule (Art College), Hitler resided in cheap rooms and hostels, eking out a living painting picture postcards. He also read avidly, including the antisemitic pamphlets which circulated widely in early-twentieth-century Vienna, and developed a disgust for the poorer Jews he encountered in the city. He was impressed by the tactics of the populist and somewhat antisemitic mayor of Vienna, Karl Lueger, and horrified by the chaotic scenes in the multinational, multilingual and inoperable Austrian parliament. Hitler moved to Germany in 1913 and enrolled in the Bavarian army when war broke out. War gave him his first truly motivating experience, and he served bravely, though never rising above the rank of corporal. When defeat came, Hitler regarded it as a calamity which, he believed, resulted from an international Jewish conspiracy against Germany.

After the war, Hitler became a political officer in the Bavarian army and in September 1919 was dispatched to observe a DAP meeting. Angered by a speaker who favoured Bavarian independence from the rest of Germany, Hitler himself began to speak with such passion and conviction in favour of German national unity that the leaders persuaded him to join the party. In the following months, Hitler developed his oratorical skills and began to address meetings as a key speaker. In an age without television and radio, political meetings were popular social events for which admission could be charged. As news spread in Munich of this talented and passionate speaker, attendances at DAP meetings grew, membership increased and the party's finances improved.

Hitler played a major role in defining the DAP's aims within its 25-point programme of 1920. From the outset there were two distinct strands to the party's aims, reflected in the longer name – *Nationalsozialistische Deutsche Arbeiterpartei* – adopted (at Hitler's suggestion) that year. *National* aims – the rejection of the *Versailler Vertrag*, the removal of Jews from German life, the inclusion of all Germans in a single state – coexisted with traditionally *socialist* goals which would strengthen workers and weaken the power of capitalist monopolies. In this way, the NSDAP hoped to rally the masses to the nationalist cause in a populist party. In practice, the party later neglected the socialist aspects of its programme and did little to alter the balance of economic power once in power. Hitler was always more committed to the programme's nationalist and antisemitic elements.

By 1921 the NSDAP was entirely dependent on Hitler, who insisted on becoming party chairman with extensive powers. Once his position was secure, Hitler began to make contact with the other **völkisch** parties and groups in southern Germany and beyond,

völkisch

For the early German nationalists who influenced Hitler's political development, the *Volk* became an almost mystical community, linked by racial characteristics. The adjective *völkisch* represented a particular racial nationalism, based on a misguided pseudo-scientific belief in notions of racial superiority and largely borrowed from Charles Darwin's work on the evolution of species and the survival of the fittest. Applied to the human race, *völkisch* agitators claimed that the Jews were an inferior, parasitic race who sought to undermine and dominate their host communities throughout the world.

which would later merge under his leadership. The party acquired a paramilitary wing, the *Sturmabteilungen* (SA), originally designed to protect party meetings. The SA's tight military formation appealed to many denied the opportunity to serve in the restricted *Reichswehr*, and to those who relished the opportunity for violence against their political opponents. The party also developed its uniforms and symbols (adopting the ancient swastika symbol, already in common use among *völkisch* groups). Hitler paid great attention to organising the party's visual and propaganda appeal, as well as ensuring strict hierarchical control over the growing party.

The turning point in the early NSDAP's development came in November 1923 with Hitler's failed putsch attempt (see p. 67). Briefly jailed in 1924, Hitler wrote the first volume of *Mein Kampf*, part flattering autobiography, part confused political tract, which served as the (usually unread) bible of the movement. While in prison, Hitler reviewed his political strategies and resolved never again to attempt to take power by force. Instead, he would seek power through the ballot box and subvert the parliamentary system he despised by its own means.

While in prison, Hitler appointed no substitute who might later challenge his leadership, and left the NSDAP to splinter into warring factions. In 1925 he was able to unite the opposing sides under his leadership and rebuild the party, now extending its reach into the rest of Germany by coopting similar groups. Hitler entrenched his position by assuming the title *Führer*. There would be no debates about the party programme and no elections to the party leadership; Hitler would appoint his own men. Hitler adopted and projected the role of a political messiah, come to redeem Germany from the ills of republican democracy and national weakness. In the following years, Hitler seems to have believed the myth which he and the party concocted of his special destiny to lead Germany.

In an attempt to extend the party's appeal beyond the working classes, who remained stubbornly loyal to the social democratic and communist parties, the party created special sections for teachers, doctors, lawyers and others, in addition to the youth group and paramilitary wings. As Chapter 3 explained, the party made little electoral headway while the *Weimarer Republik* remained outwardly stable during the 1924–29 period. However, Hitler's emergence during these years as the unchallenged leader of the *völkisch* movement and the NSDAP's creation of a strong organisational hierarchy with roots in various societal sectors enabled the party to grow rapidly when its chance came amid the Wall Street and Young Plan crises of 1929–30.

Nazi support was not evenly distributed across society. As we have noted, the largely leaderless lower middle classes (the *Mittelstand*) were disproportionately inclined to vote NSDAP, whereas the industrial working class tended to maintain their strong ties to the SPD's network of organisations, and the industrial unemployed were more likely to prefer communism as a radical solution. Religious affiliation also played a role. Many Roman Catholics remained loyal to their *Zentrum* party, with the result that the Nazis' Bavarian homeland contained disproportionately few NSDAP voters. Conversely, Protestants had fewer institutional ties, producing stronger NSDAP support in the north and east, particularly in the rural areas where farming suffered economic crisis during the late 1920s and early 1930s. Nonetheless, the Nazis found protest voters, dissatisfied with the ailing republic, across all sections of society. The young and those who had previously not voted were particularly likely to vote NSDAP, enthused by the opportunity for radical change.

The composition of the NSDAP's membership reflected these trends. Even after the party's dynamic growth began in the early 1930s, industrial workers were under-represented in the membership, while salaried workers, self-employed craftsmen and merchants – the core of the *Mittelstand* – formed a disproportionately large group among NSDAP recruits. That said, NSDAP members also came from all walks of life.

Hitler's determination to achieve complete power within the party was repeated in his refusal to accept a subordinate role in national government. There were risks in this approach, since the NSDAP was running dangerously short of money by early 1933, having already financed three national and various regional election campaigns during the previous year. Contrary to earlier beliefs, the party only became a major recipient of subsidies from the major industrialists after it had achieved power; capitalist interests were just as likely to fund other parties, and Hitler was not their pawn. Equally, the enthusiasm for Hitler's outspoken rejection of Weimar was slowly beginning to wane since he had taken no concrete actions. Still Hitler preferred to take power by legal means (while not hesitating to use the SA to intimidate political opponents). Thus Hindenburg's call to Hitler to form a government came just in time for the NSDAP, still secure in the public's affections.

Taking power: the *Machtergreifung*

Historians often refer to 30 January 1933 as the day of Hitler's *Machtergreifung* – literally, his 'seizure of power'. In fact, Hitler did not seize power but accepted it legally from the *Reichspräsident* as leader of the largest parliamentary party and supported by a third of the vote given in free elections. The real *Machtergreifung* came in the following months when Hitler acted to overturn what remained of Weimar's political order and to remove the remaining legal restraints on his power.

To fulfil his self-appointed mission as Germany's redeemer, Hitler needed to eliminate the *Reichstag* as a forum of political opposition, coopt or destroy competing political parties, remove the freedom of the *Länder* to pursue alternative policies, curtail the powers of the *Reichspräsident* and transform the NSDAP itself into an organisation which no longer agitated for radical change but instead supported stable government under Hitler. Furthermore, he needed to secure the loyalty of the army, and of the whole plethora of social and religious institutions, from trade unions to chess clubs, many of which were controlled by the Nazis' political opponents. The entire process is described by the word *Gleichschaltung*. Normally translated as 'coordination', the term reflects the way that the disparate structures and organisations of German public life were brought into line (*gleichgeschaltet*) with, and subordinated to, the structures of the NSDAP itself.

Hitler achieved these goals with breathtaking speed. He began by calling fresh *Reichstag* elections, hoping to secure a clear NSDAP majority. Before polling day, the *Reichstag* building itself burned to the ground. The government blamed the communists, but the speed of official reaction caused many to suspect that the Nazis had themselves committed arson as a pretext to hinder a free election campaign. The same night, KPD leaders and officials were rounded up and imprisoned, and the party effectively banned. Within hours a decree, 'Zum Schutz von Volk und Staat', was issued under Article 48 of the Weimar constitution. This limited the key freedoms of speech, assembly and the press. Even this degree of political intimidation did not produce an absolute NSDAP majority, though the party's share of the vote rose to 44 per cent.

Unwilling to depend on his DNVP coalition partners or to allow the opposition parties a forum in the *Reichstag*, Hitler prepared an *Ermächtigungsgesetz* ('Enabling Act'), introduced at the first formal meeting of parliament. This allowed the government full powers to take whatever measures seemed appropriate for Germany's recovery, without *Reichstag* support, for the following four years. In his speech (Document 4a), Hitler promised to preserve Germany's constitutional framework. Only the SPD voted against the Bill; the elected KPD members were prevented from taking their seats, while the other parties believed they had secured guarantees of continued influence, or feared reprisals if they resisted. With the *Ermächtigungsgesetz*, the corpse of Weimar parliamentarism was finally buried.

Within months, the competing political parties had themselves disappeared. The SPD was banned after some of the leadership emigrated to Czechoslovakia to establish a secure base for the party, enabling the government to denounce the SPD as a hostile, foreign force. The *Zentrum* dissolved itself as the price for the Concordat, the treaty between the Roman Catholic leadership in the Vatican and the German government which promised the preservation of the church's status in return for an end to its political activity. The remaining parties, faced with Hitler's dominance, either disintegrated or merged with the NSDAP. In July 1933 a law prohibited the formation of any further parties; by the end of the year, the NSDAP was declared to be one with the state. The emasculated *Reichstag* still met occasionally, but now consisted solely of NSDAP representatives elected intermittently from an unopposed list of candidates. This *gleichgeschaltete* 'parliament' legalised further changes which had not been authorised by the *Ermächtigungsgesetz*, and thereafter simply applauded government announcements.

Germany's federal system was also swiftly abolished, and with it the regional autonomies and diversity which had characterised German politics for centuries. The SA was encouraged to take forward the 'national revolution' by striking blows at the Nazis' political opponents in the *Länder*. The disturbances which ensued served as a pretext for the central government to send in *Reichskommissare* ('*Reich* commissioners') to restore order. By mid-March, Nazi-led governments were installed in the *Länder* and the *Landtage* (regional parliaments) had passed their own *Ermächtigungsgesetze*. Laws of late March and early April 1933 finalised the *Gleichschaltung* of the *Länder* to the *Reich*. The *Landtage*, already virtually powerless, were henceforth filled in the same proportions as the *Reichstag*, thus guaranteeing the NSDAP–DNVP majority throughout the country, and *Reichsstatthalter* (governors) were appointed by Hitler to impose central government's requirements in each *Land*. Early in 1934 the obsolete *Landtage* and the *Reichsrat* were abolished.

Hitler had no need to unseat the elderly *Reichspräsident*, Hindenburg, who, despite his initial unwillingness to appoint Hitler, did not hinder the *Gleichschaltung* process. When Hindenburg died on 2 August 1934, Hitler merged the offices of *Reichskanzler* and *Reichspräsident* to become *Führer*. As head of state, Hitler also assumed supreme command of the armed forces. In a referendum, a device used by the NSDAP to demonstrate public support for the regime, almost 90 per cent of voters legitimised this change.

The assumption of political power would, however, be incomplete unless the state's employees – *Beamten*, teachers, judges – implemented the new government's policies. The government enacted a law reforming the German civil service in early April 1933, providing for political opponents (principally social democrats) and Jews to be removed from office. The NSDAP installed some of its own members in important posts to ensure the civil service's political reliability, but the party lacked sufficient qualified and able members to achieve blanket control. However, many *Beamten* recognised that their best interests lay in joining the NSDAP. Not all became committed national socialists, but they nonetheless ensured a high degree of NSDAP control over Germany's administrative and judicial structures. In particular, the extensive politicisation of the law, now exercised in the interests of national socialism rather than true justice, strongly contributed to the breakdown of the *Rechtsstaat* (the rule of law).

The early months and years of the *Drittes Reich* also saw the *Gleichschaltung* of Germany's social organisations. The independent trade unions, mainly associated with the SPD and KPD, were forcibly taken over on 2 May 1933 and merged within the NSDAP-led *Deutsche Arbeitsfront* (DAF). Unlike most trade unions, the DAF regimented workers and contained rather than represented their grievances. The banning of the parties ended the independent existence of their youth groups, sports associations and similar societies. These too became *gleichgeschaltet*, the youth groups under the aegis of the *Hitler-Jugend* (for boys) and the *Bund deutscher Mädel* (for girls). Not only did these NSDAP-led youth associations enjoy a monopoly status, but by 1936 membership was made virtually (and in 1939 actually) compulsory for all under-eighteens. Similarly, the various professional organisations (for teachers, farmers, etc.) were subordinated to NSDAP-controlled institutions. Even ostensibly non-political organisations such as sports clubs and choirs were brought, at least nominally, within the Nazi fold. Roman Catholic organisations retained their independence for a little longer, initially protected by Hitler's Concordat with the Vatican, but even these were *gleichgeschaltet* as the church was increasingly restricted to purely religious activities.

In the cultural sphere, too, *Gleichschaltung* proceeded apace. Membership of the *Reichskulturkammer* (*Reich* Cultural Chamber), under Hitler's loyal ally Joseph Goebbels, became mandatory for writers and artists. The *Kammer* barred the NSDAP's political opponents and ensured that only works acceptable to the national socialist ideal appeared. Similarly, independent and opposition newspapers and magazines were either closed or taken over. Radio, film and the nascent television service were also brought under *Reich* control and deployed in an ongoing propaganda blitz, masterminded by Goebbels.

Finally, Hitler needed to rein in the NSDAP, which by mid-1933 had fulfilled its purpose as a campaigning organisation to achieve electoral victory and state power. Many Nazi activists, inspired by the original party programme's socialist elements, had aspired to a true national revolution which would entirely sweep away Germany's economic and social structures. The SA had directed this energy into the *Machtergreifung* in the regions, but once the NSDAP's power was secure, Hitler was anxious to assert his own authority over these potentially unreliable forces. As early as July 1933 Hitler asserted that the revolution was over and called on the party to support the state. Still concerned at the SA's potential rivalry and its leaders' interest in a wider social revolution, Hitler agreed to the virtual liquidation of the organisation. On 30 June 1934 – the 'Night of the Long Knives' – the more loyal **Schutzstaffeln** (SS) murdered the SA's leader, Ernst Röhm, and his associates, and took the opportunity to kill several other potential rivals to the *Führer*.

Despite the far-reaching impact of Hitler's *Gleichschaltung*, one key pocket of autonomy remained in the churches. The Nazis had little success with their attempt to form a national Protestant church in place of the traditional, regionally based Lutheran and reformist churches. Despite the installation of a '*Reichsbischof*' and efforts to breed a specifically German form of Christianity, which included ancient pagan overtones and attempted to deny Jesus Christ's Jewish origins, the *Deutsche Christen* attracted only a minority of German Protestants. In protest, many Protestants organised themselves within the *bekennende Kirche* ('confessing church') under Martin Niemöller, which upheld traditional doctrines and, where possible, defied the un-Christian aspects of Nazi rule. The Roman Catholic church, backed by a far stronger international organisation, was as formidable an opponent under Hitler as it had been during Bismarck's *Kulturkampf*. A papal letter condemning attacks on the church, 'Mit brennender Sorge' ('With burning anxiety'), was read from all Catholic pulpits during 1937. Yet neither major church risked an all-out attack on national socialism for fear of the consequences (the imprisonment of outspoken clergy was not uncommon in the *Drittes Reich*); the papacy generally preferred the authoritarian rule of fascist governments such as Hitler's to the perceived risk of communist invasion and the dismantling of the church.

Despite the neutralisation of the Nazis' real and potential rivals, Hitler's personal accumulation of ultimate power, and his status as a leader of near divine status, responsible only to God, destiny and the mystical *Volksgemeinschaft* (the national community embodied in his person), the *Drittes Reich* did not enjoy clear, strong

> ### *Schutzstaffeln* (SS)
>
> Founded in 1925 as an elite protection squad for Hitler, the SS developed under Heinrich Himmler to become the Nazis' chief instrument of political control. The SS, a party organisation fiercely loyal to Hitler, became interwoven with the state police and security forces by 1934. All were eventually brought under Himmler's central command. This 'state within the state' controlled the secret and criminal police and the *Konzentrationslager*. Its supposedly racially pure *Waffen-SS* division enforced Nazi control over the territories conquered by the army once war began.

government. Indeed, the reverse was true, since Hitler had little interest in everyday government, concerning himself mainly with the broad sweep of policy direction or matters of personal interest (such as plans for the reconstruction of his hometown, Linz). Nonetheless, Hitler – as *Führer* – was the ultimate legal authority in the system. The *Führerbefehl* (*Führer* order), written or oral, became as binding as laws passed by more traditional methods. His authority could be delegated to the subordinates he appointed in accordance with the *Führerprinzip* (*Führer* principle).

Hitler disliked being drawn into debates which forced him to decide in favour of one or another policy, much preferring to retain his mythical status by remaining above the political fray. Consequently, cabinet meetings ceased altogether by 1938. Hitler also wished to avoid the emergence of any strong power centres within the Nazi government system which might one day challenge his ultimate authority. Consequently he seems deliberately to have allowed the creation of a confused system of government ministries, agencies and special offices, some with equivalents in the party structure. Their responsibilities often overlapped (for instance, numerous offices competed for responsibility in economic policy, particularly once the war began), and there was no clear hierarchy of control. Yet despite the apparent chaos of this polycratic (multi-centred) system, Hitler was not a weak dictator. His generally acknowledged authority as the personification of the German people's national will ensured that his underlings would not attempt to oppose his known wishes or his general policy. Instead, Hitler remained strong precisely because of his distance from the often acrimonious competition to fulfil his will most effectively. Meanwhile, collective responsibility for government was abandoned as the individual ministries and special offices asserted the right to govern under the *Führerprinzip*, particularly if they could claim a *Führerbefehl* to legitimate their actions. He who had the *Führer*'s ear had real power.

This far-reaching reorganisation of German public life has often been described as a 'legal revolution'. Since the Weimar constitution of 1919 had lacked sufficient checks and balances to preserve its democratic spirit, it was easy for the NSDAP to use formal, legal devices (the presidential decree, and after March 1933 the *Ermächtigungsgesetz*) to dismantle the entire democratic system and to round up opponents as enemies of the state, many of whom were quickly put to work building the first *Konzentrationslager*. This notwithstanding, the violent intimidation of the SA and SS, both of which organisations resorted to illegal acts which undermined the state, often created the framework for the Nazi government's actions. In this sense, the 'legal revolution' represented only an extremely formal and somewhat warped legality, frequently underpinned by serious abuses of basic human rights. It is perhaps testimony to the shortcomings of the Weimar years and the Germans' frustration with democracy that so many were prepared to look away and ignore the foundations upon which the new stability was being constructed.

The *Drittes Reich* in power

What did Hitler hope to achieve once the NSDAP had consolidated its hold on state power? The answers lie deep in the roots of Hitler's *Weltanschauung*, his ideological outlook, forged in the early twentieth century and confirmed by his experience of defeat in 1918.

First, there were foreign policy goals. Initially Hitler continued the course of earlier *Reichskanzler* in attempting to throw off the remaining shackles of the *Versailler Vertrag*. In the short term this involved further strengthening the German armed forces and reoccupying the demilitarised Rhineland. Thereafter, Hitler aimed to recover the lost German territories – the Saarland, the eastern provinces – and to expand the *Reich* into the other German-speaking areas (particularly Austria, the Sudetenland and Alsace-Lorraine). In the third phase, Hitler's national aspirations became more acutely fused with his mistaken notions of German racial supremacy. Hitler believed that Germans required more *Lebensraum* ('living space'). This was to be achieved by expanding eastwards into the lands settled by the supposedly inferior Slav nations. Conquered Slavs would act as virtual slave labour for the *Reich*, and eastern Europe would secure supplies of agricultural products, fuel and other important raw materials. Hitler was well aware that eastward expansion would eventually provoke confrontation with the Soviet Union. However, he saw this outcome as inevitable in a battle for both racial and ideological dominance, since he despised communism and believed it to be part of the Jewish plot to achieve world domination. The defeat of Slav Russia would also entrench Germany's supposed racial supremacy. Some readings of Hitler's intentions suggest that he aimed for global German dominance, initially in partnership with the British Empire, with the USA eliminated as a significant power factor.

Hitler's domestic agenda was closely linked to his foreign policy goals. It was essential to rebuild the German economy to prepare the country for the inevitable war which would secure territorial expansion. Equally, Germany's racial stock must be purified and strengthened to ensure the *Volk*'s supremacy in the battle to come. Consequently, the racially impure (supposedly Jews, gypsies, negroes, homosexuals, the disabled and others fitted into this category) had to be removed from German society as far as possible, while measures should be taken to improve the physical prowess of boys and young men, Germany's future soldiers, and to enable the country's womenfolk to give birth to racially pure specimens.

These objectives, albeit based on an ignorant, irrational and bigoted view of the world and humanity, constituted a coherent long-term plan in Hitler's mind. This is not to say, however, that Hitler had already mapped out the precise course of his actions in 1933, or that he expected to achieve all he desired. Rather, specific decisions and the timing of actions were often a response to other developments, and the chaotic system of governance in the *Drittes Reich* ensured that not every initiative came from Hitler himself. Some historians have argued that the Nazis' expansionist aims formed part of a continuum in German foreign policy stretching back to the nineteenth century; others believe that the radicalisation of Nazi foreign policy reflected the movement's need to maintain a sense of dynamism, particularly as the leadership had clamped down on further reform within Germany itself by 1934 (at the latest with the 'Night of the Long Knives') and needed to divert attention from growing economic problems in the later 1930s. Nonetheless, the increasingly murderous course of Nazi policy reflected Hitler's long-term goals, as set out in his published writings and internal briefings. In the political framework of the *Drittes Reich*, the broad direction of policy was clearly in the *Führer*'s hands, however distorted the interpretation of that policy became in the hands of the deliberately chaotic administration.

On assuming power in 1933, however, notions of world domination remained a distant prospect. The initial priority was economic recovery, for the sake of internal stability as much as to lay the foundations for future German wars. In fact, the German economy had been slowly reviving since 1932, but the new government widely extended work creation schemes and subsidies to industry. Investment went into rearmament, the creation of a network of *Autobahnen* (motorways/freeways) and the extension of the motor industry, with the production of more lorries and cars. Consequently, unemployment fell rapidly. As the government had not discovered new sources of wealth, this was financed by deficit spending, with government bonds issued on the security of future tax revenues. The Nazis retained legislation introduced in the early 1930s, when the recession was at its deepest, to limit prices and wages and the repayment of foreign debts (Hitler also benefited from the ending of reparations, an achievement which predated him). However, imports of raw materials for the armaments industry vastly reduced the *Reichsbank*'s foreign currency reserves during the 1930s, and Germany relied instead on bilateral barter agreements with other countries, while also attempting to increase its level of economic autarky (self-sufficiency). These policies could not function indefinitely. By the late 1930s, it was greatly in Germany's economic interest to acquire new territory and gain access to additional resources. Historians have debated whether Hitler's expansionist policies principally reflected Hitler's political will or Germany's economic requirements. By the late 1930s Germany had also again begun to increase the paper money supply to finance expansion. However, with strict price regulations still in force, there was no new inflationary spiral. The Nazis' long-term economic policy – to the extent that any coherent plan existed – depended on the vast profits which would eventually be made when Germany expanded into eastern Europe and dominated global trade. The failure of this long-term strategy in the defeat of 1945 rendered the *Reichsmark* worthless by the end of the war.

Though Germany's economic revival was being constructed on quicksand, in the short term the ending of mass unemployment and the new prestige construction projects gave most Germans a sense of a successful national rebirth. This helped to obscure the fact that large companies rather than small businessmen were best placed to profit from the recovery, despite the Nazis' vague pre-1933 promises. However, although Hitler did not break the power of the large industrialists and redistribute economic power equally (the Marxist socialist goal) – indeed the large firms received the major government contracts – Hitler was not the puppet of big business, as Marxist historians have sometimes argued. Instead of allowing the free market to flourish, the government increasingly brought the economy under state control, notably with the Four-Year Plan of 1936, designed to enable Germany to fight a war. The Nazis' programme provided for little growth in consumer goods production which would have benefited workers, who were instead diverted by the leisure activities organised by the DAF and its subsidiaries.

Hitler's early diplomatic successes also distracted many Germans from the harsh political realities of the *Drittes Reich*. Hitler was determined to end the Versailles era of restrictions on German rights. He asserted Germany's claims to full sovereignty by demonstratively leaving the League of Nations in October 1933 over the west's un-willingness to agree equitable armament levels for Germany and her neighbours. The return of the Saarland to Germany in 1935 following a plebiscite in the region also underlined Germany's rehabilitation. In the following years Hitler used evidence of European rearmament to justify the expansion of Germany's own armed forces beyond the levels permitted at Versailles; the western allies failed to react.

Still, Hitler initially remained cautious, preferring not to attempt an *Anschluss* with Austria in 1934 while the international community remained united on this point. He also awaited the pretext of a Franco-Soviet treaty before sending German troops into the Rhineland along the sensitive French border in 1936, in defiance of Versailles. The French did not react: eighteen years after the end of the world war it was hard to argue that Germany had no right to station troops throughout her own territory. In 1936 Hitler also seized the opportunity to escape Germany's diplomatic isolation when Italy's relations with Britain and France broke down over Mussolini's occupation of Abyssinia (modern Ethiopia) and Italy's involvement in the Spanish Civil War. Hitler forged an alliance (the '*Achse Berlin–Rom*') with Mussolini, always probable given their similar ideological outlooks. Emboldened by Italy's realignment, Germany's stronger position, and the allies' failure to respond to the reoccupation of the Rhineland, Hitler executed the Austrian *Anschluss* in March 1938 (see p. 180). Again, the international community took no action; after all, the *Anschluss* appeared merely as two German-speaking coun-tries using their right of self-determination to unite.

By this point, Hitler was anxious to exploit the advantages Germany had secured from rearming before other countries could catch up, and to secure additional sources of raw materials to sustain Germany's war preparations. This latter consideration became something of a vicious circle. The greater Germany's ambitions, the greater her resource requirements; yet as Germany's resource requirements grew, so she was forced to look farther afield to fulfil her needs.

Aware by the late 1930s of Britain's unwillingness to ally with Germany, Hitler recognised also that Germany's expansionist agenda must eventually provoke war with the British Empire. He was anxious to neutralise the potential threat from Czechoslovakia before this larger war, but also keen to incorporate into the *Reich* more than three million Germans in the Sudetenland, apportioned to Czechoslovakia from Austria-Hungary after the 1918 defeat. As he also hoped to gain the region's raw materials and strong industrial base, Hitler encouraged the Sudeten Germans to demand their national liberation, confident that Britain and France would not actually go to war over this issue. Though hostilities were briefly threatened, Hitler's gamble in September 1938 paid off. Britain and France persuaded Czechoslovakia to cede the Sudetenland to Germany, while Hitler promised to guarantee the sovereignty of what remained of Czechoslovakia. Thereafter, Hitler encouraged a Slovak declaration of independence, leaving the Czech government in Prague at his mercy. In March 1939 the Czech lands became the German-dominated *Reichsprotektorat Böhmen und*

Mähren ('*Reich* protectorate of Bohemia and Moravia'). Britain and France took no action.

Though Bohemia and Moravia had once belonged to the *Heiliges Römisches Reich*, Hitler had for the first time extended into non-German-speaking territory. The British government of Neville Chamberlain was eager to avoid war, but Hitler's destruction of Czechoslovakia finally ended British patience with Germany. Chamberlain pledged Britain to defend Poland against future attack. Nonetheless, Britain did not succeed in concluding an anti-German pact with Stalin's cautious Soviet Union. Hitler, seeing an opportunity to regain lost German territory in Poland and extend the *Reich's Lebensraum* still further, concluded a *Nichtangriffspakt* (non-aggression pact) with Stalin, allowing for Poland's division between Germany and the Soviet Union (echoing earlier eras when Poland had been divided between Prussia, Russia and the Habsburg Empire). The *Nichtangriffspakt* is a good example of Hitler's willingness to subordinate long-term ideological aims (the defeat of the Slav, communist Soviet Union in the interests of German *Lebensraum*) to short-term practical advantage. Convinced that the British and French would no more intervene over Poland than they had over Austria or Czechoslovakia, Hitler again incited nationalist fervour among Poland's German population and invaded Poland on this pretext on 1 September 1939; meanwhile, Soviet troops entered Poland from the east. Though the German *Wehrmacht* (army) and *Luftwaffe* (airforce) quickly subdued Poland with *Blitzkrieg* tactics, Hitler's wider gamble failed. Britain and France declared war on Germany on 3 September.

Racial war

Initially, the war with the west appeared disastrous. German public opinion firmly opposed a new war, while the military, which had been planning for Germany's full rearmament to be achieved by 1943 at the earliest (even this date represented an optimistic target), knew it was unprepared. Fortunately for Hitler, neither Britain nor France was prepared to attack Germany, public opinion in the United States would not countenance American intervention in a European war, and Hitler had already neutralised the Soviet Union.

Hitler was anxious to avoid a *Zweifrontenkrieg*, the long-standing nightmare scenario of any German leader. It seemed imperative to defeat the western powers before turning to the Soviet Union. Having partially secured control of the northern European sealanes with the occupation of Denmark and Norway in April 1940 (control of the latter's ports was a significant tactical advantage) before the British could act, Germany launched an ambitious attack on France in May 1940, defeating Belgium, Luxemburg and the Netherlands on the way. Northern France was occupied, and the south placed under the largely compliant control of a puppet government based at Vichy. Though the Germans lacked the military strength to defeat the United Kingdom, this rapid series of victories restored German confidence and seems to have convinced Hitler of his invincibility.

Hitler's tactics now altered. Convinced that the Soviet Red Army was fairly weak, and particularly concerned to gain access to further supplies of fuel and food, Hitler

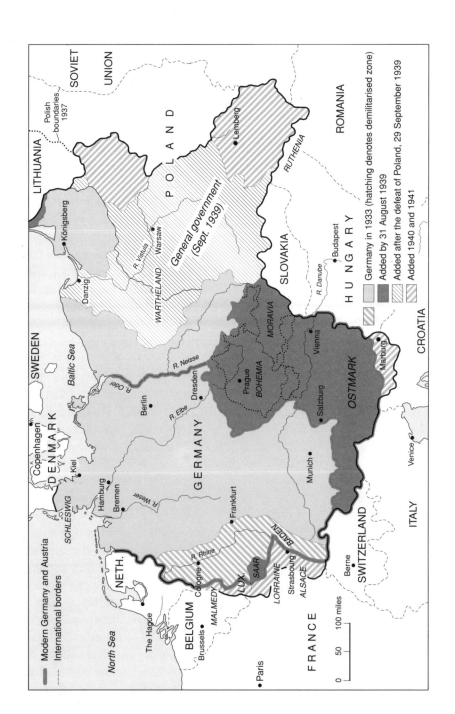

Map 4.1: *Expansion of the Drittes Reich, 1939–1941*

determined to defeat the Soviet Union first and to postpone dealing with the British and the growing American threat. In June 1941 German armies launched a surprise attack on the Soviet Union. Though they occupied much of the western part of the country, they could not take the capital, Moscow, and failed to impose a speedy *Blitzkrieg* defeat on the Polish and French models. The Soviets were stronger than Hitler had imagined and very determined to defend their homeland. As winter set in, the *Wehrmacht* found itself ill-equipped to confront the harsh conditions, particularly against an enemy used to the climate and able to draw on resources well to the east in the Soviet Union's Asian territories. Germany's ally, Japan, proved to have more pressing concerns of its own in China and Southeast Asia than pinning down the Soviets' eastern flank for the Germans' advantage. By early 1943, the German defeat at Stalingrad heralded the collapse of Hitler's war effort in the east.

Not content with the *Zweifrontenkrieg* he had initiated by invading the Soviet Union, Hitler also drew the United States into the war in December 1941, believing that a swift victory in the Soviet Union by early 1942 would release resources to turn against the British and American forces. Germany's long war in Russia merely confirmed the magnitude of Hitler's strategic blunder. Between them, the British Empire, the USA and the Soviet Union had far greater resources than Germany could muster, particularly after her Italian allies collapsed in 1943. By 1944, American and Canadian forces had joined their British allies and launched an invasion of German-occupied Europe. Within months, France and the Low Countries were liberated; Aachen was in allied hands by October 1944, and Germany's defences on the Rhine were breached the following spring. As allied armies marched on Germany from all directions during 1945, and under the widespread devastation wreaked by allied air raids, Hitler accepted that the Germans had betrayed their own nation and took his life on 30 April. The *Drittes Reich* collapsed almost without trace once Hitler was gone. Within days, Berlin surrendered. The Nazi leaders emigrated, went into hiding or, in a few cases, also committed suicide. As the allies established their occupation regimes (see Chapter 5), the NSDAP and its subsidiaries simply dissolved. It appeared that the force of Hitler's willpower had sustained the movement and the war effort, and that without the *Führer* the German people were released.

So far we have considered Hitler's military war of expansion, but the *Führer* was simultaneously leading another, related battle. The war for Germany's racial purity was perhaps the more important struggle in Hitler's mind. While targeting the neighbouring Slav countries as much for their supposed racial inferiority as for the opportunities they provided for *Lebensraum*, within Germany Hitler acted to strengthen the racial stock by progressively removing to the prisons and *Konzentrationslager* homosexuals (considered racially degenerate since they contributed nothing to the gene pool and might ensnare the racially pure) and the Sinti and Roma (more commonly known as gypsies, and also regarded as racially inferior infiltrators of the German people). The 'asocial' (alcoholics, the workshy and other persons deemed unfit or unwilling to contribute to the *Volksgemeinschaft*) could also expect arrest, imprisonment and forced labour. A full-blown campaign of 'euthanasia' – in fact state murder – of the mentally and physically disabled began in 1939, building on earlier legislation to sterilise those with hereditary diseases and later extended to other groups. The Nazis believed that the disabled were a drain on national resources as well as a blemish on the *Volk*'s racial purity. Despite a public outcry against 'euthanasia' inspired by the Catholic bishop of Münster, Galen, the killings continued in secret. Besides removing these supposed racial cankers, none of which represented a political threat to the regime, the Nazis also attempted a proactive approach by encouraging those pronounced racially pure to produce more healthy specimens for the *Vaterland*. These attempts to manipulate humanity and encourage selective breeding were governed by blind ideological motivations, often termed 'eugenics'.

Despite the attention the Nazi regime paid to the groups already mentioned, Hitler regarded the Jewish people as the most pernicious threat to the new German world order, and was determined to prevent Jews from poisoning the allegedly pure 'Aryan' race which incorporated 'thoroughbred' Germans and their near neighbours (Scandinavians, Anglo-Saxons, etc.). Despite Hitler's antisemitic convictions, and the usefulness of antisemitism in popularising Nazism, it should be noted that Jews comprised less than 1 per cent of Germany's population in 1933. Nonetheless, Hitler (along with many Germans) believed that the Jews had conspired to engineer Germany's defeat in the First World War.

Antisemitism, was by no means a new or uniquely German phenomenon. It had flourished for some two thousand years since the Romans had forced the Jewish people to leave their traditional settlements in the Holy Land and sent them into exile. Consequently, Jewish populations existed throughout the world, but retained their religious and cultural traditions, never integrating fully with their host communities and hence encouraging suspicion. The spread of Christianity deepened animosity towards the Jews, who were accused of having murdered Christ. Jewish populations were attacked in Europe during the Christian crusades to recover the Holy Land in the middle ages, and were often subjected to restrictive legislation. The ban in many countries on their owning land led many Jews into professions such as tax collection and money lending, occupations which exposed them to further popular antipathy. In tsarist Russia, such restrictions encouraged some Jews to join revolutionary movements in the late nineteenth century. The presence of Jews among the leaders of the Russian Revolution in 1917 enabled antisemites to associate Jews with bloody Bolshevik upheaval; paradoxically, as many Jews had prospered as industrialists, bankers, lawyers and merchants in the German-speaking area following their emancipation from earlier restrictions in the mid-nineteenth century, Jews were also claimed to be bleeding honest workers dry as the unacceptable face of capitalism. The contribution to the *Kaiser*'s army of many Jews who considered themselves first and foremost Germans was conveniently ignored against the overwhelming background of suspicion and hatred against the Jews after the defeat of 1918. The unscientific belief in the Jews' racial inferiority derived from the growth of post-Darwinist, *völkisch* thought, discussed above (p. 86).

The NSDAP's 1920 programme had promised to end the Jews' status as equal citizens in German society, and Hitler began the task within weeks of taking power.

Jews were quickly purged from the civil service, and banned from inheriting land or practising the law. Restrictions were placed on the numbers of Jews attending university. In two symbolic acts, the Nazis organised a day's boycott of Jewish businesses on 1 April 1933, and publicly burned books by un-German (and particularly Jewish) authors. The *Nürnberger Gesetze* launched a further radicalisation of antisemitic policy.

Antisemitic laws were introduced slowly, lest a sudden crackdown on Jewish life damage the economy. By the late 1930s, however, the Jews were being routinely excluded from economic life and induced to transfer their business interests to 'racially pure' Aryans. The Nazis aimed to make Germans aware of their distinction from Jews, and to encourage Jews to consider emigration, the simplest means of solving Germany's 'Jewish problem'. Around two-fifths of Germany's Jews emigrated between 1933 and 1939, and half of Austria's Jewish population in the year after the 1938 *Anschluss*. (Antisemitic legislation was introduced in Austria in a single wave.) Emigration was particularly encouraged by the events of the '*Reichskristallnacht*'.

The emigration policy became more difficult after western countries began blocking further Jewish immigration into their own countries. It was, however, Hitler's war which proved the greatest hindrance to Nazi plans of racial cleansing by discriminatory but mainly peaceful means. The occupation of western Poland brought millions of Jews under German rule at a stroke; millions more were added by the occupation of eastern Poland and the western Soviet Union in 1941. Clearly, cleansing the engorged *Reich* by emigration was no longer feasible; an ambitious plan to relocate Europe's Jewish population to the French colony of Madagascar was judged impractical given the other economic priorities in wartime. Instead, between 1939 and 1941 Germany adopted a policy of murder to remove the 'Jewish problem'. For committed Nazis, the Second World War was principally waged over racial supremacy.

Much debate has centred on the further radicalisation of antisemitic policy which accompanied the outbreak and development of the war. Some historians have seen in Hitler's undoubted extreme antisemitism an intention from the outset to murder European Jewry. This 'intentionalist' view is countered by those who point to a 'structuralist' interpretation, arguing that the shift from emigration to extermination was not strategically planned but resulted from the general brutalisation of the war and the competition between different agencies to fulfil Hitler's broad objectives in the chaotic government structures of the *Drittes Reich*. It is also pointed out that the campaign to persuade Jews to emigrate before 1939 would not have been pursued with such vigour had Hitler's intention always been to exterminate them later, a policy which required transporting German and Austrian Jewish émigrés from all across occupied Europe to the death camps after 1941.

No order for the systematic murder of the Jews bearing Hitler's name has ever been discovered, yet the truth probably lies somewhere between these two interpretative schools of thought. As with German expansion, the removal of the Jews was clearly one of Hitler's long-term objectives, but not one for which he made firm plans. The war made Jewish extermination possible, and even desirable in the occupied territories for Nazi authorities uncertain of how to administer a large Jewish population. While the extermination policy may well have begun at the initiative of local commanders, it could not have proceeded without Hitler's knowledge or assent, not least because the killing programme consumed valuable resources which could have been deployed elsewhere in the war effort.

> ### *Reichskristallnacht* ('The night of broken glass'), 9 November 1938
>
> Following the murder of a German embassy official in Paris by a Polish Jew whose parents had been expelled from the *Reich*, Goebbels orchestrated a 'spontaneous' wave of anti-Jewish outrage throughout Germany, which saw the burning of synagogues and the looting and destruction of Jewish businesses, mainly by committed Nazis. Around ninety Jews were killed, and thousands more arrested. The Jewish community was fined a billion marks for the material damage which the Germans had caused. Most Germans, however, were appalled at this violence on their doorsteps; the Nazis never again attempted similar actions on German soil.

The radicalisation of Nazi antisemitism began with the occupation of western Poland. The districts closest to the *Reich* were annexed to Germany itself. Non-Germans were mainly removed from these territories to the rest of occupied Poland (known as the *Generalgouvernement*) to make room for German settlers. Throughout Poland, the SS murdered or imprisoned Poles who might threaten the German occupation. Meanwhile, the Polish Jews were concentrated in closed-off sectors of the major Polish cities, such as Warsaw and Lódz, known as ghettos. Here they lived in cramped conditions with poor rations and without medical attention. Many died of starvation or the diseases which soon became rampant.

The invasion of the Soviet Union, where millions more Jews resided, took matters a step further. Here SS *Einsatzgruppen* followed behind the *Wehrmacht*, killing communist officials, Soviet Jews, Soviet Red Army leaders and other likely opponents of the Nazi occupation. However, it was quickly clear that mass shootings were inadequate as a means of executing all these groups, particularly the millions of Jews. Notions of resettling Europe's Jewish population in conquered territories further to the east became redundant once it was clear that the Soviet Union would not be swiftly defeated in a *Blitzkrieg*. The situation was exacerbated by the regional Nazi chiefs (the *Gauleiter*), who were anxious to please Hitler by ridding their districts of all Jews and who dispatched the first transports of Jews from Germany and other occupied countries to the Baltic states and the *Generalgouvernement*.

The *Generalgouvernement*, unable to absorb any further Jews into its ghettos, or to persuade the authorities further east to take any more, insisted on a more radical solution to the problem. Here historians remain uncertain of the precise chain of events. It is clear, however, that Hermann Göring, Hitler's *Reichsmarschall*, called on Reinhard Heydrich, head of the *Reich*'s security services, to make plans for a 'final solution of the Jewish question' ('Endlösung der Judenfrage') in late July 1941, and that experiments to execute Soviet soldiers by poison gas were conducted that autumn. Poison gas consequently emerged as a potential means of murdering large numbers with minimal brutality – the Nazis were not motivated by a concern to grant their victims a less horrific death, but to spare *Wehrmacht* and SS soldiers the gruesome bloodshed involved in mass shootings. It is also clear that the first *Vernichtungslager* (extermination camps) were constructed in occupied Poland in late 1941 and early 1942. The most infamous *Vernichtungslager*, Auschwitz, was developed during 1942 on the basis of an existing *Konzentrationslager*. It should be noted that the *Vernichtungslager*, none of which was situated within the pre-1937 territory of the *Reich*, had a distinctly different purpose – killing – from the *Konzentrationslager*, which were built in Germany and beyond and populated chiefly by political opponents, criminals, homosexuals, prisoners of war and other groups (including Jews) deemed noxious by the Nazis. Prisoners in *Konzentrationslager* such as Dachau, Buchenwald and Mauthausen were used as slave labour, and the death rates from execution, exhaustion or disease were high.

Even though the mass extermination of the Jews may well have developed as a response to extreme practical pressures and in the context of the brutality of the eastern front, historians agree that the policy was confirmed from Berlin no later than the autumn of 1941 and formalised in January 1942 at the Wannsee conference. This meeting, held just outside Berlin, brought together the various agencies involved in the mass transportation of Jews to the east. To maintain secrecy, the minutes of the meeting again referred simply to the '*Endlösung*' of the 'Jewish question'. History knows the outcome as the Holocaust. It is estimated that some six million Jews died in the Holocaust, though the precise figure will never be known. Many of them arrived at the *Vernichtungslager* in railway goods wagons and were murdered within hours. Even at the height of the war, the *Drittes Reich* used much-needed resources to transport Jews to their deaths, generally preferring to fulfil the ultimate ideological goal of anti-semitism rather than spare the Jews and utilise their labour in the war effort.

Since the war, debate has raged over responsibility for these excesses. While a handful of the key Nazis (those who had not committed suicide) were tried at Nuremberg in 1945–46 for crimes against humanity, it was clear that Nazi crimes – the Holocaust itself and the extraordinary levels of suffering and death inflicted on *Konzentrationslager* prisoners – would have been impossible without the active cooperation of very many military personnel and civilians. Many Germans claimed to have known nothing of the *Vernichtungslager*, believing that the Jews were merely being resettled somewhere further east. However, many – soldiers, SS men, officials, even railway workers and their relatives and friends – did know the truth and maintained the system either directly in the camps, indirectly in the offices and railway sidings where the transports were organised, or through silence and inaction. Many maintained after the war that they had only been following orders, and that disobedience would have risked their own lives and reprisals against their families. The committed Nazis depended on the apathetic and the fearful; they in turn, having allowed the destruction of Germany's democratic institutions and the creation of the dictatorship, could merely acquiesce in Nazi crimes. This said, it would clearly be misleading to suggest that any more than a relatively small number of Germans had direct knowledge of the form taken by the '*Endlösung der Judenfrage*', or that the German people as a whole enthusiastically approved of mass murder as a means of removing Jewish influence, despite the widely challenged claims made in the mid-1990s by Daniel Goldhagen in his book *Hitler's Willing Executioners.*

For Germans, the Holocaust still makes the question of *Vergangenheitsbewältigung* (dealing with the past) unusually difficult. In the late 1980s, controversy raged among West German historians in the *Historikerstreit* (historians' conflict) over the extent to which the Holocaust should be viewed as a historical event comparable with others, or as a unique occurrence which marked out the Germans as particularly evil. Historians associated with the political right and keen to resurrect a sense of German national pride argued that the Holocaust should be seen in the context of other genocides and mass murders, particularly noting the excesses of Stalinism in the Soviet Union, where millions had died in political purges and in the famine which accompanied the suppression of private farming. For their critics, often associated with the left, there was no question that the Holocaust was uniquely evil and that an attempt to view this part of German history dispassionately was grossly disrespectful to the Nazis' victims. Controversy continued in the 1990s over the best way of commemorating the victims of the Holocaust, with critics maintaining that it was time for Germany to move on and resist the perpetual burden of guilt for the sins of earlier generations.

Germany was not the first nation to embark on a genocidal war against another people (Armenians had endured enormous losses at Turkish hands and American Indians were decimated by European settlers, to give but two examples) and has not been the last (as the wars in Rwanda and former Yugoslavia testified at the end of the twentieth century). However, perhaps no similar crime in world history has been implemented on such a scale and as systematically as the Nazis' attempt to exterminate the Jews, aided and abetted by many ordinary Germans and by collaborators in the various allied and occupied countries.

Germany cannot be singled out as uniquely evil in world history. Equally, guilt applies to any murder: comparing the scale of different historical crimes (for instance, trying to determine whether Hitler or Stalin was the greater criminal) cannot relativise the injury done to the individual victim of either system. Germany bears a special responsibility for preserving the memory of the Holocaust and historians must continue to endeavour to explain how such a crime could have been perpetrated. Nonetheless, this should not allow other nations the luxury of moral superiority over their own histories – or their own futures.

Assent and dissent

How did most Germans experience the *Drittes Reich*? Most Germans were not fanatical Nazis, though many agreed with at least some parts of Nazi policy. Initially, there was enthusiasm for political stability and apparent economic growth, coupled with gratitude and pride at Germany's reemergence as a great power, particularly after the victories of 1938–40 which many saw as enabling Germany to retake her rightful place in the world. Not all German workers were content with continuing low wages (particularly as a labour shortage developed in the late 1930s), and farmers were disappointed that Nazi promises to strengthen rural communities came to naught as the industrial cities consumed ever more manpower. The early Nazi revolutionaries were also disappointed that society was not in fact revolutionised to allow the 'little man' a greater role, and that instead the old elites continued to wield power and influence once they had accommodated themselves to the new order.

However, most Germans accepted their lot. Some made careers which depended on loyalty to the regime, whatever their personal convictions. Others accepted that Hitler was the best option available, especially as the alternative might be a communist society on the model of Stalin's Soviet Union. Nearly all found it practically impossible to air their grievances since *Gleichschaltung* removed the organisations which before 1933 had marshalled the different social interest groups (particularly the trade unions and the working-class political parties). Some historians have noted a consequent 'atomisation' of society, as traditional clubs and societies were broken up, leaving most Germans as individuals rather than members of cohesive social groups. Equally, Germans could not ignore the extensive police state, which relied on the regular police, the *Gestapo* (*Geheime Staatspolizei*, secret police), the SS and Nazi loyalists prepared to denounce their neighbours to the authorities. The politicised justice system and the threat of incarceration in a *Konzentrationslager* played their part in ensuring that many Germans became *Mitläufer*, 'fellow travellers' of the regime, who believed their best interests were served in maintaining a broad outward loyalty, whatever their personal opinions. This was further bolstered by a widespread, almost religious belief in Hitler as Germany's saviour which persisted until virtually the end, even after faith in the NSDAP and the government had collapsed. The war, too, encouraged patriotic support for the *Vaterland*, even among those who despised the Nazis' politics.

Nonetheless, the war did begin a slow change of popular attitudes. Germans did not welcome renewed conflict, even if this time the diversion of supplies from occupied Europe spared them the food shortages of the First World War. Far greater impact was made by the loss of a new generation of fathers, sons and brothers at the fronts and, particularly in the cities, by devastating bombing raids. The Nazis' social organisations, which had initially provided welcome leisure opportunities, became the focus of dreary war work after 1939, particularly the *Hitler-Jugend*, whose activities became increasingly geared to military training, sapping the earlier enthusiasm for the dynamic rebirth of the nation. Nonetheless, disillusionment was not widespread until 1944, by which time most realised that the war was lost. Even then, no general active opposition to the regime emerged.

Against this background of broad acceptance of the *Drittes Reich*, some opposition did emerge, though historians have differed in its interpretation. Many scholars nowadays take a broad approach to the issue, noting that in a state which aspired to total control, and total commitment from its citizens, any deviation from the expected norm could be construed as political. Despite the police state, many Germans refused to use the expected 'Heil Hitler' greeting or display the swastika flag, and did voice grievances. There were instances of strikes and unauthorised contacts with Jews. Nonetheless, these expressions of dissent fall short of active opposition or resistance to the regime.

Active, organised resistance was somewhat rarer, and the failure of resistance groups to dent the regime significantly is also explained by their broad range of conflicting motives. Communists, for example, were often active in brave conspiratorial work against the Nazi regime on ideological grounds, but achieved little in practical terms. The same can be said of social democrats; numerous members of both groups were incarcerated in the *Konzentrationslager* system. The churches (particularly the Catholic church) opposed Nazism on religious grounds when it attacked church rights or, sometimes, broad moral values (such as Bishop Galen's public criticism of the 'euthanasia' programme), but were not consistent in opposing the system. Official church protests were notably absent when the Jews were targeted, though brave individual clergy did speak out.

Certain other groups, such as the Munich students who formed the *Weiße Rose* movement and distributed leaflets around their university (see Document 4b), were also concerned with the Nazis' abandonment of moral principles. Similarly, relatively small elite groups were horrified at the barbaric methods with which the Nazis exercised power and feared the consequences of the expansionist war once Germany was defeated. One such group, the *Kreisauer Kreis*, planned an alternative, more democratic order and attempted in vain to persuade foreign powers and the military to support them. Another group, linked to Carl Goerdeler, until 1937 the mayor of Leipzig, similarly rejected the Nazis' methods, but was led by more traditional conservative motives. Some military leaders opposed Hitler's dangerous populism, and envisaged replacing Nazism with an authoritarian form of rule. Hitler's best-known opponents, the conspirators of the Stauffenberg plot, largely fell into this latter category, believing that Hitler's removal was vital if Germany were to secure a favourable peace treaty, but with no plans for democratic renewal. Their plan to kill Hitler with a bomb planted in his military headquarters failed on 20 July 1944, launching a comprehensive crackdown on all real or suspected opponents of the regime, but leaving Hitler with a renewed sense of mystical destiny after his narrow escape.

Ultimately German resistance did not remove the Nazi regime. Only a minority of Germans actively resisted Hitler's rule, and this often from motives of self-preservation which precluded cooperation with the wider public.

Conclusion

The Nazis came to power promising a thorough revolution of German life. This largely did not occur, as the old elites generally adapted to the new order and since the Nazis' plans were often vague and contradictory. To give but two examples: the NSDAP envisaged a traditional role for women based on *Kinder, Kirche, Küche* (children, church, kitchen), but the economic demands of preparation for the war ensured that many women were not left to minister to their husbands and children, but were instead forced to work in the factories; similarly, Hitler's aspiration to keep Germany for the Germans was also undermined by the labour shortage, resulting in millions of foreign workers flooding into Germany from occupied Europe to maintain the war effort. Despite the smashing of the pre-1933 social organisations which dominated German life, the broad contours of German society remained largely intact until 1945, when the impact of defeat and allied occupation brought significant upheaval to the country's social, economic and political fabric, particularly in the areas occupied by the Soviet Union.

National socialism was born as a means of escaping the unresolved social and political questions of the *Kaiserreich* and the *Weimarer Republik*, an uneasy and unworkable compromise between the expression of popular will and strongman rule. In providing an escape from the post-1918 settlement, widely regarded as unjust, and promising a reckoning with those within Germany who appeared to have betrayed the nation (Marxist socialists, Jews, parliamentarians) in favour of a return to core national values (strong leadership, the sanctity of rural life, traditional family life), the movement had a broad appeal. In the absence of alternatives, Hitler was given free rein to pursue his extremist goals with the active or passive participation of nearly the entire population. The shortcomings and contradictions within national socialism's domestic agenda arguably made it all the more essential for Germany to pursue goals of international aggrandisement at the expense of other states and races. Ultimately Germany was changed not so much by Hitler's programme as by the devastation wreaked on the country by the enemies Germany had made in pursuing inhumane goals. The tradition of expansive German foreign policy was irrevocably undermined.

Republik Österreich and 'Ostmark', 1933–1945

Following the accidental self-destruction of the *Nationalrat* in March 1933, *Bundeskanzler* Engelbert Dollfuß abandoned Austria's chaotic parliamentary democracy and attempted to heal the country's bitter divisions under authoritarian rule. Parliamentarians who attempted to reconvene the *Nationalrat* a few days after its collapse were dispersed. Instead, Dollfuß ruled by decrees, given a shady legality by a 1917 law which permitted emergency measures necessitated by the war. Meanwhile, a new constitutional structure was elaborated, turning the Austrian republic into a *Ständestaat* ('corporate state'), with pronounced Roman Catholic influence. Under this authoritarian model, not dissimilar to that proposed in the *Korneuburger Eid* (Document 3b), parliament would consist of representatives nominated by the key elements in society (the *Stände*), including the churches, the schools and universities, and economic interest groups such as agriculture, mining, banking and industry. The government could also appoint worthy citizens of its own choice. However, parliament would have no right to propose laws, only to accept or reject those drawn up by the government. In practice, even this limited, indirect representation was never fully implemented, and the government relied instead on emergency decrees.

Dollfuß faced various challenges to his power: the socialists opposed the republic's destruction, while Austrian Nazis hoped to achieve power themselves, supported by the new German *Reichskanzler*, Hitler. The right-wing paramilitary *Heimwehr* organisations also hoped to oust Dollfuß. The *Bundeskanzler*'s only strong backer was the fascist Italian leader Mussolini, not yet Hitler's ally and hoping to establish Italy as a regional powerbroker in southeast Europe. The *Ständestaat* plan owed much to the well-established structures of Mussolini's Italy (indeed, the system became known as *Austro-Faschismus*), and Dollfuß followed Mussolini's advice in outlawing the KPÖ and the socialists' armed division, the *Republikanischer Schutzbund*. He also attempted to replicate Italy's one-party rule by creating a *Vaterländische Front* ('Patriotic Front') as a political home for all Austrian patriots. The *Front* quickly absorbed the *Christlichsoziale Partei* and the *Heimwehren* whose leader, Starhemberg, hoped to achieve power by this route.

The socialists hoped to avoid total defeat by offering far-reaching concessions to Dollfuß. However, both Mussolini and the *Heimwehren* were insistent that *Austro-Bolschewismus* ('Austrian bolshevism') be crushed. On 12 March 1934, when a *Republikanischer Schutzbund* commander fired on an army patrol inspecting illegal weapons supplies, the *Heimwehr* and the *Bundesheer* (army) began a brutal crackdown on socialists throughout Austria, sparking a second wave of civil war. Though most socialists were not radical enough to fight for their cause, there were bitter exchanges in parts of Vienna. After two days of fighting, 196 socialists and 118 of their opponents lay dead; the SDAP was outlawed, the socialist experiment in 'Red Vienna' was over, and the way was cleared for the 'Rome Protocols' which allied Austria and fascist Italy still more closely.

Dollfuß's attempts to create a new, nationalist Austria were opposed by the many German nationalists whose long-standing hopes of *Anschluss* were encouraged by Hitler's *Machtergreifung*. Hitler, Austrian-born himself, hoped for an *Anschluss* both from nationalist motivations and also to gain access to Austria's natural resources, which would be important in wartime. The possibility of German support for the *Anschluss* helped the hitherto small Austrian Nazi party to expand. Dollfuß attempted to counter German propaganda for an *Anschluss* and banned the Austrian Nazi party after it began a series of terrorist attacks; Hitler responded by imposing a thousand mark charge on Germans who wished to visit Austria, thus sabotaging the country's tourist industry. As the Austrian Nazis could not be elected to power in the *Ständestaat* (and Dollfuß would not admit opponents of independent Austria to his government), they launched a putsch attempt on 25 July 1934. It is unclear if the Austrian Nazis acted with Hitler's encouragement or independently; either way, they received no German military assistance and the badly organised plan quickly ran aground. They succeeded, however, in killing Dollfuß, left to bleed to death in his office.

The new *Bundeskanzler*, Kurt Schuschnigg (formerly the education minister), pursued Dollfuß's policy of an independent Austria, aided by international condemnation of the abortive Nazi putsch. Hitler preferred to consolidate his power in

Germany than risk foreign interventions by attempting a forcible *Anschluss*. However, though the earlier disposal of the political parties and rivalries between different factions in the *Heimwehren* enabled Schuschnigg to expand his domestic powerbase, Austria's independence was clearly predicated upon Italian support. This vanished in 1936 when Mussolini and Hitler became allies and agreed that Austria fell within the German sphere of influence. In return, Hitler, a surprisingly pragmatic German nationalist when it suited, agreed that Italy should retain the German-speaking South Tyrol it had seized in 1918.

Austria's new dependence on Germany was underlined in an agreement between the two countries in July 1936, which ended German trade sanctions against Austria. However, Germany's recognition of Austrian sovereignty was fatally undermined by Austria's agreement to act 'as a German state'. Schuschnigg admitted two German nationalists to his government; Hitler bided his time. Schuschnigg hoped to place independent Austria's relationship with Germany on a stronger footing, and was persuaded to visit Hitler in February 1938, believing that this could be achieved. Instead, Hitler accused Austria of betraying the German nation and insisted on greater Nazi involvement in the Austrian government, with wide-ranging powers for Arthur Seyß-Inquart, a Hitler trustee. Though the Austrian Nazi party was still outlawed, this encouragement sparked more open pro-German, and anti-Schuschnigg, sentiment in Austria.

With Austrian independence seriously undermined, Schuschnigg responded with a wave of propaganda for Austrian nationalism (under the slogan *Rot-weiß-rot bis in den Tod*, referring to the colours of the Austrian flag), made concessions to secure the support of the outlawed socialist leaders, and determined to call a referendum. Austrians would be invited to declare 'für ein freies und deutsches, unabhängiges und soziales, für ein christliches und einiges Österreich'. The Austrian identity which had been lacking since the republic's birth in 1918 was created only when the country was diplomatically isolated and at the mercy of an invincible opponent.

It appeared that Schuschnigg would win the referendum, demonstrating popular support for Austrian independence and making an *Anschluss* politically difficult. Hitler determined to prevent the referendum, mobilised German forces to enter Austria, and demanded that the Austrian president dismiss Schuschnigg and appoint Seyß-Inquart in his place. Seeing no alternative, Schuschnigg resigned. On 12 March 1938 German forces entered Austria to the rapturous applause which Hitler himself enjoyed in Vienna on 14 and 15 March. The Austrian army offered no resistance. By then the new Seyß-Inquart government had pronounced Austria a *Land* of the *Deutsches Reich*, soon officially dubbed the '*Ostmark*'. The *Anschluss* was complete, and given popular legitimacy by over 99 per cent of the Austrian electorate in a referendum the following month. Hitler's promises (later broken) that the church's rights would be upheld induced senior Austrian bishops to support the *Anschluss* publicly before the referendum; even Karl Renner, the leading Austrian socialist who had been instrumental in establishing the Austrian republic in 1918, confirmed his support, subordinating his hatred of Nazism to his German identity, a dilemma shared by many Austrians.

In the following months, Austria was fully integrated into the *Reich* and its independent government disbanded. Most elements of German law were introduced to the reorganised Austrian *Länder*, the principal victims were the Austrian Jews, who were humiliated and intimidated as the country's long-established antisemitic traditions were given free reign. Around half emigrated before war broke out in September 1939; most of the rest perished in the concentration and extermination camps. Nazi opponents – principally active socialists and Austrian nationalists – were also imprisoned, many of them in the Mauthausen concentration camp near Linz where some 100,000 prisoners perished.

Once the excitement of the *Anschluss*, and the release from the problems of the Austrian republic, had passed, Austrians were generally no more or less enthusiastic about Nazi rule than other Germans. Some 850,000 Austrians joined the NSDAP by 1942, and Austrians served in the *Wehrmacht* until the bitter end. Some resistance groups emerged, but they were small and mainly eradicated by the *Gestapo* early on; the communists alone, with Soviet support, maintained an active Austrian resistance, albeit with no tangible success. Only as defeat neared did Austrian politicians gather to discuss the future and to contact the advancing allied armies.

Though the Austrians themselves made no more contribution to defeating Nazism than the other Germans of the *Reich*, the disillusionment which surrounded the wartime defeat, and the disappointment with Vienna's relegation to the status of a provincial capital among others, finally stirred in most Austrians the realisation of their distinct identity within the wider cultural and linguistic German nation. Perversely, Hitler's total subjugation of Austria within Germany was the factor which made a single German state unthinkable after 1945.

Austria and the legacy of national socialism

Though Austria did not have to cope with partition between the superpowers after the war, the national socialist past has cast a shadow over the country, just as in Germany. The Austrian state, and much of the country's population, have consistently attempted to ignore responsibility for the Nazi era by maintaining that Austria was the first victim of German aggression and simply did not exist between 1938 and 1945. This explanation ignores Austrians' participation in the structures of the *Drittes Reich* and their overwhelming support for the *Anschluss* in 1938. Denazification was relatively unsuccessful in Austria, undermined as early as the late 1940s by the political parties' interest in obscuring their own forerunners' part in the transformation of the *Erste Republik* into a protofascist state. Instead the major political parties enabled most former NSDAP members to resume their posts throughout public life.

Austria has been at pains to distance herself entirely from her German past since the war, nourishing the myth of an unblemished '*Insel der Seligen*' ('island of the blessed'). Meanwhile, well into the early 1990s most of the Austrian historians who researched the country's Nazi past concentrated on Austrian resistance to Nazism, leading critical voices to identify a '*Krise der Zeitgeschichte*' ('crisis in contemporary historical research') which ignored Austria's active involvement in the Nazi past.

Austria's rather cosy consensus was first jolted when Kurt Waldheim, a former secretary general of the United Nations, campaigned to become Austria's *Bundespräsident* in 1986. Waldheim served as a *Wehrmacht* officer in Yugoslavia in the mid-1940s and, while there was no evidence to link him personally to war crimes, he was (in common with many other Austrians of his generation) vague about the precise nature of his wartime role. Despite international criticism, Waldheim refused to withdraw his candidacy and was elected by 54 per cent of the electorate, the foreign reaction perhaps having strengthened his popularity among conservative voters. Throughout his six-year presidential term, most foreign states refused to receive Waldheim on official state visits. Vienna, which had used its neutrality to act as an impartial broker in world affairs, found itself isolated.

The rise of Austria's extreme right-wing party, the *Freiheitliche Partei Österreichs* (FPÖ), in the 1990s (see Chapter 8) nurtured fears of Austrian neo-Nazism, yet this very political radicalisation has – belatedly – aroused a more critical interest in Austria's past. Austria's willingness to pay compensation to slave workers and to Jews whose property was expropriated during the *Drittes Reich* is a sign that Austria is beginning to recognise its responsibility for the past, even while the legalistic fiction of a discontinuity of seven years between the First and Second Republics is preserved.

Document 4a: Hitler's speech to the *Reichstag*, 23 March 1933

. . . Um die Regierung in die Lage zu versetzen, die Aufgaben zu erfüllen, die innerhalb dieses allgemein gekennzeichneten Rahmens liegen, hat sie im Reichstag durch die beiden Parteien der Nationalsozialisten und der Deutschnationalen das Ermächtigungsgesetz einbringen lassen. Ein Teil der beabsichtigten Maßnahmen erfordert die verfassungsändernde Mehrheit. Die Durchführung dieser Aufgaben bzw. ihre Lösung ist notwendig. Es würde dem Sinn der nationalen Erhebung widersprechen und dem beabsichtigten Zweck nicht genügen, wollte die Regierung sich für ihre Maßnahmen von Fall zu Fall die Genehmigung des Reichstags erhandeln und erbitten. Die Regierung wird dabei nicht von der Absicht getrieben, den Reichstag als solchen aufzuheben . . . Die Autorität und damit die Erfüllung der Aufgaben der Regierung würden aber leiden, wenn im Volke Zweifel an der Stabilität des neuen Regiments entstehen könnten. Sie hält vor allem eine weitere Tagung des Reichstags im heutigen Zustand der tiefgehenden Erregung der Nation für unmöglich. Es ist kaum eine Revolution von so großem Ausmaß so diszipliniert und unblutig verlaufen wie die der Erhebung des deutschen Volks in diesen Wochen. Es ist mein Wille und meine feste Absicht, für diese ruhige Entwicklung auch in Zukunft zu sorgen. Allein um so nötiger ist es, daß der nationalen Regierung jene souveräne Stellung gegeben wird, die in einer solchen Zeit allein geeignet ist, eine andere Entwicklung zu verhindern. Die Regierung beabsichtigt dabei, von diesem Gesetz nur insoweit Gebrauch zu machen, als es zur Durchführung der lebensnotwendigen Maßnahmen erforderlich ist. Weder die Existenz des Reichstags noch des Reichsrats soll dadurch bedroht sein. Die Stellung und die Rechte des Herrn Reichspräsidenten bleiben unberührt; die innere Übereinstimmung mit seinem Willen herbeizuführen, wird stets die oberste Aufgabe der Regierung sein. Der Bestand der Länder wird nicht beseitigt, die Rechte der Kirchen werden nicht geschmälert, ihre Stellung zum Staate nicht geändert.

Da die Regierung an sich über eine klare Mehrheit verfügt, ist die Zahl der Fälle, in denen eine innere Notwendigkeit vorliegt, zu einem solchen Gesetz die Zuflucht zu nehmen, an sich eine begrenzte. Um so mehr aber besteht die Regierung der nationalen Erhebung auf der Verabschiedung dieses Gesetzes. Sie zieht in jedem Falle eine klare Entscheidung vor. Sie bietet den Parteien des Reichstages die Möglichkeit einer ruhigen deutschen Entwicklung und einer sich daraus in der Zukunft anbahnenden Verständigung; sie ist aber ebenso entschlossen und bereit, die Bekundung der Ablehnung und damit die Ansage des Widerstands entgegenzunehmen.

Mögen Sie, meine Herren, nunmehr selbst die Entscheidung treffen über Frieden oder Krieg.

Source: Erhard Klöss (ed.), *Reden des Führers. Politik und Propaganda Adolf Hitlers 1922–1945* (Munich: dtv, 1967), pp. 107–8.

Document 4b: Leaflet circulated by the *Weiße Rose* group, 1943

The following is an edited version of the last illegal leaflet circulated by the *Weiße Rose* group in 1943.

Kommilitonen! Kommilitoninnen!

Erschüttert steht unser Volk vor dem Untergang der Männer von Stalingrad. Dreihundertdreißigtausend deutsche Männer hat die geniale Strategie des Weltkriegsgefreiten sinn- und verantwortungslos in Tod und Verderben gehetzt. Führer, wir danken dir!

Es gärt im deutschen Volk: Wollen wir weiter einem Dilettanten das Schicksal unserer Armeen anvertrauen? Wollen wir den niederen Machtinstinkten einer Parteiclique den Rest der deutschen Jugend opfern? Nimmermehr! Der Tag der Abrechnung ist gekommen, der Abrechnung der deutschen Jugend mit der verabscheuungswürdigsten Tyrannis, die unser Volk je erduldet hat. Im Namen der deutschen Jugend fordern wir vom Staat Adolf Hitlers die persönliche Freiheit, das kostbarste Gut des Deutschen zurück, um das er uns in der erbärmlichsten Weise betrogen.

In einem Staat rücksichtsloser Knebelung jeder freien Meinungsäußerung sind wir aufgewachsen. HJ, SA, SS haben uns in den fruchtbarsten Bildungsjahren unseres Lebens zu uniformieren, zu revolutionieren, zu narkotisieren versucht. . . . Eine Führerauslese . . . zieht ihre künftigen Parteibonzen auf Ordensburgen zu gottlosen, schamlosen und gewissenlosen Ausbeutern und Mordbuben heran, zur blinden, stupiden Führergefolgschaft. . . .

Es gilt für uns nur eine Parole: Kampf gegen die Partei! Heraus aus den Parteigliederungen, in denen man uns weiter politisch mundtot halten will! . . . Es gilt den Kampf jedes einzelnen von uns um unsere Zukunft, unsere Freiheit und Ehre in einem seiner sittlichen Verantwortung bewußten Staatswesen.

Freiheit und Ehre! Zehn lange Jahre haben Hitler und seine Genossen die beiden herrlichen deutschen Worte bis zum Ekel ausgequetscht, abgedroschen, verdreht, wie es nur Dilettanten vermögen, die die höchsten Werte einer Nation vor die Säue werfen. Was ihnen Freiheit und Ehre gilt, haben sie in zehn Jahren der Zerstörung aller materiellen und geistigen Freiheit, aller sittlichen Substanzen im deutschen Volk genugsam gezeigt. Auch dem dümmsten Deutschen hat das furchtbare Blutbad die Augen geöffnet, das sie im Namen von Freiheit und Ehre der deutschen Nation in ganz Europa angerichtet haben und täglich neu anrichten. Der deutsche Name bleibt für immer geschändet, wenn nicht die deutsche Jugend endlich aufsteht, rächt und sühnt zugleich, ihre Peiniger zerschmettert und ein neues geistiges Europa aufrichtet. Studentinnen! Studenten! Auf uns sieht das deutsche Volk! Von uns erwartet es, wie 1813 die Brechung des Napoleonischen, so 1943 die Brechung des nationalsozialistischen Terrors aus der Macht des Geistes. Beresina und Stalingrad flammen im Osten auf, die Toten von Stalingrad beschwören uns!

»Frisch auf mein Volk, die Flammenzeichen rauchen!«

Unser Volk steht im Aufbruch gegen die Verknechtung Europas durch den Nationalsozialismus, im neuen gläubigen Durchbruch von Freiheit und Ehre.

Source: Walther Hofer (ed.), *Der Nationalsozialismus. Dokumente 1933–1945* (Frankfurt am Main: Fischer, revised new edition, 1982), pp. 328–30 (shortened).

Topics
FOR DISCUSSION / FURTHER RESEARCH

■ Which of the promises made in his speech to the *Reichstag* on 23 March 1933 (Document 4a) did Hitler later break?

■ What does Document 4b reveal of the motivations which inspired the *Weiße Rose* group?

■ How justified is it to speak of a 'Nazi revolution' in the period 1933–39?

■ To what extent is German national socialism reducible to the person of Hitler?

■ How effectively was the NSDAP able to control Germany during the *Drittes Reich*?

CHAPTER 5

Parting of the ways: 1945–1949

Timeline

30 April 1945
Hitler commits suicide in Berlin

7 May 1945
Germany surrenders unconditionally

5 June 1945
Allies assume 'supreme power'

17 July –2 August 1945
Potsdam Conference

21 April 1946
KPD and SPD merge to form the SED in the Soviet zone

1 January 1947
British and American zones of occupation merge as the *Bizone*

20 June 1948
Currency reform in western zones

24 June 1948
Berlin Blockade begins

23 May 1949
West German *Grundgesetz* in force: *Bundesrepublik Deutschland* established in the western zones

7 October 1949
Deutsche Demokratische Republik proclaimed in the Soviet zone

Germany's division after 1945 symbolised the developing Cold War between the USA and the Soviet Union, the two global superpowers. Their dispute was principally ideological: the USA and its western allies upheld market capitalism and parliamentary democracy, while the Soviets' model depended on state ownership, central planning and authoritarian political control. Only opposition to Hitler had united these two sides in common cause. With his death, mutual distrust returned: the west feared communist attempts at global revolution, while the Soviets remembered western efforts to smother the 1917 Russian Revolution. Informal wartime agreements assigned western Europe to the Anglo-American sphere of influence, and eastern Europe principally to the Soviet sphere. An 'Iron Curtain' descended across Europe as Moscow established communist regimes throughout eastern Europe by the late 1940s. However, conflicts arose over some countries (Greece, Korea), and the Soviets feared the expansionist implications of the Americans' 'European Recovery Program' (the 'Marshall Plan', see p. 118). The destructive potential of atomic warfare sparked an arms race, further heightening tensions.

The allies take control

For Germany, 30 April 1945 – the date of Hitler's suicide – became the *Stunde Null* (zero hour). In practice, not everything changed (the non-criminal elites of the *Drittes Reich* and the *Weimarer Republik* survived to play important roles in the postwar era, particularly in the west), and the changes which did occur did not all take effect immediately.

By 30 April most of Germany was already under allied occupation. Within days Berlin fell to the Soviet Red Army's advance, and the new German government under *Großadmiral* Dönitz (Hitler's nominated successor) could only surrender. Determined to prevent German militarism resurfacing, as it had after 1918, the allies insisted on an unconditional surrender, which the Germans initially signed on 7 May. On 5 June the allies further declared that they had assumed 'supreme authority' in Germany. Henceforth, German authorities could only function legitimately on the orders, or with the approval, of the allied forces.

The allies had reached initial agreement on Germany's occupation before the war ended: the Soviet Union occupied the eastern zone, Britain the northwest and the Americans the south. Additionally, the allies accorded the French occupation rights in a fourth zone in the southwest. The French detached the industrial Saarland, rich in natural resources, from the rest of Germany and attempted to integrate the region into France's economic structures. Berlin, the *Reichshauptstadt*, was viewed as so important that it would be divided into sectors and occupied by all four powers. By the time the three principal allies met in Potsdam, just outside Berlin, in July 1945 to discuss the postwar order (the French were not invited to this conference), the Soviets had already created a *fait accompli*. The German population in the eastern provinces had fled or been deported before the Red Army's advance, leaving the traditional German regions of East Prussia, Silesia and Pomerania to be settled by Poles. This westward shift of Poland's border with Germany to a line along the rivers Oder and Neiße (*die Oder-Neiße-Linie*), effectively sanctioned by the British and Americans at Potsdam in view of the large population movement which had already occurred, enabled the Soviet Union also to expand westwards into former Polish territory as compensation for its wartime losses. Similarly, the German population of the Sudetenland was violently expelled by the reborn Czechoslovak state. Hitler's legacy was a significant shrinking of the boundaries of the German nation state. The remainder of Germany was forced to absorb millions of refugees from these lost provinces, a process initially accompanied by much rancour among the already impoverished Germans required to open their homes to these newcomers.

Though arguments had been presented in favour of splitting Germany permanently into two or more smaller states, to weaken the country's future strength, at Potsdam the allies agreed that Germany should be maintained as a single economic unit. An *Alliierter Kontrollrat* (Allied Control Council) would issue laws on matters which affected Germany as a whole; an interallied authority would similarly govern all four sectors of Berlin. German civil authorities with powers across the whole country were envisaged for important issues such as finance, transport and industry, and established as *Deutsche Zentralverwaltungen* (German central administrations) in Berlin by the Soviet occupation

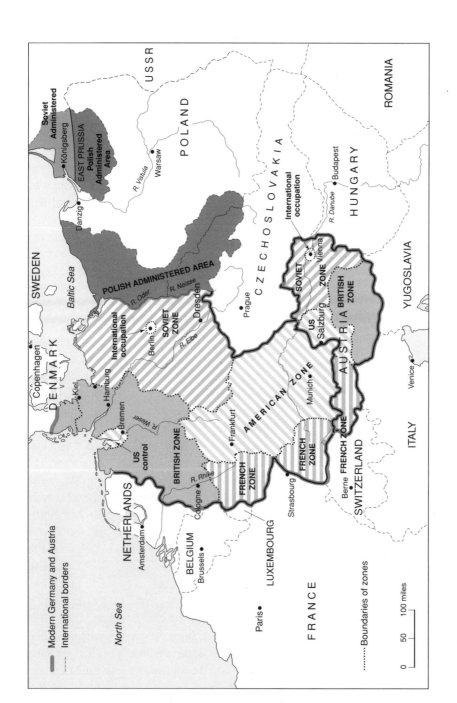

Map 5.1: Occupation zones in Germany and Austria following the defeat of the Drittes Reich

authorities. However, in each occupation zone the military commander would have ultimate power. In practice, this division of sovereignty enabled superpower divisions to be reflected in the administration of Germany. The scope for independent developments in the different zones quickly became apparent when the western allies refused to recognise the authority of the Berlin *Deutsche Zentralverwaltungen* in their zones. The French feared that they represented the recreation of a centralised and potentially powerful German nation state, while the Americans worried that they might enable the Soviets to extend their influence across the entire country. The influence of the *Deutsche Zentralverwaltungen* was henceforth limited to the Soviet zone; they formed the nucleus of the later East German ministries. Parallel structures emerged in the western zones.

Despite their differences, the allies did share some general objectives. All agreed at Potsdam that Germany must pay reparations, and that the country should be demilitarised, denazified and democratised. Demilitarisation was swiftly completed: large numbers of German troops were imprisoned (many not emerging from Soviet camps until 1955) and many armaments factories were dismantled. The allies differed in their reparations policy: while the Soviets took over many industrial plants in eastern Germany, and dismantled other machinery and installations for transport to the USSR, effectively disabling much of the east German economy, the western allies were more cautious. The Americans' 'Morgenthau Plan', drawn up before war's end, had envisaged reducing Germany to the status of a subsistence agrarian economy, but this proposal was quickly abandoned as the Americans realised the importance of a strong, industrial Germany for Europe's economic recovery. After 1951 the western allies stopped dismantling German industrial plant altogether; the removal of West German assets to the Soviet Union in lieu of reparations was halted as early as 1946. By 1948 the Americans had effectively reversed their original policy and were supplying the western zones of Germany with reconstruction aid under the **European Recovery Program**.

Denazification and democratisation proved complex and contentious. The NSDAP itself and its allied mass organisations spontaneously disintegrated along with the *Drittes Reich*, and the four allies cooperated to prosecute the most notorious Nazi leaders who had survived the war in the *Nürnberger Prozess* (Nuremberg Trial) of 1945–46. Further war crimes trials were held in the individual zones.

European Recovery Program ('Marshall Plan')

Following proposals by George C. Marshall, the American secretary of state (foreign minister) in 1947, the US government transferred almost $13 billion in aid to western Europe between 1948 and 1952. This funded postwar reconstruction projects and enabled imports of essential goods. The recovery of the European market was recognised as essential for the future health of the American economy. Grants were made dependent on recipient countries' willingness to establish free market economies, widening the gulf between western Europe and the Soviet-dominated east, where planned economies reigned. Marshall Aid significantly assisted the revival of the west German economy, but effectively deepened the division between east and west Germany, as the Soviets did not allow their zone to participate in the scheme.

However, dealing with the eight million individual former NSDAP members proved far more problematic. Initially the allies simply removed from the public administration and leading roles in the economy all senior officials who had belonged to the party, and interned those who had held significant rank in the NSDAP and its associated organisations. In the west this procedure was systematised by requiring all key postholders to complete an extensive *Fragebogen* (questionnaire) on their activities in the *Drittes Reich* to determine whether or not they should be sacked or imprisoned. The Soviets were particularly concerned to remove as many Nazis as possible from the education and legal systems in their zone.

Inevitably, public administration was greatly hindered by this approach, since most of the individuals qualified for such work had been NSDAP members during the *Drittes Reich*, and could not easily be replaced. Partly to address this practical difficulty, but also recognising that NSDAP membership did not necessarily reveal an individual's motivations or political outlook, the allies soon distinguished between 'nominal' Nazis (those who had joined the party opportunistically or been forced to join, but had taken no part in criminal activities) and those who had compromised themselves in supporting Hitler's aims. The allies differed in their criteria for determining the gravity of an individual's record; generally speaking the Americans and the French were more assiduous in removing public officials than the British.

What of the wider public? In the Soviet zone, following vigorous purges during the first two postwar years, the denazification of individuals was effectively halted by 1948 in the interests of integrating the whole of society behind the new political order (discussed below). In the west, the Americans issued shorter questionnaires to all adults in their zone, hoping to identify further Nazis liable for punishment or exclusion from important jobs. The British and French did not undertake blanket checks on the population, enabling some high-ranking Nazis to begin new respectable careers unpunished. Those implicated of involvement in the Nazi regime were brought before tribunals, where many produced testimonials of their Christian rectitude written by character witnesses, sometimes priests. Denazification of Germany's key structures gradually turned into a system to rehabilitate former NSDAP members. In the process many redefined their previous activities as honourable and inconsequential endeavours for the national cause or claimed that their actions had amounted to no more than obeying orders from above. By the late 1940s, the process had effectively ground to a halt, except where war criminals could be identified. The German authorities recognised the impossibility of ostracising such a large proportion of the population and of checking the details given in the questionnaires. The bureaucracy alone rendered a comprehensive denazification unfeasible. Ironically it was the difficult cases of those more deeply implicated in the Nazi regime which were dropped as the system was abandoned in the late 1940s. In the west, many of the dismissed civil servants were reappointed by the early 1950s; in the Soviet zone this generally did not occur, their places often taken by communist functionaries. Though denazification was widely regarded as a failure, it did at least make clear the boundaries of acceptable political activity; the overwhelming majority of rehabilitated NSDAP members made no attempt to revive the old ideology in later years.

More than personal consequences, the Soviets believed that structural changes were needed if Nazism were to be stamped out completely. Marxist-Leninist ideology had been developed to explain fascism as the highest form of capitalism, and it was believed (mainly erroneously) that businessmen had been a prominent source of Hitler's support. Thus, monopoly capitalism must be disempowered to secure an antifascist future. In the Soviet zone of occupation, therefore, denazification also entailed the wholesale expropriation of assets belonging to high-ranking Nazis and armaments manufacturers, and the nationalisation of key industries and branches of commerce. The power of the landed *Junker* aristocracy was also broken in a far-reaching *Bodenreform* (land reform). All landowners with more than 100 hectares lost their entire holdings under the slogan 'Junkerland in Bauernhand'. In most cases, small parcels of this land were distributed to smallholders and agricultural labourers, as well as to the homeless Germans from the lost eastern provinces.

The rebirth of German politics

While political power was firmly in allied hands following the unconditional surrender, the allies depended on German politicians and bureaucrats to operate the administration in the localities and provinces of the separate zones. Initially the allied commandants called on former members of the pre-1933 parties or on known Nazi opponents to fill positions as mayors and ministers. For the longer term the allies wished the Germans to develop their own political parties which could eventually contest elections, so that political power could be exercised by democratically legitimate authorities under allied supervision, first locally and regionally, and ultimately nationally.

On 10 June 1945, the Soviet military authorities were the first to permit the formation of German political parties. The first party to reappear was the *Kommunistische Partei Deutschlands* (KPD), with a programme (see Document 5) which called for antifascist unity in the rebuilding of Germany, but was careful to avoid mentioning socialism, and even insisted that it would be wrong 'to force the Soviet system on Germany'. By contrast, the reborn *Sozialdemokratische Partei Deutschlands* (SPD) was far more forthright in calling for the speedy establishment of socialism, and for a merger of the two working-class parties. The *Christlich-Demokratische Union* (CDU) was an entirely new party. Though its heritage was partly that of the pre-1933 Roman Catholic *Zentrumspartei*, the CDU attempted to draw Catholics and Protestants together into a single party which would promote Christian values, while not excluding non-Christians. In the immediate aftermath of the Nazi defeat, the CDU espoused notions of central economic planning and a 'Christian socialism'. The pre-1933 liberal parties were finally united in the *Liberal-Demokratische Partei Deutschlands* (LDPD). The LDPD subscribed to the antifascist consensus, but was more vocal in defending a place for private enterprise.

The Soviet authorities refused to license any further political parties, and insisted that all four cooperate in the Soviet zone within an 'antifascist democratic bloc' which would agree strategies for rebuilding Germany on the basis of unanimity – a settlement which effectively allowed the KPD a veto over the political wishes of the other parties in the Soviet zone.

The four-party model was essentially replicated in the western zones, though the western liberals coalesced under the title *Freie Demokratische Partei* (FDP), and the Bavarian Christian party retained a separate identity, as it had in the Weimar years, under the name *Christlich-Soziale Union* (CSU). Nonetheless, the CDU and CSU quickly forged an enduring partnership in the west. The western powers also allowed a variety of smaller parties, some regionally based, others representing those expelled from the eastern provinces. However, none of the zones licensed a specifically right-wing party, let alone a successor to the NSDAP.

Initially the allies did not permit the parties to organise nationally, preferring to restrict their activities to the zonal level where they could more easily be observed. Against this background east and west Germany went different ways within a year. The KPD had expected to benefit from the backlash against Nazism which followed Germany's crushing defeat and to become the leading German party on the basis of its committed antifascist record. Instead its growth was hindered by Germans' long-standing fears of the effects of communist rule on personal freedom and property, combined with resistance to support a party so closely linked with the Soviet Union, a state consistently vilified in Nazi propaganda. It became quickly apparent that the SPD would become the larger of the two working-class parties. Election results in Austria and Hungary, where the communists were heavily defeated, confirmed the KPD's fears that it would be marginalised if challenged in free elections in Germany. By autumn 1945, the communist leaders began pressing for a merger with the social democrats. The argument that the merger would secure the unity of the working classes against any future fascist threat, and thus correct the damaging divisions of the Weimar years, was supported by many social democrats and, crucially, by the Soviet military authorities in their zone. Nonetheless, other social democrats opposed the plan: the communists had been determined in the previous months to exclude social democratic influence by any means possible from local antifascist committees and regional govern-ments, and many SPD members feared they would be outmanoeuvred in a united workers' party. In particular the SPD leader in the western zones, Kurt Schumacher, was deeply sceptical about the communists' intentions, and firmly opposed a merger.

Schumacher, however, did not face the same pressures as social democrats in the Soviet zone, where a campaign to merge the two parties was in full swing by Christmas. The Soviet military authorities pressurised reluctant social democratic leaders and assisted those who supported a merger. The Soviet zone SPD under Otto Grotewohl initially insisted that the two parties should merge only on a national basis (a proposition unacceptable to the western allies), but faced with an orchestrated campaign of pressure from local party groups to merge with the KPD, and abandoned by their western comrades, the eastern SPD executive finally agreed to the union by Easter 1946. The *Sozialistische Einheitspartei Deutschlands* (Socialist Unity Party of Germany, SED) was born. No poll of the membership of either party was permitted to sanction the merger in the Soviet zone, and as dissident social democrats were not permitted to continue the SPD in the Soviet zone alongside the SED, many felt that the merger in fact represented a *Zwangsvereinigung* – a merger by force. This view is strengthened by the far greater popularity of the SPD over the SED in the western sectors of Berlin, the only part of Germany where the two parties competed openly.

Communists quickly dominated the SED, supported by the Soviet military authorities, as Schumacher had predicted. In 1948, when the Yugoslav communist party insisted on its autonomy from Moscow, Stalin initiated a general crackdown on other communist parties throughout eastern Europe to avoid any further losses to the Soviet buffer zone being created in these countries. This coincided with the SED's decision to become a *Partei neuen Typus* ('party of a new type') – effectively a Leninist party on the model of the Communist Party of the Soviet Union (CPSU). Social democrats in the Soviet zone could either retire from politics, leave the Soviet zone or adopt the communist line (Grotewohl and many others, some from conviction, others from expediency, chose the latter alternative). Those who attempted to maintain openly social democratic positions in the Soviet zone were purged from the SED or arrested for illegal party activity.

The SED's creation not only laid the foundations for eastern Germany's later development, but also divided the party political landscape between east and west. Other divisions also became apparent, as the 'Christian socialist' faction within the western CDU found itself outnumbered by more conservative elements around Konrad Adenauer, the mayor of Cologne. He and the economist Ludwig Erhard rejected socialist politics and favoured free enterprise over public ownership and central planning. Meanwhile, the Soviet zone CDU remained wedded to antifascist cooperation, not least because the Soviet military command intervened to remove senior eastern CDU leaders who opposed the *Bodenreform* and cooperation with the SED. Similar developments divided the Soviet zone LDPD from the western FDP. Inexorably the sister parties in east and west grew further apart, a process encouraged by the tendency for activists with no political home in the Soviet zone to leave for the west.

Superpower tensions and the division of Germany

More significant still for Germany's future were relations between the allied powers. The British and Americans shared so much common ground that they merged the administration of their zones into a *Bizone* on 1 January 1947; though the French initially resisted moves to restore a German nation state, their zone was administratively incorporated into the *Bizone* in April 1949.

Nonetheless, insuperable difficulties emerged between the Soviets and the western allies against the backdrop of growing Cold War tensions. As the western powers tired of Soviet refusals to make progress on Germany's future, they made contingency plans for a new German state based initially on the western occupation zones alone. When the Soviets were not invited to discussions on this subject held in March 1948 between the western allies and the Benelux countries (Belgium, the Netherlands and Luxembourg), the Soviet representative left the *Alliierter Kontrollrat* in protest, rendering the allied instrument for interzonal government inoperable. Matters came to a head in June 1948 when the western allies instituted the long necessary currency reform to replace the worthless *Reichsmark* with a new currency, the *Deutsche Mark*. As this reform was implemented in the western zones only, the Soviets were obliged to instigate a currency reform of their own several days later to avoid a flood of old *Reichsmarks* into their zone. As the new Soviet zone currency was also introduced in Berlin, the western allies also brought the *Deutsche Mark* to west Berlin.

The currency reform crystallised the separate development of the two parts of Germany: the Soviets initially closed the border between their zone and the western zones, claiming that this was necessary to stop black marketeering before the Soviet zone currency reform was in place. However, the borders remained closed, blocking land access between the western zones of Germany and the western sectors of Berlin. It became apparent that the Soviets were effectively holding west Berlin hostage to dissuade the western allies from establishing a separate west German state. Rather than changing minds in London and Washington, however, the Berlin Blockade galvanised western politicians and public opinion alike to support west Berlin against Soviet aggression. Within three years, west Berlin's population had been transformed from dangerous Nazi enemies to champions of democratic freedoms. Refusing to allow west Berlin to be supplied from, and effectively incorporated into, the Soviet zone, the Americans and British organised an airlift (*Luftbrücke*) of essential supplies from western Germany to west Berlin. The operation was maintained for eleven months, with planes landing every two minutes at peak times. During the blockade, the citywide Berlin government collapsed, as the Soviet representative left the interallied authority in protest at the west's unilateral currency reform, and the German politicians who represented the western sectors on Berlin's city council decamped in November 1948 to form their own separate administration for west Berlin, citing antidemocratic SED tactics.

By the time the Soviets lifted the blockade in May 1949, a separate West German state had become an established fact. In the *Frankfurter Dokumente*, published on 1 August 1948, the western allies had instructed the prime ministers of the *Länder* in their zones to draw up a constitution for a West German state, stipulating that it should be democratic and federal in character. The work was carried out by a *Parlamentarischer Rat* (Parliamentary Council), consisting of representatives of each *Landtag* in the western zones of occupation. Though these German politicians were keen to create a fully fledged German state, they insisted that the new constitution should not be termed a *Verfassung*, the usual German word, but instead a *Grundgesetz* (Basic Law). Though this made very little practical difference to the new state's structures, the terminology implied that the new state was a temporary measure – a *Provisorium* – and left the way clear for a complete German state to be created once the divisions between the Soviet and the western occupation zones could be healed. Similarly, the choice of a sleepy provincial town, Bonn, as the new West German capital underlined the envisaged impermanence of the new structures. Many German politicians still hoped that the unified German state would also contain the territories east of the *Oder-Neiße-Linie* which had been part of Germany in 1937. The western allies approved the *Grundgesetz* (discussed in Chapter 6) in May 1949, and the *Bundesrepublik Deutschland* (BRD, or Federal Republic of Germany, FRG) was created.

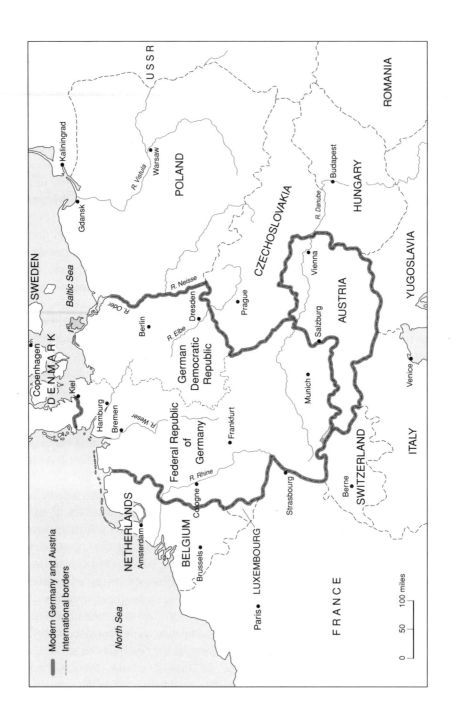

Map 5.2: Central Europe, 1949–1990

Meanwhile, parallel developments in the Soviet zone also led to the formation of a separate state. As early as 1946 the SED had drawn up a draft constitution, originally intended for a united German state, and this formed the basis for further discussions within the zone once it became clear that no agreement would be reached with the west. The framework for the constitutional debate was the *Volkskongressbewegung* ('People's Congress Movement'), which assembled unelected representatives from the various political parties and other organisations (such as the trade unions and the youth movement). Shortly after the *Grundgesetz* became law in the west, elections were held in the Soviet zone to a third *Volkskongress*. However, the influence of the Soviet military authority and the SED over the CDU and LDPD in particular led to the various parties and organisations presenting a single, jointly agreed list of candidates who stood for 'German unity and a just peace treaty with Germany'. Though these were almost universally shared aspirations, only 66 per cent cast a *Ja* vote, 34 per cent preferring not to legitimise an election which offered no real alternative. The duly elected *Dritter Volkskongress* selected a smaller *Volksrat* (People's Council) to carry out detailed work on the new constitution; once the *Bundestag*, the *Bundesrepublik*'s parliament, was constituted, the *Volksrat* proclaimed the constitution of the new *Deutsche Demokratische Republik* (DDR, or German Democratic Republic, GDR) in the Soviet zone on 7 October 1949, and declared itself the *provisorische Volkskammer*, the new state's provisional parliament.

Who divided Germany?

By 1949 Germany had lost large areas of the territory it had occupied when Hitler came to power in 1933. The remaining area had been divided into two entirely separate states with different currencies and increasingly divergent economic systems. Both states initially claimed to speak for the entire German nation, but the creation of neither had been formally legitimised by a referendum, and neither state recognised the other's right to exist. Furthermore, the old *Reichshauptstadt*, Berlin, was itself divided both politically and economically: the GDR claimed that the Soviet sector of Berlin was its own capital, while the western allies maintained that the whole of Berlin remained under four-power control, jealously guarding their rights in West Berlin as a toehold within the Soviet bloc.

The question of responsibility for Germany's division was often presented in very black and white terms during the Cold War. Official GDR histories blamed western *Spalter* ('splitters') for the division, correctly noting that the west made every significant first move (the currency reform which introduced the western '*Spaltermark*', the *Frankfurter Dokumente*, the creation of the *Bundesrepublik*) and claiming that the western allies' decision to negotiate Germany's future without the Soviet Union represented a breach of the 1945 Potsdam Agreement. The west, meanwhile, blamed the Soviet authorities and the SED for pursuing their political agenda in an undemocratic fashion which made agreement impossible, forcing unilateral progress. The Berlin Blockade and the SED's intimidation of the elected Berlin city council in 1948 are taken as evidence of this.

Certainly there was intransigence on all sides. Each of the wartime allies recognised the crucial importance of Germany to Europe's future development, and each wished to make a decisive contribution to the shape of the future state. However, the incompatible aspirations of the Soviet Union and the western powers fractured Germany along the borders between the separate occupation zones. For the French in particular, Germany's division was in any case desirable, as it weakened a state which had invaded France on three occasions (1870, 1914 and 1940) in the previous eighty years. Churchill also initially took this view, arriving at the Potsdam Conference with maps showing different scenarios for dividing Germany into two or more separate states.

Debate continues particularly about the Soviet Union's policy objectives for postwar Germany, with suggestions that Stalin had always intended to turn the Soviet occupation zone into a communist puppet state. While Soviet archival records on this issue are still inaccessible, the debate is necessarily rather speculative. It certainly seems likely that Stalin wished to extend Soviet influence across Germany, but improbable that he would have provoked conflict with the western powers, particularly so soon after the highly costly Second World War, by attempting a communist takeover of the entire country. But the transformation of just the Soviet zone into a separate communist state was also not in Stalin's interests. The Soviet zone seemed unviable as an independent state, as it was poor in natural resources and had an underdeveloped infrastructure; furthermore, the division of Germany impeded the Soviet Union's access to the reparations it had been promised from the western zones. Finally, the inclusion of the strong West German state in the west's anti-Soviet defensive alliance, the North Atlantic Treaty Organisation (NATO), was the worst possible outcome for the Soviet Union as it tried to rebuild and consolidate after the Second World War. The USSR's attempts during the 1950s to overcome Germany's division by offering to sacrifice the GDR (see p. 163) testify to this.

Germany's division was, however, in the interests of many German politicians themselves. The alternative socialist society postulated by the communists was incompatible with the free market democracy based on Christian values favoured by many after the war. Dividing the country along ideological lines removed the need for either side to compromise with the other. The SED's leader, Walter Ulbricht, was no more prepared to compromise Marxist-Leninist doctrine than were the leaders of the two principal western parties, Konrad Adenauer and Kurt Schumacher, to make concessions to the Soviet occupation authorities and their communist protégés. Though both sides frequently spoke of securing German unity, each meant a German unity on their own terms. Thus the communists and more radical social democrats built their state in the east, where they had traditionally been strongest, under Soviet protection, while the western state developed along the liberal democratic lines preferred by its occupiers. The predominantly Catholic nature of the south and west of Germany, *Bundesrepublik* heartlands, cemented this tendency. The SED could never have secured popular support for monopoly rule across the whole of Germany, and furthermore faced opposition from the western powers in their zones. Equally, the western CDU, which dominated the early development of the *Bundesrepublik*, would have been proportionally weaker and forced to make concessions had it attempted to extend its power into predominantly Protestant and traditionally more leftward-leaning eastern Germany. Partition seemed to serve each party's best interests.

Though Germany's division between east and west, communist and capitalist, was not consciously planned as a punishment for the crimes of the *Drittes Reich*, ultimately this outcome must be traced back to Germany's unconditional surrender in 1945, made necessary by the war of aggression which Hitler launched and which many Germans fought with dedication.

The rebirth of Austria

In 1938 most Austrians had welcomed the long-awaited *Anschluss* with Germany, and in the following years many served willingly in the armed forces of the *Drittes Reich*. However, by 1945 the catastrophe of Nazism had finally created what Austria had lacked since 1918: a separate identity, built on a widespread desire to distance Austria from the criminal German state.

The allied powers concurred in this view to a certain extent. In 1943, in the 'Moscow Declaration', they had already declared that they considered the *Anschluss* of 1938 null and void. However, they did not give Austria the status of a liberated country. Instead, like Germany, Austria was occupied as part of the defeated *Drittes Reich* and divided into four zones of occupation. The capital, Vienna, was divided into five sectors: one for each allied power and the fifth, within the central *Ring*, occupied jointly by all four. Unlike Germany, Austria was immediately permitted to reestablish a central government. As in 1918, the task of creating the new state, quickly known as the *Zweite Republik* (Second Republic), fell to Karl Renner, initially appointed for the task by the Soviets. He reinstated the pre-Dollfuß constitution of the *Erste Republik* and constructed a coalition government of the principal political groupings (the socialists, Christians and communists). At the first elections in November 1945, the communists received a humiliating 5 per cent of the vote, while the conservative Christians, reorganised in the *Österreichische Volkspartei* (ÖVP), just scraped an absolute majority. However, the two principal parties – the ÖVP and the social democrats – continued in coalition (with the communists until 1947) until 1966.

The decision for coalition reflected the perceived need for national unity during the occupation period. As in Germany, the occupying powers could not agree on a common policy for the country. Austria's relatively insignificant size also meant that deciding its future was not an allied priority. However, Austria escaped Germany's fate of partition. In 1946 the allies gave the central government full powers in all but constitutional matters, though they reserved the right to veto any Austrian laws to which all objected, an increasingly unlikely scenario as the Cold War deepened. Austria also benefited from the Marshall Plan.

Nonetheless, significant differences did emerge between the Soviet and the western zones of Austria. The Soviets were unable to establish the KPÖ as the nucleus for a Soviet satellite state in Austria (the repressive communist takeovers in Austria's eastern neighbours quickly disillusioned most KPÖ adherents), but profited economically from their occupation. Although the western allies vetoed Soviet proposals to take $250 million in reparations from Austria, the Soviets claimed 'German' assets in their zone, defining these as companies run by the old *Reich*, even if they had been confiscated from their previous Austrian owners or nationalised by the Austrian state. The Soviets thus controlled the Austrian oil industry and many of the key enterprises in their zone; they employed 10 per cent of the Austrian workforce in the Soviet firms created from these assets, and removed profits estimated at up to $1 billion from the country by 1955.

Particularly given this background, the Austrian government was anxious to secure full sovereignty. The Soviets delayed progress in talks between Austria and the four allies until after Stalin's death in 1953. In 1955, however, the Soviets agreed to remove their occupation troops from Austria and lift remaining allied rights. In return they required compensation for the 'German' assets, a guarantee that there would be no renewed *Anschluss*, and permanent Austrian neutrality. In abandoning their attempts to bring Austria within their sphere of influence, the Soviets were probably attempting to wrest concessions from the west over the still undecided, and more significant, question of Germany's postwar status.

For the Austrians, the terms were acceptable: there was no desire for *Anschluss*, and the Swiss example of neutrality had been proposed by some Austrian politicians soon after the end of the war. However, the Austrian government was careful to ensure that the vow of *immerfortwährende Neutralität* (perpetual neutrality) was made as a sovereign Austrian decision, not as a prerequisite of a peace treaty with the allies. Further underlining this point, the treaty of 1955 was not a peace treaty but a *Staatsvertrag* (state treaty).

Though initially not universally welcomed by the Austrian public, a strong consensus quickly grew around neutrality, and enabled the country to act as a link between east and west throughout the Cold War. Even though Austria developed politically and economically as a 'western' country, successive governments jealously guarded the country's neutral status, which was only seriously challenged after the Soviet bloc collapsed in 1989–91.

Document 5: *Aufruf des Zentralkomitees der Kommunistischen Partei Deutschlands*, 11 June 1945

Schaffendes Volk in Stadt und Land!

Männer und Frauen! Deutsche Jugend!

Wohin wir blicken, Ruinen, Schutt und Asche. Unsere Städte sind zerstört, weite ehemals fruchtbare Gebiete verwüstet und verlassen. Die Wirtschaft ist desorganisiert und völlig gelähmt. Millionen und aber Millionen Menschenopfer hat der Krieg verschlungen...

Und wer trägt daran die Schuld?

Die Schuld und Verantwortung tragen die gewissenlosen Abenteurer und Verbrecher, die die Schuld am Kriege tragen. Es sind die Hitler und Göring, Himmler und Goebbels, die aktiven Anhänger und Helfer der Nazipartei. Es sind die Träger des reaktionären Militarismus, die Keitel, Jodl und Konsorten. Es sind die imperialistischen Auftraggeber der Nazipartei, die Herren der Großbanken und Konzerne, die Krupp und Röchling, Poensgen und Siemens. . . .

Nicht nur Hitler ist schuld an den Verbrechen, die an der Menschheit begangen wurden! Ihr Teil Schuld tragen auch die zehn Millionen Deutsche, die 1932 bei freien Wahlen für Hitler stimmten, obwohl wir Kommunisten warnten: »Wer Hitler wählt, der wählt den Krieg!«

Ihr Teil Schuld tragen alle jene deutschen Männer und Frauen, die willenlos und widerstandslos zusahen, wie Hitler die Macht an sich riß, wie er alle demokratischen Organisationen, vor allem die Arbeiterorganisationen, zerschlug und die besten Deutschen einsperren, martern und köpfen ließ. . . .

Jetzt gilt es, gründlich und für immer die Lehren aus der Vergangenheit zu ziehen. *Ein ganz neuer Weg muß beschritten werden!*

Werde sich jeder Deutsche bewußt, daß der Weg, den unser Volk bisher ging, ein falscher Weg, ein Irrweg war, der in Schutt und Schande, Krieg und Verderben führte!

Nicht nur der Schutt der zerstörten Städte, auch der reaktionäre Schutt aus der Vergangenheit muß gründlich hinweggeräumt werden. Möge der Neubau Deutschlands auf solider Grundlage erfolgen, damit eine dritte Wiederholung der imperialistischen Katastrophenpolitik unmöglich wird.

Mit der Vernichtung des Hitlerismus gilt es gleichzeitig, die Sache der Demokratisierung Deutschlands, die Sache der bürgerlich-demokratischen Umbildung, die 1848 begonnen wurde, zu Ende zu führen, die feudalen Überreste völlig zu beseitigen und den reaktionären altpreußischen Militarismus mit allen seinen ökonomischen und politischen Ablegern zu vernichten.

Wir sind der Auffassung, daß der Weg, Deutschland das Sowjetsystem aufzuzwingen, falsch wäre, denn dieser Weg entspricht nicht den gegenwärtigen Entwicklungsbedingungen in Deutschland.

Wir sind vielmehr der Auffassung, daß die entscheidenden Interessen des deutschen Volkes in der gegenwärtigen Lage für Deutschland einen anderen Weg vorschreiben, und zwar den Weg der *Aufrichtung eines antifaschistischen, demokratischen Regimes, einer parlamentarisch-demokratischen Republik mit allen demokratischen Rechten und Freiheiten für das Volk.*

Source: Dokumente zur Geschichte der SED (Berlin: Dietz, 1986), Vol. 2, pp. 7–12 (shortened).

Topics

FOR DISCUSSION / FURTHER RESEARCH

■ According to the KPD's first postwar declaration (Document 5), who was responsible for the catastrophe of national socialism?

■ How did the KPD propose to overcome the Nazi legacy?

■ By what point did Germany's division become unavoidable?

■ Discuss the view that partition was the only viable solution to the German question in the immediate postwar era.

■ How does the imposition of SED rule in eastern Germany compare with the emergence of communist-dominated states elsewhere in eastern Europe after 1945?

CHAPTER 6

Rehabilitation, restoration and reform: West Germany, 1949–1989

The rivalries which had sparked two world wars inspired western European politicians to unite the different states in a common interest after 1945. The Cold War, which overshadowed this period, prevented a pan-European settlement, but in 1949 gave rise to a western military alliance, NATO (North Atlantic Treaty Organisation), including the United States and Canada. Joint institutions also countered economic rivalries: the multinational common market for coal and steel (*Montanunion*) of 1951 expanded into the European Economic Community (EEC) in 1958. By 1989 the renamed European Community's (EC) twelve member states shared political, cultural and legal norms, and were building an open market for goods and services. A new political consensus also favoured unity: once Spain and Portugal had removed right-wing dictatorships in the mid-1970s, all western Europe was characterised by stable democracies. The period saw unprecedented economic prosperity, and accompanying environmental damage.

Structures of the *Bundesrepublik*

None of the German states, and none of the chronological periods we have discussed so far, has been characterised by stability. At least with the benefit of hindsight, each of the pre-1949 regimes seemed to contain the seeds of their own destruction. Even Bismarck's *Reich* lasted for less than fifty years, doomed by its military nature and its attempt to exclude democratic participation in an age of mass politics.

By contrast, the Federal Republic of Germany has emerged as one of the most stable states in postwar western Europe, proving strong enough to see off internal challenges from extremists and terrorists, and to absorb a former communist state, the GDR (see Chapter 8). The foundations for this success have been the inclusiveness of its structures and the firm lead given by its first *Bundeskanzler* (federal chancellor), Konrad Adenauer. Nonetheless, particularly in the early years, these policies attracted criticism that stability had been bought at the price of national unity and full freedoms, and that the legacy of the past had not been fully addressed.

During its first decade, the contours of the *Bundesrepublik Deutschland* were defined by three principal factors, whose influence is still apparent today: its constitution, the *Grundgesetz* (Basic Law); *Bundeskanzler* Adenauer; and the *soziale Marktwirtschaft* (social market economy) which produced the *Wirtschaftswunder* (economic miracle) on which, arguably, both the country's prosperity and its political stability ultimately rest.

The authors of the *Grundgesetz* (see Document 6a), drawn up during 1948 and 1949 according to broad allied requirements, consciously drew both on the attempts made since 1848 to establish a democratic *Rechtsstaat* (state based on the rule of law), and on the shortcomings and failures of earlier constitutional settlements, principally those of the 1919 *Reichsverfassung* which had culminated in Hitler's legal subversion of the state. As we have seen in previous chapters, these earlier shortcomings had included unaccountable governments, structurally weak parliaments and overbearing heads of state, able to override the democratic framework at will. The new *Grundgesetz* was designed to avoid these pitfalls.

The two guiding principles of the *Grundgesetz* are democracy and federalism. Federalism not only safeguards the regional identities which have been so important in German history, but also upholds democracy by providing a strong counterweight to the role of central government. One of the two houses of parliament – the *Bundesrat* – represents the governments of the different *Länder* and its approval is required for a number of laws. Article 20 of the *Grundgesetz* stipulates that neither of these guiding principles may be abandoned, and that Germans have the right to resist (*das Recht zum Widerstand*) anyone who attempts to subvert the democratic order; furthermore, this article may not be legally altered. This formulation is a response to 1933, designed to prevent any future attempt to undermine democracy.

The structures of government equally reflect the lessons of the weak *Weimarer Republik*. In the *Bundesrepublik*, the centre of power is unambiguously the *Bundeskanzler*, while the head of state, the *Bundespräsident*, is not directly elected and has only representative functions (such as receiving heads of state and counter-signing laws). The *Bundeskanzler* is elected by the lower house of parliament, the *Bundestag*, and not dependent on the *Bundespräsident*'s support. However, the *Bundestag* may not act irresponsibly: normally a *Bundeskanzler* may only be removed by the *Bundestag* if it simultaneously proposes an alternative candidate (Article 67). This *konstruktives Misstrauensvotum* ('constructive vote of no confidence') ensures that parliament cannot abrogate responsibility for government, and insulates the *Bundeskanzler* from the passing whims of *Bundestag* members (the *konstruktives Misstrauensvotum* has only once successfully unseated a *Bundeskanzler*). The *Bundeskanzler*'s role is so dominant within the *Grundgesetz* (Article 65) that some commentators have spoken of a *Kanzlerdemokratie* ('chancellor democracy') rather than a parliamentary democracy.

The *Bundestag* itself is elected by a complex method in which each elector has two votes. The first is for a local constituency representative, elected by a simple majority (the candidate in each constituency with the most votes wins). The second vote elects candidates from party lists. It is thus possible to vote for a social democrat as a constituency representative, but to cast one's second vote for the liberal party's candidate list. The *Bundestag*'s overall composition is determined by the *Zweitstimmen* (second votes), giving smaller parties with little hope of winning individual con-stituencies greater chances of representation. However, to avoid a plethora of tiny parties gaining parliamentary seats and the difficulties this presents in forming coalition governments (another lesson of the Weimar years), political parties must normally achieve at least 5 per cent of the *Zweitstimmen* to win *Bundestag* seats. This *Fünfprozenthürde* (5 per cent barrier) can prevent small extremist parties from gaining a parliamentary platform for their political message – as the NSDAP did in the late 1920s. However, the *Fünfprozenthürde* cannot alone prevent extremist parties with wide support from being elected. To date, though, no radical right-wing party has ever won *Bundestag* seats.

The potential threat of extremist parties is countered in other ways, partly through the education system and organs such as the federal and regional *Zentralen für politische Bildung* ('political education centres'), which exist to cement support for the democratic parliamentary order. The *Grundgesetz* itself also provides mechanisms to prevent extremism: all political parties are constitutionally required to uphold the *Grundgesetz* (Article 21), and a *Bundesverfassungsgericht* (Constitutional Court) can ban parties or other groups which infringe this law. Any organisation or individual can also invoke the *Bundesverfassungsgericht* to rule on whether a law or official ruling breaches the *Grundgesetz*. On occasion the court has overturned controversial laws, or insisted that they be modified. Some critics have seen in this system, designed to preserve the democratic order, a weakening of the *Bundestag*'s rights. However, the judges who form the *Bundesverfassungsgericht* are elected by the *Bundestag* and *Bundesrat* and thus derive their powers from a democratic base. Between them, the various safeguards in the *Grundgesetz*, the *Fünfprozenthürde* and the *Bundesverfassungsgericht* effectively limit certain aspects of absolute democracy to ensure that democracy itself is preserved.

Political parties of the *Bundesrepublik Deutschland*

Christlich-Demokratische Union (CDU): successor to the Roman Catholic *Zentrum*, but now a non-denominational, broadly based party of family values, and proponents of free economics linked to a strong welfare state.

Christlich-Soziale Union (CSU): Bavarian sister party of the CDU.

Sozialdemokratische Partei Deutschlands (SPD): broadly based centre-left party, which abandoned its traditional Marxist tenets after 1959.

Freie Demokratische Partei (FDP): successor to the prewar liberal parties (see p. 141).

Die Grünen: ecological party formed in 1979–80; fused with the East German dissidents' party, *Bündnis 90*, after German unification in 1992–93.

Kommunistische Partei Deutschlands (KPD) / *Deutsche Kommunistische Partei* (DKP) / *Partei des demokratischen Sozialismus* (PDS): the KPD, successor to the pre-1933 party, was banned in the *Bundesrepublik* in 1956 but reformed (legally) as the DKP in 1968. Since 1990 the PDS, successor to the ruling East German communist party (SED), has been the principal party of the radical left.

Nationaldemokratische Partei Deutschlands (NPD) / *Republikaner* / *Deutsche Volksunion* (DVU): parties of the far right; their policies have included racist and neo-Nazi elements, but none has yet won *Bundestag* seats.

The *Grundgesetz* is also notable for placing basic human rights (*Grundrechte*) in its first nineteen articles, giving them a prominence not seen in earlier German constitutions. As a direct repudiation of the crimes of national socialism, the *Bundesrepublik* is committed to upholding the freedom and value of each individual, and equality of race, gender, religion and opinion. The principles of the 1848/49 *Frankfurter Parlament*, enriched by the lessons of the mid-twentieth century, have found renewed expression in the *Grundgesetz*.

1949–1969: Defining moments

With the *Grundgesetz* in force by late May 1949, the first *Bundestag* elections were held in August. The CDU/CSU had a narrow lead over the SPD and formed a coalition with the liberals of the FDP and a small right-wing party centred on Lower Saxony (Niedersachsen), the *Deutsche Partei*. The CDU's leader, **Konrad Adenauer**, was duly elected as *Bundeskanzler* by the *Bundestag* with a slender majority of one vote. Ludwig Erhard, who had already masterminded the beginnings of economic recovery with the currency reform in the western zones during 1948, became *Wirtschaftsminister* (economics minister). The alternative – a grand coalition (*große Koalition*) of the CDU and SPD – was rejected, with decisive consequences for the *Bundesrepublik*'s development: Adenauer was determined to set the state on an unambiguous course of western integration and economic growth based on a market economy, and believed that the SPD would endanger both goals.

The new government was not, however, entirely the master of its own destiny. Not only was Germany divided and the Saarland occupied, but the *Bundesrepublik*'s sovereignty was limited in its early years by the remaining rights of the western allies, set out in a

TABLE 6.1: *BUNDESTAG* ELECTION RESULTS (SEATS WON), 1949–1998

	1949	1953	1957	1961	1965	1969	1972	1976	1980	1983	1987	1990	1994	1998
CDU/CSU	139	243	270	242	245	242	225	243	226	244	223	319	294	245
FDP	52	48	41	67	49	30	41	39	53	34	46	79	47	43
SPD	131	151	169	190	202	224	230	214	218	193	186	239	252	298
Grüne/B90	—	—	—	—	—	—	—	—	—	27	42	8	49	47
KPD/DKP/PDS	15	—	—	—	—	—	—	—	—	—	—	17	30	36
Other parties*	65	45	17	—	—	—	—	—	—	—	—	—	—	—

Note: * not including the single seat allocated to representatives of the Danish minority in Schleswig-Holstein.

Source: compiled from *Bundestag* statistics.

Konrad Adenauer (1876–1967)

As a Catholic Rhinelander, Adenauer grew up close to France and with a deep distrust of rule from Prussian Berlin. He trained as a lawyer and became *Oberbürgermeister* (mayor) of Cologne in 1917. He stamped his mark on the city and was sometimes viewed as a potential *Reichskanzler*, but was forced from office by the Nazis in 1933, and arrested in 1944 in the wake of the Stauffenberg plot (see p. 105). A prewar member of the *Zentrum*, he emerged as leader of the western CDU after 1945 and was already 73 when he became *Bundeskanzler* in 1949. He resigned, his policies somewhat discredited, only in 1963, aged 87, and continued to lead his party until his death four years later.

Besatzungsstatut (Occupation Statute). The *Bundesrepublik* was not permitted a foreign ministry or armed forces, nor permitted to control its own foreign trade. The allies could veto any laws, and resume full powers if they saw fit.

Rather like Gustav Stresemann in the *Weimarer Republik*, Adenauer aimed principally at reestablishing Germany's full sovereignty and independence, with the additional challenge of reuniting the eastern GDR with the western *Bundesrepublik*. Adenauer believed that German independence could best be secured in alliance with the western powers, which must be persuaded that a new democratic Germany would never again threaten world peace. As a conservative Catholic, Adenauer's politics were in any case diametrically opposed to those of the communist Soviet Union. He resisted compromises with the Soviets, even if they might enable a speedier German unification, recognising the danger of German subordination to the Soviet superpower. Instead, Adenauer believed that a strong, clearly superior West German state would exert a magnetic attraction on the GDR: unification would be achieved by a *Politik der Stärke* ('policy of strength') and the future united Germany would become a western parliamentary democracy, preferably guided by Adenauer's own Christian democracy.

Taking the long view, Adenauer's policy might be deemed successful: when the GDR finally collapsed into the arms of the stronger *Bundesrepublik* in 1990 under his CDU successor as *Bundeskanzler*, Helmut Kohl (see Chapter 8), the *Politik der Stärke* seemed vindicated. In the shorter term, however, Adenauer's dogged refusal to concede an inch to the Soviet leadership or the GDR government in East Berlin deepened German divisions, encouraged the SED to retaliate by building the Berlin Wall in 1961, and prevented most contacts between the two sides over two decades. It is with this background in mind that we must consider Adenauer's policies for the *Bundesrepublik* itself.

Adenauer began lobbying at once for a reduction in the scope of the *Besatzungsstatut*, with some success. The *Petersberger Abkommen* (Petersberg Agreement), signed by the *Bundesregierung* and the western allies just weeks after Adenauer had become *Bundeskanzler*, allowed West German participation in the international body which controlled coal and steel production in the *Ruhrgebiet*, and reduced the scale of industrial dismantling for reparations. By 1951, the *Bundesrepublik* had its own *Auswärtiges Amt* (foreign ministry); the autocratically minded Adenauer appointed himself *Außenminister*.

The western allies were beginning to appreciate not only that Adenauer could be relied upon to deliver a democratic and pro-western German state, but also that the deepening Cold War made the *Bundesrepublik's* participation in western defence a necessity. This was underlined with the outbreak of the **Korean War** in 1950. Though only five years had passed since the *Wehrmacht's* defeat, Adenauer saw that a fully sovereign Germany would require its own armed forces, and that the *Bundesrepublik's* participation in a western defence alliance could be made dependent on the restoration of German sovereignty by the allies.

Korean War, 1950–1953

Like Germany, Korea was divided after the Second World War. After the Soviet Union's north Korean client state invaded the south (under US protection) in June 1950, an indecisive war raged for three years until a truce was signed. The war symbolised superpower conflicts and represented a scenario which many feared would be repeated in Europe over Germany. The *Bundesrepublik* benefited economically from its exports of the iron and steel required for weapons production, an important boost to the country's recovery.

Negotiations about the size, role and command structures of West German armed forces began within months of the *Bundesrepublik's* creation. Predictably, given the experience of German invasion, France attempted to place West German troops under allied authority; this led to the proposal of a 'European Defence Community' (EDC) alongside NATO, in which troops would be subordinate to international command. The western European states agreed to establish the EDC in 1952, and at the same time the western allies signed a related treaty with the *Bundesrepublik*, the *Deutschlandvertrag*, which would lift the *Besatzungsstatut* and transfer all but residual allied rights to the *Bundesrepublik*.

The prospect of German rearmament appalled many prominent West Germans, including Adenauer's *Innenminister* (minister for the interior), Gustav Heinemann, who resigned over the issue in 1950. Some believed (correctly) that German unity was being sacrificed to Adenauer's *Westintegration*, while others, particularly the pacifists inspired by the great loss of life in the recent world war, launched the '*ohne mich*' ('without me') movement and swore to take no part in remilitarisation. Nonetheless, the CDU's election victory in 1953 strengthened Adenauer's hand.

The EDC treaty required ratification by all member states; the process ground on for two years until the French Senate finally rejected the plan in October 1954, still perturbed by the prospect of German forces. Though Adenauer's policy seemed in ruins, the west still required a West German defence contribution. An alternative solution – West German membership of NATO – was adopted by 1955, the French having come under strong American pressure to agree. This consequently enabled ratification of the *Deutschlandvertrag* by which the *Besatzungsstatut* was lifted. The *Bundesrepublik* created its own *Bundeswehr* (preparations had been under way for some years), partly led by experienced former *Wehrmacht* officers, and introduced conscription.

The status of the Saarland was resolved shortly afterwards. As the population rejected French proposals to integrate the region into France, the Saarland was incorporated into the *Bundesrepublik* on 1 January 1957 under Article 23 of the *Grundgesetz*, which allowed any part of Germany to accede to the territory covered by the Basic Law.

Agreement with France over mutual defence and the Saarland was part of a broader movement to involve the *Bundesrepublik* in an integrated western Europe. This had begun with the *Bundesrepublik*'s membership of the Council of Europe (*Europarat*) in 1951, and progressed through the agreements between France, Italy, West Germany and the Benelux countries to pool their coal and steel resources in an open market, the European Coal and Steel Community (*Montanunion*), in 1952. The first stage of this process was completed when these six countries signed the Treaty of Rome to create the EEC (*Europäische Wirtschaftsgemeinschaft*, EWG) on 1 January 1958.

The contrast with the victors' treatment of Germany after 1918 could not have been clearer: while the *Weimarer Republik* was saddled with reparations and war guilt, the *Bundesrepublik* was – cautiously – accepted into the international community and given a stake in its success. However, the GDR was not involved in any of these western organisations, and instead became tied into parallel eastern equivalents. The *Bundesrepublik*'s sovereignty was secured at the cost of Germany's deepening division.

The *Bundesrepublik*'s stability depended on economic success as well as its international status. Despite significant destruction in bombing raids, and the dismantling of some industrial plant on allied orders after 1945, much of the wartime investment in the economic infrastructure remained intact, providing entrepreneurs with a relatively strong starting base. Nonetheless, given the scale of defeat in 1945, West Germany staged a remarkable recovery in the first postwar decade, often described as a *Wirtschaftswunder*. This resulted from a group of related policies, including the 'European Recovery Program' (see p. 118), the successful currency reform of June 1948 and the introduction of the *soziale Marktwirtschaft*, principally associated with Ludwig Erhard ('*Vater des Wirtschaftswunders*').

Before June 1948, producers had been storing goods, rather than selling them for restricted prices in a worthless currency (the old *Reichsmark*). The lifting of most price controls and the introduction of the *Deutsche Mark* (*D-Mark*) released these goods for sale, rendering the black market largely redundant and giving workers an incentive to earn. However, market forces were not given entirely free rein: cartels of producers were outlawed to prevent price fixing, and a strong social security safety net was introduced, with employer contributions and guaranteed protection for the unemployed and sick. The law also required a degree of *Mitbestimmung* (workers' codetermination) in the running of most companies; arguably this reduced tensions between employers and employees, limiting strikes and protecting productivity. Wage levels remained relatively low during the 1950s, as the westward migration of some three million East Germans (many of them young, skilled workers) prevented labour shortages. Profit levels were consequently higher, and taxation policy encouraged businesses to reinvest the surplus in additional capacity and production. The West German economy was also geared to exports of high-value manufactured goods and boosted by the Korean War. Underpinning the whole policy was monetary caution. The *Bundesbank* (central bank) was independent of the government, and required by law to protect the value of the *D-Mark*. This ensured that money supply was carefully limited and avoided the hyper-inflation which had undermined earlier governments when paper money had flooded the market.

Erhard's reforms took several years to take root, but unemployment fell and personal wealth grew steadily during the 1950s, enabling many West Germans to afford cars, foreign holidays and the new domestic appliances (fridges, televisions and the like) by the end of the decade. During this period, public expenditure on housing also largely resolved the accommodation shortages created by wartime damage. However, some West Germans benefited from the recovery more than others. Although the 1948 currency reform had originally provided the same amount of *Startgeld* (initially just DM 40) to each citizen, and written off most of the devalued savings in *Reichsmark* accounts, those with material assets had a head start; any debts they had incurred in acquiring these assets were also written off in the reform. The government attempted to reallocate wealth to the many Germans who had arrived from the lost eastern provinces with no property by a *Lastenausgleich* ('equalisation of burdens' law). This redistributed the revenue from an additional income tax to the poorest citizens, though it could not entirely redress the imbalances within West German society.

The overall success of this economic policy not only kept the CDU at the head of government until the late 1960s (the architect of the 'miracle', Erhard, himself succeeded Adenauer as *Bundeskanzler* in 1963), but increasingly wedded West Germans to the *Bundesrepublik* and the broader western European structures, while weakening interest in any negotiated reunification with the GDR which might imperil this prosperity. Though relatively successful with its own economic reconstruction, the GDR's planned economy could not keep pace (see Chapter 7): increasingly, the affluent *Bundesrepublik* exerted a magnetic attraction over the less wealthy East Germans. The consensus which supported the *soziale Marktwirtschaft* was best symbolised by the SPD's decision to adopt this economic system, and move away from adherence to Marxist planned economics, at its conference in Bad Godesberg in 1959. The party's *Bad Godesberger Programm*, which also accepted Adenauer's policy of *Westintegration*, marked the beginning of the SPD's transformation from a party representing a specific interest group (the working class) into a broader party of principle (essentially, social equality) to which people of all backgrounds could subscribe. The emergence of these two *Volksparteien* (mass parties) – the CDU/CSU and the SPD – proved a key source of political stability in the *Bundesrepublik* and marked a clear break with the political parties of narrow interest which had dominated the *Kaiserreich* and the *Weimarer Republik*.

The successful implementation of *Westintegration* and economic recovery by the Adenauer government – against the strong opposition of traditionalists, pacifists, those who prioritised Germany's national unity and, initially, the SPD – could only be achieved by a strong government. Threats (real or imagined) to the new order were dealt with robustly: two political parties, the far-right *Sozialistische Reichspartei* and the KPD, were banned by the *Bundesverfassungsgericht* in 1952 and 1956 respectively.

Adenauer's style of rule was often somewhat authoritarian: he ensured in the early days that the allied commanders dealt exclusively with him, not his ministers, and failed to consult his cabinet on foreign policy initiatives, preferring to create *faits accomplis*. This personal approach sometimes led to misjudgements which slowly undermined confidence in the *Bundeskanzler*. For example, in 1960 Adenauer hoped to establish a new commercial television channel, controlled by CDU supporters who could be expected to broadcast favourable reports on government policy. The opposition of the *Länder* and ultimately the *Bundesverfassungsgericht* prevented the plan. In 1959, Adenauer announced his intention of resigning the chancellorship and becoming *Bundespräsident*. He withdrew his candidacy when persuaded that the presidency could not constitutionally be transformed into a position of executive authority (as de Gaulle had achieved in France in 1958).

The sometimes high-handed nature of the Adenauer government is best illustrated by two further examples. One concerns Hans Globke, the controversial secretary of state in Adenauer's own chancellery. In 1935 Globke had written the official commentary on the implementation of the racist *Nürnberger Gesetze* (see p. 100). Adenauer refused to dismiss him, and attracted further criticism when his government passed legislation in 1951 requiring the vast majority of the *Beamten* who had lost their positions in the denazification process to be reinstated. Large numbers of former NSDAP members were henceforth appointed to the revived foreign and defence ministries. To some observers – particularly the GDR's propagandists – the policy smacked of a restoration of the old regime, an accusation underpinned by the renewed economic muscle of many of the industrialists who had prospered under the Third Reich. However, there could be no suggestion that the *Bundesrepublik* pursued specifically Nazi policies (even the *Bundeswehr* was limited to an exclusively defensive role), and Adenauer's policy had the benefit of giving the non-criminal adherents of the former regime a stake in the new democracy, rather than attempting to exclude them and risking their dogged opposition. Tacitly, a form of internal reconciliation was taking place, albeit one which initially avoided a clear reckoning with the Nazi past in favour of rebuilding the country. Arguably Adenauer's approach was essential to maintain order and achieve progress in the difficult post-war environment. His rule firmly cemented the notion of the *Bundesrepublik* as a *Kanzlerdemokratie*. However, the provisions of the *Grundgesetz* ensured that democratic rule prevailed.

The '*Spiegel* affair' of 1962 also highlighted the authoritarian streak which many perceived within the government. Following its publication of sensitive information about the *Bundeswehr* and rumours of plans by the CSU defence minister, Franz-Josef Strauß, to equip the *Bundesrepublik* with nuclear weapons, the influential weekly news magazine *Der Spiegel* was accused of treasonous behaviour. The magazine's offices were raided by the police, and its publisher and deputy editor arrested. Strauß and

Adenauer instigated and approved these actions, and kept the justice minister, a member of the **FDP**, the junior coalition party, in the dark. The wave of public protest about this blatant attack on press freedom forced Strauß's resignation, and nearly broke the coalition. The episode underlined that in the *Bundesrepublik*, governments could not act at will outside the law.

Ultimately Adenauer's political strength depended on his electoral support. When this waned after the *Spiegel* affair, and once the GDR cemented Germany's division by building the Berlin Wall in 1961, seemingly contradicting the wisdom of Adenauer's *Politik der Stärke*, the FDP insisted that Adenauer resign the chancellorship, to the relief of many in his own party who felt that the 87-year-old *Bundeskanzler* should make way for a younger man.

The end of the Adenauer era coincided with the coming of age of the first postwar generation, and this generated two decades of challenges to the rather staid founding establishment of the *Bundesrepublik*. The first signs of change, however, were prompted by a relatively minor economic downturn in the mid-1960s which undermined the government of Adenauer's successor, his popular economics minister Ludwig Erhard. The prospect of tax rises to cover public expenditure prompted the FDP to abandon its coalition with the CDU/CSU in 1966; the CDU instead negotiated a grand coalition (*große Koalition*) of the two *Volksparteien*, the CDU/CSU and SPD. Kurt Georg Kiesinger, the CDU leader in Baden-Württemberg, was appointed *Bundeskanzler*, though his work as a radio propagandist for the NSDAP during the Third Reich caused controversy.

> ### *Freie Demokratische Partei* (FDP)
>
> The FDP represents the liberal tradition in German politics. A sometimes uneasy combination of those who principally favour economic liberalism (with minimal restrictions on business freedom, the heirs to the *Nationalliberalen* of the *Kaiserreich*) and those who emphasise personal liberties (successors to the *Fortschrittlichen*), the party has swung between support for the CDU and the SPD. As the proportional representation system makes it difficult for any party to achieve an absolute majority in the *Bundestag*, the FDP has been the natural junior coalition party for most of the *Bundesrepublik*'s history. Its shifting internal consensus has enabled both the SPD (in 1969) and the CDU (in 1982) to take power with its support. When in government, the party has often been rewarded with control of the important *Auswärtiges Amt*. In the late 1990s FDP support dwindled as the party increasingly seemed indistinguishable from the CDU/CSU. The emergence of a fourth major party, the Greens, enabled the SPD to form a coalition without FDP support in 1998.

The SPD's arrival in national government for the first time since 1930 began a process which altered the *Bundesrepublik*'s character, without dismantling the constitutional and economic framework. In particular, the dynamic new *Außenminister*, the SPD's Willy Brandt, embarked on a new *Ostpolitik* which built bridges to the GDR and eastern Europe, and is discussed fully in Chapter 8. The *große Koalition* lasted only three years. In itself this was not surprising, as it united two parties with very different outlooks. However, the political and social consensus experienced vast upheaval during this period. The very existence of the *große Koalition* itself sparked unrest, as the only parliamentary opposition party between 1966 and 1969 was the small FDP. With no opportunity for concerted opposition to the government within the *Bundestag*, opponents began to organise protests outside parliament. The emergence of an *außerparlamentarische Opposition* ('extraparliamentary opposition'), principally comprising left-wingers, established a new political framework with long-lasting effects. Meanwhile, the *Nationaldemokratische Partei Deutschlands* (NPD) presented a short-lived far-right threat to the established order, and won seats in some *Landtage*.

The *große Koalition* incited widespread opposition by introducing a system of 'emergency laws' (*Notstandsgesetze*) which could be invoked if the *Bundesrepublik* ever faced a serious threat. Though there was no immediate danger to avert, such laws were needed if the *Bundesrepublik* were to end the last restrictions on its sovereignty: the western allies had retained the right to intervene and resume power in West Germany in a crisis, unless the state developed its own systems for dealing with such eventualities. This constitutional change had been delayed for many years, as the SPD, when in opposition, had denied the measures the necessary two-thirds majority in the *Bundestag*. The *große Koalition* presented an opportunity to reach agreement on laws which were controversial because they provided for the central government to take additional powers, raising the prospect that a future government might subvert the democratic constitution on the pretext of an emergency as Hitler had done. The issue particularly enraged students and young radicals, who were beginning to question the conservative ethos which prevailed in the economy and society of the *Bundesrepublik*, and also to question the actions of their parents' generation under national socialism. This critical trend coincided with new historical research into the origins of the *Drittes Reich* and the publication of Fritz Fischer's book which claimed Germany's guilt in the outbreak of the First World War (see p. 47). Attention had already been focused on German guilt by the trial in Frankfurt am Main between 1963 and 1965 of some twenty former staff of Auschwitz, and in 1960–62 by the arrest and subsequent execution in Israel of Adolf Eichmann, who had masterminded the deportation of Europe's Jews.

Students were already angered by the undemocratic traditions which persisted in German universities, and, in common with students in the USA and other western European states, firmly opposed western attempts to bring down the communist regime of Ho Chi Minh in Vietnam. The *Bundesregierung*'s role as a chief ally of the USA caused as much unrest as its support of the undemocratic regime of the Shah of Iran. Protests in West Berlin against the *Bundesregierung*'s warm reception for the Shah on a state visit in 1967 were countered by heavy police attacks, during which one student, Benno Ohnesorg, was killed by a police bullet. Students regarded the shooting as symptomatic of an authoritarian state. Protest marches erupted again in spring 1968, fuelled particularly by the Vietnam War. The right-wing *Axel Springer Verlag*, publisher of the populist *Bild-Zeitung* and numerous other right-wing newspapers, condemned the left-wing students in articles which suggested their radical repression. When a leading protester, Rudi Dutschke, was seriously injured in April 1968 students believed that his assailant, a young nationalist, had been incited by these articles. Consequently the students directed their attacks against the publisher's printing houses, claiming that Springer's dominance of the West German press market prevented freedom of speech.

Though the protests died away once the *Notstandsgesetze* were finally passed, and after the inspirational hopes for a reformist 'socialism with a human face' in Czechoslovakia (the 'Prague Spring') had been dashed by the invasion of Soviet tanks, the movement had made its mark, and not just in the universities where cautious reform began. The national mood was for change: the SPD made gains in the 1969 *Bundestag* elections, and with FDP support Brandt finally formed an SPD-led government.

1969–1989: New challenges

Brandt's priorities were twofold. The continuation of *Ostpolitik* was a principal task, and is discussed in Chapter 8. In domestic politics, Brandt announced (see Document 6b) a policy of 'mehr Demokratie wagen' ('daring more democracy'). Though Brandt was forced to resign in 1974 over the discovery of a GDR spy in his private office, his domestic policies were mainly continued by his SPD successor as *Bundeskanzler*, Helmut Schmidt.

Under the Brandt and Schmidt governments workers' rights of *Mitbestimmung* (codetermination) were extended in most firms, and social legislation included the decriminalisation of abortion and homosexuality. The coalition also hoped to reform the education system to enable greater equality of opportunity. In the universities there were attempts to introduce internal democratisation, and a student loans system (the *Bafög*) was established to expand the higher education system and enable students from poorer families to attend university. The other key plank of these reforms was intended to be the introduction of *Gesamtschulen* (comprehensive schools) in place of the three-tier secondary education system of *Gymnasium* (grammar school for the academically gifted), *Realschule* (for those of average academic ability) and *Hauptschule* (for students destined for manual occupations).

This controversial reform package was still incomplete when Brandt left office in 1974. The new abortion laws were challenged in the *Bundesverfassungsgericht*, and then tightened, since Article 1 of the *Grundgesetz* asserted that 'Die Würde des Menschen ist unantastbar' ('Human dignity shall be inviolable'), and could be applied to unborn children; the extension of *Mitbestimmung* was much delayed by employers' resistance. In education policy, the *Länder* exerted their rights so that university reforms were half-hearted in some regions, while the CDU/CSU-ruled *Länder* refused to introduce *Gesamtschulen*, dividing the uniformity of the national secondary school system.

The Brandt and Schmidt governments did achieve some significant social reforms, and enabled some of the angry generation of 1968 (the *68er*) to begin their *langer Marsch durch die Institutionen* ('long march through the institutions'), taking posts within the German civil service and initiating reform from within. However, a dis-affected minority preferred to remain outside the political mainstream and organised itself in extreme left-wing terrorist organisations, principally the *Rote Armee Fraktion*

('Red Army Faction'), otherwise known as the *Baader-Meinhof-Gruppe* ('Baader-Meinhof Group') after its best known leaders, Andreas Baader and Ulrike Meinhof. To preserve political stability against both the radical left and the neo-Nazi right, the Brandt government introduced the so-called *Radikalenerlass* ('Radicals' Decree'), guidelines which required state employees to refrain from activities which could be interpreted as undermining the order enshrined in the *Grundgesetz*. The measure affected only a tiny minority of the vast workforce in the German public sector (principally communists and assorted other radical left-wingers), but was widely criticised as implementing a form of *Berufsverbot* (debarment from an office or profession) which forced citizens to choose between their career and their political convictions. By 1976 the *Radikalenerlass* was generally no longer enforced.

Though the state organisation itself was bolstered, the terrorist threat proved a major challenge in the mid-1970s. Following the kidnap in 1975 of the West Berlin CDU chairman, Peter Lorenz, set free only after six terrorists were released from prison, the cycle peaked in 1977. The murders of the chairman of the Dresdner Bank, Jürgen Ponto, and the *Generalbundesanwalt* (chief state prosecutor), Siegfried Buback, were followed by the kidnap of the chairman of the employers' and industrialists' associations, Hanns Martin Schleyer. The kidnappers again demanded the release of further terrorists from West German prisons. The Schmidt government had already strengthened its legal powers against terrorists. Its determination to uphold democratic rule against the violent, politically motivated threats of an extremist minority remained intact even when Arab terrorists hijacked a West German plane in support of Schleyer's kidnappers and murdered its pilot. Special German troops stormed the plane, releasing the hostages. Though Schleyer was murdered and three imprisoned terrorists (including Baader) committed suicide, the *Bundesregierung* could claim credit for having withstood this challenge to democracy far more determinedly than the Weimar governments of the early 1920s. Terrorism never again posed the systemic threat of 1977, despite a resurgence of attacks in the late 1980s and early 1990s. These included the high-profile murder of the chairman of the agency responsible for privatising the east German economy.

Besides the terrorist minority and the majority of *68er* who committed themselves to reform from within the system, a third group emerged to pursue radical societal and economic change throughout the 1970s and beyond. Originally inspired by causes such as *antiautoritäre Erziehung* ('anti-authoritarian education'), free love and fuller equality for women and disadvantaged minorities, these groups became increasingly concerned with environmental threats as the 1970s progressed. This mood especially reflected growing concerns over nuclear power, to which the *Bundesregierung* increasingly committed itself during the energy crisis of 1973, when the Arab countries of the Middle East drastically increased world oil prices and sparked a general recession. The mid-1970s saw mass demonstrations at the sites of proposed nuclear power plants.

This wave of protest was heightened by developments in military policy which accompanied a cooling of superpower relations. The Soviet Union had already deployed medium-range missiles in eastern Europe; Schmidt was foremost among western

European leaders in demanding a 'twin track policy', the *Doppelbeschluss*. NATO must deploy similar, modern weapons of its own to resist the perceived Soviet threat, but also pursue talks with the Soviet Union and its allies to achieve nuclear arms control. However, the Soviet invasion of Afghanistan in 1979 and the threat of a similar solution in communist Poland, where martial law was imposed following revolts in 1980–81, precluded warm relations, as did the election of US President Ronald Reagan, a dedicated Cold Warrior, in 1980. The impending deployment of a new generation of nuclear weapons caused outraged public responses in several European countries, and spurred the movement against nuclear power in the *Bundesrepublik*. In 1979 protest groups began fighting local elections; in 1980 they coalesced as a new political party, *Die Grünen*, and won seats in local and regional parliaments. In 1983 they entered the *Bundestag* for the first time, an unconventional group of politicians who distanced themselves from the traditional tactics of the established parties.

Besides the political threat posed by *Die Grünen*, who benefited from a growing dissatisfaction with the SPD among its own pacifist and environmentally concerned members, the Schmidt government had increasingly to address serious economic problems. The reform of public services, especially the expansion of education, had increased state indebtedness just as the economy was beginning to slow, hit both by the trade unions' increased wage demands and the oil crisis. In the late 1970s the *Bundesrepublik* experienced higher rates of inflation and unemployment than those to which the West German public had grown accustomed since the days of the *Wirtschaftswunder*. Though the West German economy remained among the strongest in Europe, not least because of industrialists' strategy of long-term investment, it was clear that some response was necessary. To the dismay of many SPD members, the Schmidt government preferred to cut the state budget for social security payments and to reduce taxes on business while increasing the *Mehrwertsteuer* (purchase tax, or VAT) on goods, rather than to attempt to stimulate the economy with public spending projects which would also increase the national debt.

These measures, however, did not go far enough for the right wing of the FDP under *Wirtschaftsminister* Otto Graf Lambsdorff. His party also feared that opposition amongst SPD members to Schmidt's course in foreign affairs (the *Doppelbeschluss*), nuclear energy and economic policy would soon bring policy changes which much of the FDP could not support. By September 1982 the *sozialliberale Koalition* had broken down, again causing divisions along the well-established faultlines within the FDP.

Schmidt hoped to call elections to secure a new mandate for his government, but before these could be arranged the FDP agreed terms for a new coalition with the CDU/CSU. On 1 October 1982 the *konstruktives Misstrauensvotum* was used successfully for the first time in the *Bundesrepublik*'s history when CDU, CSU and some FDP *Bundestag* members voted to remove Schmidt and replace him as *Bundeskanzler* with the CDU leader, Helmut Kohl. As this change of government occurred without the involvement of the electorate, Kohl engineered an early dissolution of the *Bundestag* the following year by contriving to lose a vote of confidence in his own administration. In elections on 6 March 1983 the CDU/CSU made impressive gains which confirmed Kohl's coalition government with the FDP in office.

Several important trends had altered West Germany since the days of the previous CDU-led administration. The development of a new relationship with the GDR through Brandt's *Ostpolitik* (see Chapter 8) had achieved consensus support among all political parties and was no longer the divisive issue which had soured West German politics in the 1960s and early 1970s. As the *Bundesrepublik* appeared more permanent once the German question was no longer high on the international agenda, the country's role in the EEC was also enhanced. Relations with France had grown ever warmer, enabling the Paris–Bonn axis to become central to the western European alliance. In economic terms, the strength of the West German economy led most other EEC states to peg their currencies against the *D-Mark* in the European Monetary System of 1978. The aim was to stabilise international trade by preventing wild fluctuations of the exchange rate. These developments cemented Adenauer's policy of *Westintegration* and represented the logical continuation of the postwar generation's attempt to end the threat of war by linking Europe's common economic interests in a structural framework.

Gastarbeiter ('guest workers')

As the *Wirtschaftswunder* created a labour shortage by the mid-1960s, the *Bundesregierung* began inviting workers from southern Europe (particularly Italy, Yugoslavia, Spain, Portugal and Turkey) to take jobs (often menial and poorly paid) in the *Bundesrepublik* on short-term contracts. If they were no longer needed, these *Gastarbeiter* would return home. However, by the economic downturn of the late 1970s, many foreign families had become established in the *Bundesrepublik* and been granted residence rights, especially in cases where their children had been born there. The population of *Gastarbeiter* and their families totalled some four and a half million by the end of Schmidt's term of office. However, German citizenship laws prevented *Gastarbeiter* from acquiring full legal rights; the resolution of this issue caused great political unrest in the late 1990s (see pp. 194–5).

Finally, the nature of West German society had been changed not only by the advent of 'alternative lifestyles' and a reduced willingness to conform to established modes of behaviour, but also by the growing numbers of **Gastarbeiter**, perceived as a threat to the German way of life by conservatives and nationalists unwilling to accept an immigrant population.

The 1982 change of government was hailed as a *Wende* ('turn') as significant as that which had occurred in 1969. In fact, there were significant continuities between the Schmidt and Kohl governments, particularly in the realm of foreign policy. The *Bundesrepublik* remained committed to the *Doppelbeschluss* and worked hard to deepen western European integration, a matter of great concern to Kohl who saw himself firmly in Adenauer's tradition. During this first phase of Kohl's chancellorship the Single European Act (*Einheitliche Europäische Akte*) was agreed by the EEC states, enabling the further relaxation of restrictions on trade and movement and the prospect of a common currency under a European central bank at a later date.

In domestic policy, the Kohl government attempted to reduce state spending on social security, and to rearrange the tax system to favour commercial investment. It did not, however, embark on a radical overhaul of the subsidy system which kept some uncompetitive industries afloat; nor did it undertake a wave of privatisations or effectively tackle waste and overmanning in the extensive public sector as Margaret Thatcher attempted in the United Kingdom. The West German economy nonetheless remained sound, despite the high unemployment rate of over two million. As the SPD's left-wing traditionalists who had opposed Schmidt's concessions to economic stability were in the ascendant within their party, there appeared no clear alternative to the CDU at the 1987 *Bundestag* elections for an electorate grown cautious of extensive social spending by the state.

The SPD was further challenged by the continued growth of *Die Grünen*, who were able to expand their *Bundestag* representation in 1987. However, in a sign that the FDP's days of holding the balance of power might be numbered, in 1985 the SPD had already entered into the first *Rot–Grün* coalition in Hessen. Meanwhile, a new party of the far right, *Die Republikaner*, emerged in 1983, disappointed by what they perceived as the CDU/CSU's failure to espouse a truly nationalist agenda. The *Republikaner* particularly highlighted the presence of *Gastarbeiter*, deplored the increasing loss of West German sovereignty to European institutions, and attacked the general consensus which seemed to have accepted the permanence of Germany's division.

The political landscape was, however, about to be disrupted by a far greater force than the gradual splintering of the party spectrum. In late 1989, quite unexpectedly for most observers, the communist-ruled East German state began to disintegrate. This offered Helmut Kohl an unprecedented opportunity to fulfil the aspiration to German unity enshrined in the *Grundgesetz* and thereby to secure both his immediate political future and a long-term place in the history books. Kohl was able to transform his hitherto respectable but generally uninspiring record as *Bundeskanzler* into a career which would, he hoped, rival that of Adenauer or even Bismarck.

Conclusion

The 'Bonn Republic', the *Bundesrepublik* as it existed during the period of Germany's division, established a formidable and enviable record for political and economic stability over a period of forty years. This was achieved despite the incomparably poisoned political legacy of national socialism, and despite the economic hardships which accompanied the *Bundesrepublik*'s early years and the global downturn which characterised the late 1970s. Although the democratic system was imposed by the allied forces after 1945, it was adopted enthusiastically by a new generation of politicians whose careers came to depend on the three-party system of the 1960s–1980s, and accepted by a population whose material needs were, for the first time, secured by the *soziale Marktwirtschaft*. Despite the authoritarian, conservative beginnings of the *Bundesrepublik*, arguably necessary to cement the new system, by the 1970s West German society offered greater opportunities for social mobility than ever before. The price to be paid for the West German success story and the associated *Westintegration* was the ongoing division of the German nation, as the *Bundesrepublik*'s politicians remained unprepared to endanger democracy and prosperity by making concessions to the GDR. By the 1970s at the latest, this mattered little to most West Germans, particularly the younger generations for whom cities such as Dresden and Leipzig seemed almost as distant and foreign as Paris or Vienna. However, as we shall see in Chapters 7 and 8, there were other German histories running concurrently with that of the Bonn Republic.

Republik Österreich, 1945–1989

On the surface, Austria's postwar political development marked a resumption of the trends apparent in the *Erste Republik* before 1934. Apart from the KPÖ, almost from the outset a splinter party and without *Nationalrat* representatives after 1959, three principal parties emerged. One, the *Sozialistische Partei Österreichs* (SPÖ), was a direct successor to the pre-1934 SDAP. There was greater change on the right: the old *Christlichsoziale Partei* ended its links with the Roman Catholic church and was replaced by the new *Österreichische Volkspartei* (ÖVP). Finally, former Nazis and a disparate band of others who felt no allegiance to the SPÖ or ÖVP made a new home in the *Verband der Unabhängigen* (VdU), reorganised as the *Freiheitliche Partei Österreichs* (FPÖ) in 1955 following internal wrangles. Though the VdU/FPÖ was not a neo-Nazi party, its existence was in clear contrast to developments in the *Bundesrepublik* where no special political home for former NSDAP members was permitted. The votes for these three parties divided much as they had for the *Christlichsozialen*, the SDAP and the *Deutschnationalen* during the *Erste Republik*: well into the 1980s, the FPÖ took under 10 per cent, while the remainder was shared more or less equally by the two major parties.

However, Austrian politicians of the *Zweite Republik* had no desire to return to the ideological warfare of the interwar years which had ultimately condemned many of them to Hitler's *Konzentrationslager*. Instead, moderates controlled both main parties. After 1945, neither won an absolute majority in the *Nationalrat* until 1966, leaving a *große Koalition* of ÖVP and SPÖ in office for twenty-one years. Though each party jostled for advantage at successive elections, they shared broadly common goals for economic growth within a system which embraced both the largest publicly owned industrial sector in Europe and a generous system of welfare benefits.

In a system dominated by these two parties, Austrian politics operated on a system of *Proporz*, in which political and other public posts were filled by each party in proportion to their share of the vote at the most recent election. The system extended from cabinet seats to civil service appointments, the directors of the Austrian broadcasting system (ÖRF), the management of the extended public sector, and much else besides. In most of the nine Austrian *Länder*, regional governments were constitutionally required to include representatives of all the elected parties. In practice this meant that the *Proporz* system was maintained after 1966 since the parties were compelled to cooperate at regional and local level while first the ÖVP and then the SPÖ controlled central government.

The consensus between the SPÖ and ÖVP rendered the *Nationalrat* practically superfluous, as all important decisions were agreed between the parties in advance. This tendency was exacerbated by Austria's unusual system of economic management, which was based on the principle of *soziale Partnerschaft* ('social partnership') of all the key economic interest groups. The *soziale Partner* met in the *Paritätische Kommission für Lohn- und Preisfragen* (Joint Commission on Wages and Prices), established in 1957. The *Kommission* included representatives of the Chamber of Labour and the Austrian Trade Union Federation (the employees, linked equally closely to the SPÖ) and the Chambers of Commerce and Agriculture (the employers, with close links to the ÖVP). Government observers were present, but could not vote. The *Kommission* made binding rules on wage and price increases. As unanimous decisions were required, and as membership of the three Chambers was compulsory for anyone within the three principal areas of the economy, the system established cooperation and harmony within postwar Austria by ensuring that policies were formulated by consensus and in the common interest.

Only after the late 1970s did the system begin to fray as the country's budget deficit grew. This resulted from the oil crisis, Austria's heavy expenditure on government officials and welfare payments, and inefficiencies in parts of the economy, as political considerations sometimes outweighed sound business decisions, especially in the extensive public sector. The emergence of a Green Party, in common with similar movements in the *Bundesrepublik* and elsewhere, threatened the delicate electoral arithmetic which had sustained the *Proporz* system. The radicalisation of the FPÖ after 1986 proved a greater challenge to the consensus. The party's liberal wing had dominated in the mid-1980s, enabling an SPÖ/FPÖ coalition after 1983, but the election as *Bundesparteiobmann* (the specifically Austrian term for party leader) of the radical young nationalist Jörg Haider marked a shift towards nationalist politics and forced the SPÖ again to join forces again with the ÖVP, restoring the traditional *große Koalition* to national government in 1986.

Document 6a: *Grundgesetz für die Bundesrepublik Deutschland, 23. Mai 1949* (excerpts)

Art. 1

(1) Die Würde des Menschen ist unantastbar. Sie zu achten und zu schützen ist Verpflichtung aller staatlichen Gewalt.

(2) Das Deutsche Volk bekennt sich darum zu unverletzlichen und unveräußerlichen Menschenrechten als Grundlage jeder menschlichen Gemeinschaft, des Friedens und der Gerechtigkeit in der Welt. . . .

Art. 3

(1) Alle Menschen sind vor dem Gesetz gleich.

(2) Männer und Frauen sind gleichberechtigt.

(3) Niemand darf wegen seines Geschlechtes, seiner Abstammung, seiner Rasse, seiner Sprache, seiner Heimat und Herkunft, seiner religiösen oder politischen Anschauungen benachteiligt oder bevorzugt werden.

. . .

Art. 20

(1) Die Bundesrepublik Deutschland ist ein demokratischer und sozialer Bundesstaat.

(2) Alle Staatsgewalt geht vom Volke aus. . . .

(3) Die Gesetzgebung ist an die verfassungsmäßige Ordnung, die vollziehende Gewalt und die Rechtsprechung sind an Gesetz und Recht gebunden.

(4) Gegen jeden, der es unternimmt, diese Ordnung zu beseitigen, haben alle Deutschen das Recht zum Widerstand, wenn andere Abhilfe nicht möglich ist.

Art. 21

(1) Die Parteien wirken bei der demokratischen Willensbildung des Volkes mit. Ihre Gründung ist frei. Ihre innere Ordnung muß demokratischen Grundsätzen entsprechen. Sie müssen über die Herkunft und Verwendung ihrer Mittel sowie über ihr Vermögen öffentlich Rechenschaft geben.

(2) Parteien, die nach ihren Zielen oder nach dem Verhalten ihrer Anhänger darauf ausgehen, die freiheitliche demokratische Grundordnung zu beeinträchtigen oder zu beseitigen oder den Bestand der Bundesrepublik Deutschland zu gefährden, sind verfassungswidrig. Über die Frage der Verfassungswidrigkeit entscheidet das Bundesverfassungsgericht. . . .

Art. 31

Bundesrecht bricht Landesrecht.

. . .

Art. 65

Der Bundeskanzler bestimmt die Richtlinien der Politik und trägt dafür die Verantwortung. . . .

Art. 67

(1) Der Bundestag kann dem Bundeskanzler das Mißtrauen nur dadurch aussprechen, daß er mit der Mehrheit seiner Mitglieder einen Nachfolger wählt und den Bundespräsidenten ersucht, den Bundeskanzler zu entlassen. Der Bundespräsident muß dem Ersuchen entsprechen und den Gewählten ernennen.

. . .

Art. 79

. . .

(3) Eine Änderung dieses Grundgesetzes, durch welche die Gliederung des Bundes in Länder, die grundsätzliche Mitwirkung der Länder bei der Gesetzgebung oder die in den Artikeln 1 und 20 niedergelegten Grundsätze berührt werden, ist unzulässig.

. . .

Document 6b: *Regierungserklärung von Bundeskanzler Brandt vor dem Deutschen Bundestag, 28. Oktober 1969* (excerpts)

... Unser Volk braucht wie jedes andere seine innere Ordnung. In den 70er Jahren werden wir aber in diesem Lande nur so viel Ordnung haben, wie wir an Mitverantwortung ermutigen. Solche demokratische Ordnung braucht außerordentliche Geduld im Zuhören und außerordentliche Anstrengung, sich gegenseitig zu verstehen.

Wir wollen mehr Demokratie wagen. Wir werden unsere Arbeitsweise öffnen und dem kritischen Bedürfnis nach Information Genüge tun. Wir werden darauf hinwirken, daß nicht nur durch Anhörungen im Bundestag, sondern auch durch ständige Fühlungnahme mit den repräsentativen Gruppen unseres Volkes und durch eine umfassende Unterrichtung über die Regierungspolitik jeder Bürger die Möglichkeit erhält, an der Reform von Staat und Gesellschaft mitzuwirken.

Wir wenden uns an die im Frieden nachgewachsenen Generationen, die nicht mit den Hypotheken der älteren belastet sind und belastet werden dürfen; jene jungen Menschen, die uns beim Wort nehmen wollen – und sollen. Diese jungen Menschen müssen aber verstehen, daß auch sie gegenüber Staat und Gesellschaft Verpflichtungen haben. ...

Mitbestimmung, Mitverantwortung in den verschiedenen Bereichen unserer Gesellschaft wird eine bewegende Kraft der kommenden Jahre sein. Wir können nicht die perfekte Demokratie schaffen. Wir wollen eine Gesellschaft, die mehr Freiheit bietet und mehr Mitverantwortung fordert. ...

Meine Damen und Herren! Diese Regierung geht davon aus, daß die Fragen, die sich für das deutsche Volk aus dem Zweiten Weltkrieg und aus dem nationalen Verrat durch das Hitlerregime ergeben haben, abschließend nur in einer europäischen Friedensordnung beantwortet werden können. Niemand kann uns jedoch ausreden, daß die Deutschen ein Recht auf Selbstbestimmung haben, wie alle anderen Völker auch. Aufgabe der praktischen Politik in den jetzt vor uns liegenden Jahren ist es, die Einheit der Nation dadurch zu wahren, daß das Verhältnis zwischen den Teilen Deutschlands aus der gegenwärtigen Verkrampfung gelöst wird. Die Deutschen sind nicht nur durch ihre Sprache und ihre Geschichte – mit ihrem Glanz und Elend – verbunden; wir sind alle in Deutschland zu Haus. Wir haben auch noch gemeinsame Aufgaben und gemeinsame Verantwortung: für den Frieden unter uns und in Europa. 20 Jahre nach der Gründung der Bundesrepublik Deutschland und der DDR müssen wir ein weiteres Auseinanderleben der deutschen Nation verhindern, also versuchen, über ein geregeltes Nebeneinander zu einem Miteinander zu kommen. Dies ist nicht nur ein deutsches Interesse, denn es hat seine Bedeutung auch für den Frieden in Europa und für das Ost-West-Verhältnis. ...

Source: 'Verhandlungen des Deutschen Bundestages, V, 28.10.1969', reproduced in Irmgard Wilharm (ed.), *Deutsche Geschichte 1962–1983*, 2 vols (Frankfurt am Main: Fischer, 1985), Vol. 2, pp. 27–8.

Topics
FOR DISCUSSION / FURTHER RESEARCH

■ With reference to Document 6a, discuss which factors strengthened the political system of the *Bundesrepublik* by comparison with that of the *Weimarer Republik*.

■ To what extent did the first twenty years of the *Bundesrepublik*'s history represent a restoration of earlier German traditions?

■ How valid is the view that the *68er* broke the mould of West German politics and society?

■ Were the aspirations of Brandt's 1969 *Bundestag* speech (Document 6b) matched by the *Bundesrepublik*'s development under the SPD–FDP coalition?

■ What was the principal guarantor of postwar West German stability?

■ How effectively were the weaknesses of the Austrian *Erste Republik* addressed in the *Zweite Republik* after 1945?

CHAPTER 7

'Auferstanden aus Ruinen': East Germany, 1949–1989

Timeline

After 1945, the Soviet Union used its military predominance to create undemocratic communist buffer states in Poland, Czechoslovakia, Hungary, Bulgaria, Romania and eastern Germany, linked with the USSR by economic and military alliances. Secret police suppressed the churches and opposition groups, though serious resistance sometimes occurred: Soviet tanks quelled uprisings in the GDR in 1953, a Hungarian rebellion in 1956, and Czechoslovak reformers' attempts at 'communism with a human face' (the 'Prague Spring') in 1968. In Poland martial law was introduced after 1980 to suppress the opposition trade union, Solidarity. Communist economics, based on inefficient state-owned enterprises and inflexible central planning, did not produce prosperity. As Soviet leader after 1985, Mikhail Gorbachev introduced economic and political reforms which were intended to revitalise communism, but instead unravelled the whole system. Facing enormous difficulties at home, the USSR was no longer prepared to protect communist regimes in its eastern European empire, which duly collapsed during 1989.

Though formed in a small part of the former *Reich* with relatively few natural resources, and with a population which until recently had been mobilised for Nazism, the GDR became the most successful of the socialist states of eastern Europe. Under the firm control of the SED, and the watchful eye of the Soviet Union and its occupation forces, the GDR existed as an ideological counterweight to the *Bundesrepublik*. Its *raison d'être* was antifascism. For German communists and others this meant embarking on a socialist experiment which quickly transformed political, economic and social structures. Yet the system depended on the repression of its opponents and, after 1961, a closed border which prevented the flow of disgruntled citizens to the west. Hindsight may give the GDR's eventual collapse in 1989/90 an air of inevitability; yet, though the state's existence was predicated on the wider contours of the Cold War, 'socialism in the colours of the GDR' proved stable over forty years, and laid roots which survived into united Germany after 1990.

Structures of the GDR

The essential characteristic of the GDR's political and economic systems was the monopoly of power which the SED enjoyed within them. The party, and its leadership in particular, claimed to be the revolutionary advance guard which would transform society for the good of all. As representatives of the working class, they would counter reactionary threats from other strata of society within the '*Klassenkampf*' ('class struggle'). According to Marxist theory, the working class's numerical superiority legitimised the party's claim to supreme power, and the apparently scientific nature of Marxist-Leninist teachings, as laid down in works such as *Das Kapital*, supported an official creed that the SED was infallible in its policies. The party leadership was entrusted with the task of interpreting prevailing conditions according to Marxist-Leninist teaching and developing corresponding policy to achieve the ultimate goal of socialism. This theory was reflected in the refrain of an SED song, 'Die Partei hat immer recht' ('The party is always right'). Faith in the primacy of SED dogma was so strong among many party activists in the 1940s and 1950s in particular that many of those who were unjustly punished for alleged infractions of the party line remained loyal to the system and worked for the ultimate goal.

The sovereign rights of the Soviet occupation power enabled its SED allies to implement a political system for the GDR which eradicated challenges to the party's leading role. However, the outward appearance of a pluralist democracy was essential, both to avoid open comparisons with the Third Reich and to defend the GDR against criticism from the west. Thus the multiparty system which emerged in the 1945–49 period was retained.

The GDR's first constitution, which came into force on 7 October 1949, could have been equally well applied to a western parliamentary democracy. It included firm guarantees of basic human rights, including freedom of movement, pledged the right to strike, the right of association in clubs, societies and parties, and freedom of expression, conscience and religion. Postal and telephone secrecy were confirmed, and the rights of the churches assured. However, all these constitutional rights could be limited by individual laws.

The supreme organ of the republic was its parliament, the *Volkskammer*, whose members would be elected by secret ballot under a system of proportional representation. Initially, a separate chamber of parliament, the *Länderkammer*, represented the governments of the five *Länder*. A president exercised only symbolic powers and was elected jointly by the two chambers of parliament, rather than directly by the people as in the discredited Weimar model. This system was somewhat modified by 1960 when the first president, Wilhelm Pieck, died. The presidency was replaced by a collective *Staatsrat* (Council of State), also with few real powers. By this point the GDR had become a more centralised state in which the partially autonomous *Länder* were replaced by fifteen smaller *Bezirke* ('counties') which existed merely to administer central policy; consequently the *Länderkammer* was abolished.

While all these provisions bore a strong resemblance to the *Bundesrepublik*, there were two key differences. First, the GDR's constitution stipulated not only that the leader of the party with the largest number of seats in the *Volkskammer* would form a government, but also that each political party with more than forty *Volkskammer* seats must normally be included in the government. This mechanism was designed partly to ensure governments with strong parliamentary support and to exclude the possibility that, as in the *Weimarer Republik*, large parties would evade their political responsibilities. Equally, though, this requirement associated all the parties with government policy. This effectively forced the Christian and liberal parties to make common cause with the communist-led SED. Second, the provisions in the *Grundgesetz* for an independent constitutional court as a check on the government were entirely absent from the GDR constitution. The GDR's government therefore had a fairly free hand to determine how the constitution was to be interpreted. In practice, a number of basic rights were limited, allegedly on the grounds of state security: new political parties, clubs or societies required permits from the *Ministerium des Innern* (Interior Ministry), and these were only granted to groups sanctioned by the SED; furthermore, a provision designed to protect 'democratic institutions and organisations' enabled the state and the courts to suppress critics of the government and the GDR's permitted political parties – themselves the arbiters of what could be defined as 'democratic'.

While the system appeared on paper to ensure democracy, the electoral system operated to guarantee that the SED was the sole powerbroker, working in tandem with the USSR to realise Soviet policy in the GDR even after the Soviets renounced their formal occupation rights in 1955. Citing the need to ensure the unity of all democratic forces so soon after the defeat of national socialism, the SED called upon the four other '***Blockparteien***' ('bloc parties') to join it in presenting a single manifesto and a single list of candidates at the first *Volkskammer* elections in 1950. The *Demokratische Bauernpartei Deutschlands* (DBD) and the *National-Demokratische Partei Deutschlands* (NDPD) – both created by SED members – willingly agreed, as did those members of the CDU and LDPD who believed in the importance of antifascist unity. Senior members of these parties who dissented were intimidated into agreement, silence or emigration by the SED-dominated press, and in some cases by the Soviet occupation power.

The GDR's *Blockparteien*

Though firmly under the SED's control until 1989, the GDR boasted four other political parties. The five parties agreed common policies in the *Demokratischer Block* (hence the term *Blockparteien*) and presented a joint list of candidates at elections as members of the *Nationale Front*. The multiparty system enabled the GDR to present a façade of democratic pluralism, while also providing political homes outside the SED but within the socialist system for groups like Christians and nationalists who would never join a Marxist party. The historian Hermann Weber described the bloc parties as *Transmissionsriemen*: like the transmission in a car, the bloc parties were the gears which enabled the SED to present its policies to all parts of the population.

Sozialistische Einheitspartei Deutschlands (SED): created in 1946 from a merger of the *Kommunistische Partei Deutschlands* (KPD) and the *Sozialdemokratische Partei Deutschlands* (SPD), but from 1948 predominantly a communist party.

Christlich-Demokratische Union (CDU): a political home for Christians in the GDR; recognised the SED's leading role in 1952.

Liberal-Demokratische Partei Deutschlands (LDPD): originally championed liberal, market economic principles; membership drawn principally from small business owners, *Beamten* circles, etc.; recognised the SED's leading role in 1953.

Demokratische Bauernpartei Deutschlands (DBD): founded in 1948 by the SED to represent farming and rural interests, once it became clear that farmers resisted joining the SED.

National-Demokratische Partei Deutschlands (NDPD): founded in 1948 by the SED; for German nationalists and reformed NSDAP members who wished to help rebuild Germany.

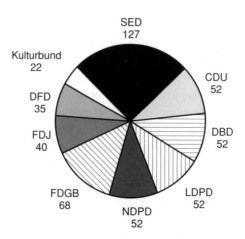

Figure 7.1: Distribution of Volkskammer seats, 1985

The five parties, joined by several of the SED's allied *Massenorganisationen* (mass organisations), campaigned under the banner of the *Nationale Front des demo-kratischen Deutschland* on a manifesto which emphasised the aims of peace and antifascist reconstruction. Voters were encouraged to demonstrate their conviction in these objectives by casting their votes publicly and openly; those who sought the secrecy of the booths at polling stations faced suspicion of voting against antifascist renewal and, by extension, of harbouring Nazi sympathies. With voting compulsory, and no alternative candidates, the *Nationale Front* regularly won in excess of 99 per cent of the vote at *Volkskammer* and local council elections from 1950 to 1989.

The bloc parties and mass organisations agreed before the elections how the parliamentary seats should be divided. Typically, the SED itself took only around a quarter of these seats, but when the SED members among the parliamentary representatives

The GDR's *Massenorganisationen*

The GDR had an elaborate, if restrictive, system of *Massenorganisationen*. Only one association was permitted for each group within society, and each organisation was controlled by SED trustees. Thus young people in the GDR could only join the SED-controlled monopoly youth organisation. Structurally, the system resembled that operated by the NSDAP in the Third Reich (see p. 90). The *Massenorganisationen* also fulfilled the role of *Transmissionsriemen* with their respective target audiences, presenting SED policies to women, children, trade unionists, etc. As the organisations stood for praiseworthy goals like world peace as well as socialism, a refusal to join suggested opposition to core societal values. Conversely, membership appeared to demonstrate acceptance of, even loyalty to, the socialist GDR. Some organisations were also principal organisers of leisure time pursuits and attracted large memberships. However, the opportunism and lack of true political commitment to socialism among members were revealed when the SED collapsed in 1989 and most organisations simply dissolved. The main groups were:

Freier Deutscher Gewerkschaftsbund (FDGB): as a trade union in socialism, the FDGB's task was to persuade workers of management and party policies, assuage local grievances and avert strikes. The union's chain of hotels and holiday homes, available to members at cheap rates, was a principal supplier of holidays in the GDR. It had 9.1 million members in 1983.

Freie Deutsche Jugend (FDJ): practically all 14–18 year olds belonged to the youth organisation. With the associated *Pionierorganisation* for younger children, the FDJ organised leisure activities and supported youngsters' ideological education. Politically loyal and talented members were groomed for roles in the SED.

Demokratischer Frauenbund Deutschlands (DFD): mobilised women for world peace and socialism.

Kulturbund (KB): an umbrella group for intellectuals and a variety of cultural pursuits from amateur opera to chess and local history.

Gesellschaft für deutsch-sowjetische Freundschaft (DSF): for the Society's six million members, the DSF was an effective way of demonstrating loyalty to socialism through friendship with the mother country of world communism.

of the mass organisations were also counted, the party had an absolute majority in the *Volkskammer* and all the local parliaments. By 1953 the CDU and LDPD had in any case declared their acknowledgement of the SED's 'leading role' and thus effectively ended any independent political role.

Though the SED grew quickly to embrace a mass membership (with more than two million members by the early 1980s), the power which the party enjoyed in the GDR's political structures was concentrated in very few hands. At the apex of the system was the SED's *Politbüro* ('political office', often translated simply as politburo), a committee of some twenty high-ranking party officials, led by the party's *Generalsekretär* ('general secretary', known as *Erster Sekretär*, 'first secretary', from 1953 to 1976). The *Politbüro* drew its legitimacy as the party's ruling council from a series of elections within the SED's membership. Every four or five years, elected delegates from the local party groups met at the *Parteitag* (Party Congress) to elect around 200 members to a *Zentralkomitee* (Central Committee) which formally acted as the party's leadership between the *Parteitage*. The *Zentralkomitee* in turn elected the *Politbüro* to direct overall policy and day-to-day business. Once appointed, the *Politbüro* relied on the system of *demokratischer Zentralismus* (democratic central-ism) for its authority. This principle required every level of the party to obey and carry out the decisions of the next highest party authority. Thus decisions of the *Politbüro* were binding on all the lower levels of the party. The *Generalsekretär* similarly occupied a position of authority over the other *Politbüro* members. The internal party democracy which supposedly accompanied this centralism was under-mined by the *Politbüro*'s power within the system to determine which party members were suitable candidates for election to the *Parteitag*, the *Zentralkomitee* and the *Politbüro* itself, as well as the regional and local party leaderships. In practice, the large *Zentralkomitee* was unable to act as a check on the *Politbüro* and the *General-sekretär*. Instead, the SED's supreme leadership became a self-perpetuating elite, and the *Politbüro* ensured that only those who supported its line advanced within the party. As the SED's leaders were generally unwilling to resign and make way for younger blood, the *Politbüro* grew increasingly elderly, out of touch and unable to react to new challenges during the 1980s.

The SED's grip on power was further facilitated by the principle of *Parteidisziplin* ('party discipline'), according to which party policy and instructions were binding on every member. In this way, the SED's elected ministers and local councillors were bound to exercise their power in the state system according to instructions from the party apparatus. At national level, an SED *Zentralkomitee* department existed parallel to nearly every government ministry. Generally speaking, the party departments decided policies which were then recommended to the government for implementa-tion. Under the principle of *Parteidisziplin* individual ministers and civil servants obeyed these instructions. Similarly, SED departments existed to guide the work of the party's members in the mass organisations, so that the *Freie Deutsche Jugend* (FDJ) and the *Freier Deutscher Gewerkschaftsbund* (FDGB) had no practical independence. The central system was replicated in each of the provinces, such that regional govern-ment officials were expected to carry out the instructions of their opposite numbers in party offices and, under *demokratischer Zentralismus*, the orders from the central Berlin ministries. By these means regional autonomy was excised, and the power of the *Politbüro* in general and the *Generalsekretär* in particular became binding throughout the GDR's political and social systems. This accumulation of central power was formalised in the GDR's new constitution of 1968 (see Document 7a), in which Article 1 asserted that the GDR stood 'unter Führung der Arbeiterklasse und ihrer marxistisch-leninistischen Partei' ('under the leadership of the working class and its Marxist-Leninist party').

The SED's power extended beyond political and social structures into the economic sphere. Economic restructuring was essential to the SED project as Marxist theory argues that ownership of the means of production is the key determinant in power relationships. As the economic system which the SED inherited was seen as dependent on the exploitation of the working classes by the factory owners, the party was determined to break the capitalist classes and transfer their assets to the state. In theory, state ownership of factories, mines and other businesses would ensure that workers worked for their own benefit, particularly if the state were controlled by a socialist party which redistributed wealth fairly throughout the population. As we saw in Chapter 5, the state acquired significant economic assets from Nazis and companies which produced armaments during the war, and redistributed agricultural land to smallholders in the *Bodenreform*. Essential industries (coal, steel, banking, etc.) were nationalised.

By the early 1950s the bulk of the GDR's industry was under state control. A system of central economic planning for the Soviet zone was established soon after the war, culminating in the appearance of a six-month economic plan for the latter half of 1948, and a two-year plan for 1949–50. The GDR's first five-year plan took force on 1 January 1951. Thereafter, five-year central plans became the norm. In the early postwar years those private firms which had escaped expropriation found themselves heavily disadvantaged by central planning, which diverted scarce resources to the publicly owned sector. Cut off from the industrialised areas of western Germany by the Cold War, the GDR also embarked on ambitious plans to develop its own heavy industry in the early 1950s and to rebuild the housing stocks destroyed in the war, also within the state sector. The creation of a state-owned trading organisation, the *HO* (*Handelsorganisation*), also with privileged access to goods, forced many private retailers out of business. By the mid-1950s the state sector dominated all major parts of the economy, and the predominant form of ownership was the *Volkseigener Betrieb* ('people's own company', VEB).

The nationalisation of most of the GDR's economy strengthened the SED's grip on power still further. The VEBs were mainly under the direct control of the central Berlin ministries, while the central plan was elaborated by a *Staatliche Plankommission* (state planning commission). In practice, these organs of power were dominated by SED ministers who followed the policies laid down by the *Politbüro* and took their detailed instructions from the *Zentralkomitee* departments responsible for economic planning. The managers of the individual VEBs were chosen as much for their *Parteidisziplin* as for their technical competence. While the attempt to allocate resources and plan production centrally was understandable in the immediate postwar era of rebuilding, the system was inevitably bureaucratic and inflexible, and consumers' wishes were usually ignored. Fulfilling or overfulfilling the targets of the economic plan became the watchword for each factory (not least as a means of demonstrating political loyalty and reliability), and encouraged firms to concentrate on producing quantity at the expense of quality.

Finally, the SED's power was underwritten by the justice and security apparatus. Besides the *Volkspolizei* ('people's police'), under the direct control of the *Ministerium des Innern*, the *Ministerium für Staatssicherheit* (Ministry for State Security, MfS), more usually known as the *Stasi*, worked conspiratorially to observe, uncover and imprison enemies of the state. While security services of this nature are common to most states, the MfS acted in the specific interests of the SED's hold on power, rather than in the more general interests of the state, and defined itself as *Schild und Schwert der Partei* ('shield and sword of the party'). Composed almost entirely of SED members, and organised along military lines, the *Stasi's* full-time staff and its extensive network of informers (*Informelle Mitarbeiter, IMs*) infiltrated all key installations and kept tabs on citizens whose loyalty to the SED was in question. In the early years, the SED's political opponents were prosecuted under laws originally designed to prevent any resurgence of fascism; by the 1960s new GDR laws widened the scope of political crimes. As the 1968 constitution specifically wedded the GDR to socialism, opposition to socialism, as defined by the SED, became unconstitutional. Judges and lawyers were also selected according to the SED's criteria and implemented *sozialistisches Recht* ('socialist justice') in accordance with the strictures of the SED-led *Justizministerium* (Ministry of Justice) and, thus, ultimately the SED's *Politbüro*. Formally, justice in the GDR was exercised according to legal norms, and in theory the GDR was a *Rechtsstaat*. However, the highly politicised nature of GDR law and the *Parteilichkeit* of those responsible for its implementation have led many commentators to categorise the GDR instead as an *Unrechtsstaat*.

The systems described above were so comprehensive that there were no opportunities for political, social or economic activity which was not regulated by SED structures. Opposition was impossible within the legal framework. Career advancement depended on loyalty to the system, and clearly demonstrated commitment to SED goals (for example, work in the *Massenorganisationen*) was a yardstick for the authorities when judging job promotions, university entrance and the allocation of accommodation. Alongside the many committed socialists in the GDR, far greater numbers of *Mitläufer* either maintained an outward attitude of conformity, even if this meant only keeping their opinions to themselves and taking part in one of the SED-led mass organisations, while others opportunistically joined the SED itself and rose within its ranks to make careers in the state and party or in the management of the economy. Ideological commitment to Marxism-Leninism as defined by the *Politbüro* was often incomplete or lacking, as the political uncertainty of ordinary party members at times of crisis and ultimately the swift collapse of the entire edifice in 1989–90 revealed. Nonetheless, the SED arguably effected a more complete *Gleichschaltung* of society than even the NSDAP had achieved.

1949–1971: From crisis to consolidation

Most East Germans felt little enthusiasm for their new state at its creation in 1949. The majority were too preoccupied with the continuing shortages of food, fuel and housing to pay much attention to wider political developments, but some were hostile to Germany's division and the imposition of an SED government by the Soviet occupiers without free elections. For others, though, the GDR represented an opportunity to make a new start and there was optimism among antifascists and the young for the state's major rebuilding projects.

Nonetheless, the GDR was in a precarious position, dependent on the aims of Soviet foreign policy. In 1952 the western allies' aim of rearming the *Bundesrepublik* within a western military alliance (see p. 137) prompted the Soviet leader, Stalin, to propose reuniting Germany as a neutral state. The western leaders suspected a Soviet attempt to extend communist power throughout Germany and proceeded with their plans regardless. With Soviet approval, the SED leadership responded with measures to place the GDR on a firmer footing, while arguing that the west was responsible for the division of Germany. For the party's *Generalsekretär*, Walter Ulbricht, this was a welcome development. Ulbricht recognised that the SED's only hope of retaining power and building socialism was in the GDR under Soviet protection, and that the party could never win a majority through free elections in a united Germany.

Citing the likely threat from a remilitarised West Germany, the GDR sealed its border with the *Bundesrepublik* (though not that with West Berlin) in May 1952 and introduced tight regulations along a 5 km strip all the way down its side of this border. These included a curfew, restrictions on who could enter the border zone, and the forcible removal of citizens who might facilitate a West German incursion or otherwise weaken the GDR on its borders. More significantly still, at the SED's Second Party Conference of July 1952 Ulbricht announced that the conditions were suitable for the building of socialism (*Aufbau des Sozialismus*) in the GDR, and warned that this would inevitably mean an intensification of the *Klassenkampf* – the neutralisation of real or potential enemies of the socialist programme, such as private entrepreneurs, active Christians and nationalist forces.

The *Aufbau des Sozialismus* involved not only further investment in the GDR's industrial infrastructure, at the expense of consumer goods production, but also a campaign to remove active young Christians from the *Oberschulen* (sixth-form colleges), and a drive to merge the small GDR farms into *Landwirtschaftliche Produktionsgenossenschaften* (agricultural collectives, LPGs), which the state could more easily control. Similarly, private farmers and business owners faced higher taxes and the loss of their food ration cards. In an attempt to save money, the government even removed the subsidies for workers' return tickets on public transport. Discontent grew in the following months, not least because of food shortages exacerbated by the departure of private farmers to the west in the face of pressure to merge their farms within the new LPGs. Workers became disillusioned that these measures were being imposed by what claimed to be a workers' government. Already under pressure to work additional voluntary shifts and to overfulfil the requirements of the central plan, the final straw came in late May 1953 when the SED announced plans to increase the *Arbeitsnormen* (production quotas) by 10 per cent for no additional pay.

The Soviet occupation authorities were well aware of the potential for unrest in the GDR, and in early June 1953 the SED leadership was instructed by Moscow to recognise its errors and rescind the harshest measures. In a clear demonstration of the SED's subservience both to the Soviet Union as the occupation power and to the political authority of the Communist Party of the Soviet Union (CPSU), the *Neuer Kurs* ('New Course') was announced on 9 June. Farmers and Christians who had left for the west to escape the political pressure were invited back, while the *Ministerpräsident*, Otto Grotewohl, met church leaders to build bridges. Significantly, though, the increased *Arbeitsnormen* were not withdrawn but instead restated in a newspaper article on 16 June. Consequently, construction workers on Berlin's prestigious *Stalinallee* project spontaneously downed tools and marched to the ministry complex. Though a junior minister eventually emerged to retract the disputed increase, a call for a general strike was taken up in Berlin and in towns and villages throughout the country on 17 June. The *Juni-Aufstand* did not occur everywhere, and was beginning to peter out even before martial law was declared and Soviet tanks intervened to restore order. No opposition leaders emerged to focus opposition to the SED (likely candidates for the role were quietly arrested and removed), and with the controversial *Arbeitsnormen* already rescinded the demonstrators and strikers lacked clear goals, despite calls in many areas for the removal of Ulbricht and the SED leadership, for free elections and, in some cases, for unification with the west. In many ways, the June uprising gave vent to the many frustrations which had built up during the difficult postwar years. Nonetheless, the uprising represented a clear challenge to the SED, which sometimes attempted in later years to pursue its goal of restructuring society by less antagonistic means. The population at large concluded that the GDR and its SED leaders could not be removed by popular unrest while Soviet troops remained in the country. The lesson was reinforced by determined Soviet military intervention during the unsuccessful uprisings against communism in Hungary in 1956 and Czechoslovakia in 1968. Overall the 1953 experience became a stabilising force in the GDR's development, though the role of Soviet troops in restoring the SED's power and the sight of workers protesting against a supposedly workers' state undermined the system's legitimacy.

In the short term, the 1953 uprising assisted Walter Ulbricht to reinforce his position as SED leader. Ulbricht, an uncompromising bureaucratic communist who insisted on absolute obedience to the central leadership along the party's hierarchical principle, had already presided over the SED's transformation into a Leninist party on the CPSU model. Former social democrats who remained loyal to their political roots and renegade communists who resisted Moscow's line had been largely purged or intimidated into conformity during a *Parteiüberprüfung* (party inspection) of 1950/51. While the new Soviet leadership might have preferred to remove the unpopular Ulbricht following Stalin's death in March 1953, it could not risk the appearance of bowing to popular demands by replacing him after the uprising, for fear of destabilising similarly disliked leaders elsewhere in eastern Europe. The power struggle for Stalin's succession in Moscow was decisive in this respect: Stalin's interior minister, Lavrenti Beria, was arrested in late June 1953 and later executed for allegedly plotting to undermine socialism in the Soviet Union and to abandon the GDR. Ulbricht seized this opportunity to isolate and remove his moderate opponents in the *Zentralkomitee*, some of whom had also considered sacrificing the GDR in favour of German national unity. These included Rudolf Herrnstadt, the editor of the SED's official newspaper *Neues Deutschland*, who had criticised the party's hard-line policies in the paper's columns, and the minister for state security, Wilhelm Zaisser. Both were accused of plotting together and with the disgraced Beria to undermine party and state. Max Fechner, who as justice minister had defended workers' right to strike, was also ousted.

Ulbricht fully consolidated his leadership by 1958 despite ideological turmoil in the intervening years, sparked by the unmasking of Stalin's regime of terror in a 'secret speech' made to the Twentieth Party Congress of the CPSU in March 1956 by the emergent Soviet leader Nikita Khrushchev. Destalinisation proceeded cautiously in the GDR, where Ulbricht wished to avoid any reforms which would endanger the SED's grip on power, but the speech, quickly revealed in full in the west and reported back to the GDR by western media, unleashed reform calls by socialist intellectuals in East Berlin, chief among them the philosopher Wolfgang Harich. These reformers envisaged greater democracy within the socialist system and reforms to the socialist economy. However, a wave of strikes in Poland and the attempt to overthrow socialist rule in Hungary in late 1956 revealed the dangers of relaxing political control, and resulted in a Soviet crackdown, strengthening Ulbricht's hand. Harich, who had compromised his position by discussing his reform proposals with the western SPD, was arrested along with his associates. By early 1958 Khrushchev had further strengthened his position in the Soviet leadership. Ulbricht, who had earned Khrushchev's trust by ensuring stability in the GDR during 1956, could follow suit: his supporters accused moderates and would-be reformers in the *Politbüro* and *Zentralkomitee* of conspiring against the agreed party line. As factionalism was an unpardonable crime in the hierarchical structures of a Marxist-Leninist party, Ulbricht was able to remove further high-ranking opponents. His position as leader was not challenged again until the early 1970s when, finally, he lost the Soviet leadership's confidence. Meanwhile, though far from all the SED's members were convinced by Ulbricht's approach to constructing socialism, the high-level purges of the late 1950s reinforced their recognition that the privileges of party membership depended on loyalty within democratic centralism.

The challenges of the 1953 uprising and destalinisation did not significantly hinder the policy of socialist restructuring during the 1950s. The state itself was given a more permanent status in 1954 when the Soviet Union formally extended sovereignty over internal affairs to the GDR government; following the FRG's incorporation within NATO in 1955 and the formal lifting of the *Besatzungsstatut* by the western allies, the GDR also received full sovereignty, though the Soviet Union continued to determine the country's broad policy framework, not least through the SED's political subordination to the CPSU within the world communist movement. The GDR acquired further trappings of permanence in 1956 with the creation of a *Nationale Volksarmee*, integrated into the eastern bloc's military alliance, the Warsaw Treaty Organisation, as a response to the creation of the West German *Bundeswehr*.

The SED also aimed to secure the state's long-term foundations by attempting to win over young people to socialism. Increasing efforts were made to ensure the political reliability of teaching staff, particularly those responsible for politically sensitive subjects like history. Russian became a compulsory part of the curriculum, alongside *Staatsbürgerkunde* (civics), which taught the essential principles under-pinning the socialist state. University students of all subjects also studied Marxism-Leninism and Russian. In 1959, the school system was overhauled with the creation of the *zehnklassige allgemeinbildende polytechnische Oberschule* ('ten-year comprehensive polytechnical secondary school') for all pupils aged 6–16. Its curriculum was designed to ease all pupils into the world of work and included weekly practical work experience in the last four years. The SED's aim was that the centrally organised school system should ensure the development of the *allseitig entwickelte sozialistische Persönlichkeit* ('rounded socialist personality').

Another strategy involved a relatively successful attempt to remove young people from the influence of the churches, traditionally firm opponents of socialism. Besides effectively banning religious education from the school curriculum, in 1954 the SED sponsored the introduction of the *Jugendweihe*, a secular coming of age ceremony for 14-year-olds. In training sessions young people were presented with a materialist view of the world and mankind's place in it. This conflicted with the traditional Christian views of the Creation and mankind's responsibility before God which were emphasised in the preparation classes for the confirmation ceremony in the Protestant and Roman Catholic churches. The churches viewed the *Jugendweihe* oath as espousing atheism and initially refused to allow those who swore it also to attend confirmation. However, with the support of the schools and the FDJ, the *Jugendweihe* became an expected part of every young person's development and replaced religious confirmation in most fami-lies. In later years, the *Jugendweihe* oath (Document 7b) committed young people to fight for socialism alongside the Soviet Union. However, its real ideological force should not be overstated: the generations who swore the oath also took to the streets in 1989 to overthrow SED rule. Parallel attempts to introduce socialist alternatives to Christian baptisms and funerals were far less successful.

In the economy, the continuing expansion of the state and collective sectors placed more power in the hands of the SED-led central planning authorities. Though the drive for agricultural collectivisation had been abandoned after the June uprising, the policy was reintroduced in the late 1950s, in the hope of removing private farmers as a potential source of political opposition, and of obtaining higher agricultural yields. The many farmers who refused to abandon their independence were exposed to a relentless campaign in early 1960. By Easter 1960, all the GDR's privately owned farmland had been organised in LPGs. Though collective farming methods took root only slowly, many farmers came to appreciate the benefits of the division of labour which collectivisation allowed. *Handwerker* (electricians, carpenters, plumbers, hairdressers, etc.) were also encouraged to form collectives, though the state was not so insistent about bringing this sector of the economy under its control. From 1956, the state also acquired shares in many of the remaining private firms, most of which were bought out fully by 1972.

Though the GDR experienced dynamic economic growth during the 1950s – albeit from a very low base – the overly ambitious second five-year plan (1956–60) was abandoned in favour of a new seven-year plan in 1959, itself unfulfilled. Food shortages remained a characteristic of everyday life and by the early 1960s it was manifestly obvious that Ulbricht's claim of 1958 that the GDR's economy would overtake the *Bundesrepublik* by 1961 could not be realised.

Political constraints and economic shortcomings in the GDR, combined with the opportunities for a better lifestyle in the FRG, led almost three million citizens to leave the GDR for the west between 1949 and 1961. As skilled, well-educated young people were the largest group to commit the crime of *Republikflucht* ('fleeing the republic'), the SED realised that the country's economic future was endangered by the continuing exodus. Following the closure of the GDR's border to the FRG in 1952, West Berlin, still governed by the western allies and closely allied with the FRG, represented the only remaining escape hatch for discontented citizens. The continuing existence of a single German citizenship and the FRG's *Alleinvertretungsanspruch* (see p. 181) meant that East Germans who crossed the open border to West Berlin could either stay in the city or travel along the transit routes to West Germany where they had the right to settle, work and acquire a West German passport.

To prevent the economic drain on the GDR caused by this emigration and the flourishing black market which exploited the GDR's subsidised prices for essential goods, but also to end the west's use of Berlin as a centre for espionage activities directed against the Soviet bloc, in November 1958 Khrushchev presented the western powers with an ultimatum to leave West Berlin within six months, arguing that the territory lay within the Soviet zone of Germany; West Berlin would become a 'free city'. The western allies, determined to uphold their rights, recognised that West Berlin would be in no sense 'free' surrounded by the GDR and Soviet troops. The west ignored the ultimatum. The Soviets took no further action until August 1961. With the number of *Republikflüchtige* steadily rising, Ulbricht persuaded Khrushchev that a solution was imperative if the GDR were to remain viable and fulfil its trade commitments to the rest of eastern Europe.

Anxious to avoid a confrontation with the west which might lead to atomic warfare in the charged atmosphere of the Cold War, Khrushchev insisted that the GDR do nothing to impede western rights. The solution was to erect a fortified border on GDR territory around West Berlin, while guaranteeing transit between West Berlin and the *Bundesrepublik* for West Germans, West Berliners and the western allies on the designated road and rail access routes. In the early hours of 12–13 August 1961 all access points between West Berlin and the GDR were sealed, and a wall was erected in the following days. Thereafter an elaborate defensive system was constructed along the wall and down the long fortified border between the two German states; would-be escapers were fired on by border guards. The western powers reacted with rhetoric and symbolic military manoeuvres, but took no practical action. The *Berliner Mauer* (Berlin Wall) symbolised the acceptance by both Cold War superpowers of the status quo in divided Germany. The SED claimed that the *Mauer* had not only protected the GDR against incursions from the west, but had also secured peace in Europe by clearly delineating the boundary between the capitalist and socialist world systems. In official GDR parlance, the *Mauer* became the *antifaschistischer Schutzwall* ('antifascist defence wall'). The price for this Cold War stand-off was paid by the many Germans on both sides of the border cut off from their friends and relatives, and by the East Germans (would-be escapees and a much smaller number of border guards) who were shot during attempts to leave the GDR.

The closure of the borders alienated many East Germans from their state, but also emphasised that the GDR and SED were there to stay. The new population stability enabled economic growth and increased prosperity during the 1960s, seen in hindsight by some as the GDR's 'golden age'. With his own political position secure, Ulbricht himself began to experiment with reforms designed to introduce economic flexibility and greater response to consumer demands. The *Neues ökonomisches System der Planung und Leitung* ('New Economic System of Planning and Management') of 1963 (soon known simply as the NÖS) allowed state firms a certain autonomy within the central planning system, and attempted to apportion costs more realistically, though the system of state subsidies on many goods hindered a thorough application of this principle. Successful firms were allowed to make profits which could be used for capital reinvestment or paid as bonuses to workers. Simultaneously, Ulbricht emphasised the importance of embracing the *wissenschaftlich-technische Revolution* ('scientific technical revolution') if the GDR and the rest of the Soviet bloc were to keep up with and out-perform the capitalist west. Nonetheless, a combination of factors quickly undermined the NÖS. The economic demands placed on the GDR by the Soviet Union and the lack of necessary expertise to operate the NÖS were compounded by the suspicion of many party leaders about surrendering ideological control over the economy. Before the NÖS was able to bear proper fruit, it was watered down in 1967 by the restrengthening of central planning, and finally abandoned altogether after Ulbricht's fall from power.

By the late 1960s, Ulbricht was already in his late seventies and considered himself the elder statesman of the eastern bloc. This translated into an arrogant attitude towards the new Soviet leader, Leonid Brezhnev. Ulbricht's economic reforms and his determi-nation to embark on improved relations with the *Bundesrepublik*, in the mistaken belief that German unification might now be possible on the strengthened GDR's terms, worried his

Erich Honecker (1912–1994)

A communist functionary in the *Weimarer Republik*, Honecker was arrested by the *Gestapo* in 1935 for illegal political activities. Released from prison in 1945, he founded the FDJ and ensured its unbending obedience to the SED. Honecker's loyalty to Ulbricht and his efficient organisation of the Berlin Wall's construction made him a clear candidate for the party leadership. After succeeding Ulbricht in 1971, Honecker embarked on a short-lived reform era before his regime stagnated. A benevolent dictator who resisted reforms which threatened party authority, his position remained unchallenged until the peaceful revolution of 1989. Poor health prevented Honecker's prosecution over the shootings at the Wall; he died in Chilean exile in 1994.

more cautious *Politbüro* colleagues. The Soviet leadership, itself not yet quite resolved to improve relations with the west, was also concerned at the GDR's independent approach. Ulbricht's likely successor, **Erich Honecker**, agreed with Brezhnev during 1970 that Ulbricht must go, and succeeded in winning the approval of most of the *Politbüro* for the change of leadership. Confronted with the demand that he resign as *Erster Sekretär*, Ulbricht bowed to *Parteidisziplin* himself and accepted the honorary, and powerless, office of SED president. Though he remained as chairman of the *Staatsrat* until his death in 1973, Honecker ensured that Ulbricht achieved nothing in this role, a clear illustration of the primacy of party over state.

1971–1989: Abortive new start, stagnation and decline

Honecker's accession to power sparked hopes of a new start, particularly as it coincided with a wider thaw in superpower east–west relations, generally known as *détente*. The early 1970s saw the establishment of formal relations with the *Bundesrepublik* (a topic discussed fully in Chapter 8), but while this enabled far easier contacts between east and west, and even enabled some GDR citizens to visit western relatives, Honecker was determined to underline the GDR's autonomy as a sovereign state, for which the *Bundesrepublik* was as much a foreign country as Denmark or France. To this end, Honecker embarked on a policy of *Abgrenzung* (demarcation). The constitution was altered in 1974 (see Document 7a) to avoid any reference to a common German heritage, and to strengthen the GDR's bonds with the Soviet Union. Prohibitive minimum currency exchange charges were introduced for western visitors, and border installations were refined. The period also saw the increasing militarisation of society, with *Wehrkundeunterricht* (compulsory military education) introduced for young people aged 14–16 in 1978.

Nonetheless, the normalisation of relations between the two German states enabled the GDR to establish diplomatic ties with the many countries which had hitherto preferred to ally themselves with the FRG, and permitted both German states to join the United Nations in 1973. Thereafter the GDR demonstrated its importance and seeming permanence to the world at large, and its own citizens, by playing an active part in international affairs. Honecker received visiting heads of state from around the world and undertook numerous state visits, including trips to western states. The strategy peaked in 1987 when Honecker was received in Bonn as head of state. GDR citizens were also encouraged to take pride in their state by the impressive run of sporting triumphs at successive Olympic events, though it later transpired that these achievements resulted in part from illegal performance enhancement drugs. In one way, however, the GDR's activities on the international stage raised expectations which were unfulfilled: in 1975 the GDR signed the Helsinki Treaties (see p. 185), which incorporated human rights guarantees, including the freedom of travel. The GDR's failure to implement these resolutions created much resentment among East Germans.

Other promises also went unfulfilled. Honecker's assurance in 1971 that there would be 'keine Tabus' ('no taboos') in the cultural sphere led to a brief and partial lifting of the censorship which had restricted GDR writers in the 1950s and 1960s. However, the party's unwillingness to allow direct criticism proved stronger. In 1976 the singer Wolf Biermann was refused readmission to the GDR after performing songs critical of the state during a tour of the *Bundesrepublik*. The crackdown sparked a wave of protest among writers, artists and performers and symbolised the limits of free speech in the GDR.

In economic policy, Honecker quickly reimposed central control over the GDR's firms following Ulbricht's experiments. Honecker also redefined priorities, and emphasised the 'Einheit von Wirtschafts- und Sozialpolitik' ('unity of economic and social policy'): henceforth, the population would benefit more directly from economic growth. In practice this meant an ambitious programme of building new flats and renovating old houses to solve the chronic housing shortage, and increased pensions and childcare benefits. The production of consumer goods increased and though there were still lengthy waiting lists for luxury items like cars, living standards rose steadily during the 1970s. However, the oil crisis of the mid-1970s hit the GDR once the Soviet Union passed on the increased world prices, and the SED's policy of higher social spending and heavy subsidies on essential goods required substantial foreign loans, leaving little capital to invest in modern equipment or research and development projects. By the late 1980s the economy was slowing as the underinvestment of previous years left the GDR uncompetitive in the world market. Though those responsible for the country's economy later claimed to have recognised the long-term unsustainability of the situation, restricting price subsidies and social benefits would have been politically impossible. As the foreign debt mountain grew, the GDR reduced imports (leading to shortages of various goods and certain foodstuffs) and began extensive, and environmentally disastrous, mining operations to recover the country's natural resources of brown coal (lignite), a dirty alternative to importing black coal, and uranium for export. However, these operations, and the suspect international trade in arms and antiques, could only delay, but not avert, the looming economic crisis.

In the late 1970s, the internationally recognised and still economically successful GDR seemed destined to remain a permanent feature of the European map. There was little open dissent among the population: most citizens outwardly accepted SED rule, while watching western television and speaking more freely in the privacy of their own homes, a situation often termed by historians as the 'niche society'. The SED's confidence was reflected in an agreement with church leaders in 1978 which permitted the churches a certain autonomy within society, providing they respected the parameters of the socialist state. Indeed, this *Kirche im Sozialismus* ('church in socialism') was the only institution outside the SED's direct influence.

Nonetheless, tensions grew during the 1980s, initially largely inspired by the protest movements against environmental pollution and nuclear weapons in the west. Though the SED subscribed to world peace as a tenet designed to unite the population, the nascent independent peace movement in the GDR demanded the abolition of the Warsaw Pact's weaponry as well as NATO's. The protesters were angered by renewed tensions between the superpowers in the early 1980s which led to the stationing of new nuclear weapons in both German states. Similarly, at a time of increasing public concern in the west about acid rain and nuclear reactors, it was impossible to ignore the poor air quality and other environmental damage caused by the GDR's economy, which placed fulfilment of the plan above all other considerations. The explosion at the Chernobyl nuclear plant in Ukraine (then part of the Soviet Union) in 1986 significantly increased these concerns.

Slowly, independent protest movements grew in the GDR, often under the protective wing of the churches. Though they drew together only a tiny proportion of the population, they were given great attention in the western broadcast media and thus became more widely known. While the *Stasi* could infiltrate these groups and largely prevent their expansion, a far greater threat was posed to the SED by reforms in the Soviet Union. Mikhail Gorbachev's reforms of the Soviet communist system provoked calls for similar changes in the GDR, fiercely resisted by Honecker, who correctly recognised the threat to communist power if liberalisation were introduced.

Emboldened by Gorbachev's reforms, and frustrated by the SED's refusal to follow suit, the number of opposition groups grew steadily during 1988 and 1989. These groups were strong enough by May 1989 to send observers to the count of ballots in local elections; their calculations confirmed that the GDR government was falsifying results. Public anger was further fuelled in mid-1989 by the SED's support for the communist Chinese government following the massacre of student protesters in Beijing. While the SED refused to embrace change, the communist government in neighbouring Poland lost power in partially free elections in August, demonstrating to East Germans that political change would no longer be impeded by Soviet troops; more significantly, the reformist Hungarian government opened its borders to the west. GDR citizens, who could travel freely to Hungary, began crossing into Austria and travelling on to West Germany in large numbers. Meanwhile, many other East Germans began occupying West German embassies in eastern European capitals and demanding the freedom to emigrate to the west.

Though only a very small percentage of GDR citizens took these new opportunities to leave their country, the determination of so many individuals to turn their backs on the GDR created an impression of crisis. When the SED belatedly responded, it arrogantly denounced those who had left as traitors for whom no tears should be shed. This high-handed attitude appalled many East Germans, including SED members, who felt the party leadership should finally consider why so many had felt constrained to leave.

In this charged atmosphere, the SED orchestrated celebrations to mark the GDR's fortieth anniversary on 7 October 1989. Gorbachev was warmly greeted by cheering crowds in East Berlin; Honecker's speech at the official banquet celebrated the GDR's achievements and made no mention of any need for reform. Crowds who gathered outside the *Palast der Republik* on the evening of 7 October began spontaneously demonstrating for change before the police and the *Stasi* brutally intervened. By this point weekly demonstrations were already taking place in Leipzig following a prayer meeting on Monday evenings in the *Nikolaikirche*. Numbers grew rapidly during September as the crisis deepened and as East Germans began to believe that they could achieve the changes already being implemented elsewhere in the Soviet bloc. Some 70,000 marched in Leipzig on 9 October; despite preparations for a military response, ultimately the SED and *Stasi* did not implement the Chinese solution and the demonstration passed off peacefully. The way was clear for similar demonstrations in towns and cities throughout the country. The *Wende* had begun and was unstoppable.

The SED *Politbüro* finally realised that a clear response was essential. Just as Honecker had ousted Ulbricht in 1971, his own protégé Egon Krenz (also a former FDJ leader) secured Gorbachev's approval to oust the *Generalsekretär*. Honecker was forced to resign by his *Politbüro* comrades on 18 October. However, as much of the old SED leadership remained in office, and as Krenz enjoyed little popularity, most East Germans regarded this as a half-hearted change, and remained sceptical about Krenz's proposed reforms, including his promise to permit travel to the west. Pressure from mass demonstrations in the following weeks forced the resignation of numerous regional SED leaders, and the chairmen of the bloc parties and mass organisations; on 7 November the government also resigned. Members of the parties and organisations also resigned in their tens of thousands, either through disappointment over the revelations of the system's failure, or because membership was ceasing to secure advantages in the collapsing GDR.

As the old structures disintegrated, new parties and organisations grew up. The small protest groups and *Bürgerbewegungen* (citizens' groups) of the 1980s became magnets for disenchanted East Germans and ballooned in size. Alongside protest groups such as *Neues Forum, Demokratie Jetzt* and *Demokratischer Aufbruch*, the SPD reappeared and a new Green Party emerged. Most of these groups initially called for the reform of a socialist GDR. The demonstrators chanted 'Wir sind das Volk!' and, in contrast to those who were heading west, 'Wir bleiben hier!'. The SED initially refused to grant these new organisations legal status, but was eventually forced to enter negotiations at a *Runder Tisch* (round table) which grouped all the bloc parties, mass organisations and new groups.

The GDR had been underpinned since 1961 by the closed borders which had prevented the disaffected from leaving; as Krenz felt obliged to bow to calls for freedom of travel, the SED drafted a new *Reisegesetz* (travel law) which would enable all East Germans to travel abroad for thirty days a year. The hasty announcement of the new regulation at a chaotic press conference on 9 November led large numbers of East Berliners to head for the crossing points along the *Berliner Mauer*. Faced with overwhelming numbers, the border guards eventually allowed the crowds through to West Berlin. The scenes of jubilation on both sides of the border marked the practical end of the SED's hold over the GDR; hours later the borders to West Germany were also opened, and within days large sections of the *Mauer* were being demolished. The SED's remaining power structures crumbled as the bloc parties reasserted their independence and forged alliances with parties in the *Bundesrepublik*. On 1 December the *Volkskammer* voted to repeal the SED's constitutional leading role. Amid revelations of corruption, incompetence, economic mismanagement and blatant disregard for human rights, many SED members called for their own party to be dissolved; instead reformers installed a lawyer, Gregor Gysi, as the new leader and expelled the discredited former leadership from the party for infractions of the party statutes. By early February 1990 the SED had become the *Partei des demokratischen Sozialismus* (PDS).

The SED/PDS's internal developments mattered little to most East Germans after December 1989. As the extent of the GDR's economic problems became clear, enthusiasm mounted for a speedy unification with the prosperous *Bundesrepublik*, encouraged by *Bundeskanzler* Helmut Kohl. Demonstrators began to chant 'Wir sind ein Volk!', despite the warnings of *Neues Forum* and other former dissidents that unification would represent a sell-out to the west and the abolition of the GDR, rather than the reform they had championed. In free *Volkskammer* elections in March 1990, victory fell to a coalition led by the East German CDU, which had quickly abandoned socialism and embraced its western namesake, along with Kohl's promises to introduce the *D-Mark* to the east. *Neues Forum* and the other dissident groups were already obsolete, their work in dismantling SED rule done. Expectations that the SPD would do well in its prewar east German strongholds were confounded: the party paid the price for its cautious approach to German unity. Though its warnings about the difficult and costly road ahead quickly proved accurate, the party's message was not in tune with the popular mood for speedy abandonment of the past. The *Wende* had reached its climax; in the following months it remained only to negotiate the terms on which the GDR would unite with the *Bundesrepublik*.

Conclusion

Particularly since its demise, the GDR has often been regarded as a state comparable to the *Drittes Reich*. Some commentators have argued that eastern Germany experienced a continuous dictatorship from 1933 to 1990. In this view, both the NSDAP and the SED operated similarly totalitarian regimes. The concept of totalitarianism highlights the similarities between different authoritarian systems (particularly between Hitler's *Drittes Reich* and Stalin's Soviet Union), but does not distinguish between the political objectives of that rule. Conversely, left-wing commentators in particular have high-lighted the positive theoretical aims of socialist ideology as differentiating the GDR quite distinctly from the *Drittes Reich*, with its emphasis on antisemitism. In this view, socialist rule was a justified experiment, albeit undermined by the repressive, sometimes criminal, means which were employed to achieve otherwise worthwhile ends. Comparisons between NSDAP and SED rule are rejected as relativising the horrors of Nazism while unduly criminalising the GDR.

Ultimately, judgements on the GDR boil down to subjective opinion and a personal choice of whether to emphasise the system's humanitarian goals or the injustices meted out to its opponents. Nonetheless, despite the political rhetoric, some observations can be made with relative safety.

SED rule did depend on severe abuses of human rights and political repression; the *Stasi* developed a far more comprehensive network to observe the population than the *Gestapo*. However, the SED did not harbour aggressive foreign policy ambitions and did not launch any equivalent of the Holocaust. Though its treatment of political prisoners was sometimes sadistic, imprisonment methods were not as inhumane as the *Konzentrationslager* system. Ultimately, the SED was weak enough to be overthrown from within. It is not possible to make a clear comparison with the *Drittes Reich* in this respect, since the patriotic motivation of wartime may have unnaturally preserved NSDAP rule.

The SED revolutionised politics, society and the economy in the GDR to a far greater extent than the NSDAP in the *Drittes Reich*, though neither party achieved the total dominance to which it aspired, and policies were often weakened between their formulation in Berlin and their implementation in the localities. Clearly the SED had far longer to secure these structural changes, but was also far more determined to revolutionise society than the NSDAP, which was more quickly satisfied with cementing its monopoly of political power. Nonetheless, the goals of both the GDR and the *Drittes Reich* lived (and to some extent live) on after their demise in the political aspirations of significant sections of the German population.

Perhaps the greatest indication of perceived differences between the *Drittes Reich* and the GDR has been the general reaction to both states following their demise. While Germans were generally silent about the Nazi era after 1945, just as adults prefer to ignore the indiscretions of their youth, public discourse was far freer about the GDR after 1990. Chapter 8 will note the emergence of a popular, often humorous, nostalgia for the GDR past (*Ostalgie*) which remains entirely unthinkable about the Nazi period. The SED's successors in the PDS maintain a vigorous public opposition in the united *Bundesrepublik* and, though denounced by many west German politicians, do so within the democratic framework of the *Grundgesetz*, also an impossibility for avowedly neo-Nazi parties. In short, for all the heated rejection of the SED past in both parts of Germany, especially immediately after 1989/90, the GDR has not attracted anything approaching the same degree of opprobrium as the *Drittes Reich*.

Assessing individuals' involvement in, and responsibility for, the preservation of SED rule has become as complex as the denazification issue discussed in Chapter 5. SED membership, often opportunistic, is not itself a clear indication of personal culpability for repression in the GDR. As practically the entire East German population belonged to a political party or one or more SED-dominated organisations, in practice responsibility has been passed back to the *Politbüro* and other senior functionaries, and the East German population generally exonerated on the principle that the GDR, though operated and perpetuated by East Germans themselves, was imposed by the Soviet Union.

It is hard to escape the conclusion that the GDR survived only as long as it remained in the Soviets' interests for it to do so, and that despite the positive aspirations and memories associated with the state, it was incapable of securing the economic and personal freedom to which East Germans aspired and did not enjoy as much popular support as its western counterpart. The *Bundesrepublik*, economically successful and highly democratic, succeeded in presenting itself as the natural successor to the German nation state; the GDR, meanwhile, achieved internal stability (in part at the price of the *Berliner Mauer*) but never escaped the shadow of the Soviet Union to appear either to its own population or the outside world as a 'normal' state.

Document 7a: Extracts from 1968 GDR Constitution, incorporating 1974 amendments

In Fortsetzung der revolutionären Traditionen der deutschen Arbeiterklasse und gestützt auf die Befreiung vom Faschismus hat das Volk der Deutschen Demokratischen Republik in Übereinstimmung mit den Prozessen der geschichtlichen Entwicklung unserer Epoche sein Recht auf sozial-ökonomische, staatliche und nationale Selbstbestimmung verwirklicht und gestaltet die entwickelte sozialistische Gesellschaft.

Erfüllt von dem Willen, seine Geschicke frei zu bestimmen, unbeirrt auch weiter den Weg des Sozialismus und Kommunismus, des Friedens, der Demokratie und Völkerfreundschaft zu gehen, hat sich das Volk der Deutschen Demokratischen Republik diese sozialistische Verfassung gegeben.

. . .

Artikel 1

Die Deutsche Demokratische Republik ist ein sozialistischer Staat der Arbeiter und Bauern. Sie ist die politische Organisation der Werktätigen in Stadt und Land unter Führung der Arbeiterklasse und ihrer marxistisch-leninistischen Partei. . . .

Artikel 2

. . .

3 Die Ausbeutung des Menschen durch den Menschen ist für immer beseitigt. Was des Volkes Hände schaffen, ist des Volkes Eigen. Das sozialistische Prinzip „Jeder nach seinen Fähigkeiten, jedem nach seiner Leistung" wird verwirklicht.

Artikel 3

1 Das Bündnis aller Kräfte des Volkes findet in der Nationalen Front der Deutschen Demokratischen Republik seinen organisierten Ausdruck.
2 In der Nationalen Front der Deutschen Demokratischen Republik vereinigen die Parteien und Massenorganisationen alle Kräfte des Volkes zum gemeinsamen Handeln für die Entwicklung der sozialistischen Gesellschaft. Dadurch verwirklichen sie das Zusammenleben aller Bürger in der sozialistischen Gemeinschaft nach dem Grundsatz, daß jeder Verantwortung für das Ganze trägt.

. . .

Artikel 6

1 Die Deutsche Demokratische Republik hat getreu den Interessen des Volkes und den internationalen Verpflichtungen auf ihrem Gebiet den deutschen Militarismus und Nazismus ausgerottet. . . .
2 Die Deutsche Demokratische Republik ist für immer und unwiderruflich mit der Union der Sozialistischen Sowjetrepubliken verbündet. Das enge und brüderliche Bündnis mit ihr garantiert dem Volk der Deutschen Demokratischen Republik das weitere Voranschreiten auf dem Wege des Sozialismus und des Friedens.
Die Deutsche Demokratische Republik ist untrennbarer Bestandteil der sozialistischen Staatengemeinschaft. . . .

Document 7b: *Jugendweihe* oath, 1968–1989

Liebe junge Freunde!
Seid ihr bereit, als junge Bürger unserer Deutschen Demokratischen Republik mit uns gemeinsam, getreu der Verfassung, für die große und edle Sache des Sozialismus zu arbeiten und zu kämpfen und das revolutionäre Erbe des Volkes in Ehren zu halten, so antwortet:
Ja, das geloben wir!
Seid ihr bereit, als treue Söhne und Töchter unseres Arbeiter-und-Bauern-Staates nach hoher Bildung und Kultur zu streben, Meister eures Faches zu werden, unentwegt zu lernen und all euer Wissen und Können für die Verwirklichung unserer großen humanistischen Ideale einzusetzen, so antwortet:
Ja, das geloben wir!
Seid ihr bereit, als würdige Mitglieder der sozialistischen Gemeinschaft stets in kameradschaftlicher Zusammenarbeit, gegenseitiger Achtung und Hilfe zu handeln und euren Weg zum persönlichen Glück immer mit dem Kampf für das Glück des Volkes zu vereinen, so antwortet:
Ja, das geloben wir!
Seid ihr bereit, als wahre Patrioten die feste Freundschaft mit der Sowjetunion weiter zu vertiefen, den Bruderbund mit den sozialistischen Ländern zu stärken, im Geiste des proletarischen Internationalismus zu kämpfen, den Frieden zu schützen und den Sozialismus gegen jeden imperialistischen Angriff zu verteidigen, so anwortet:
Ja, das geloben wir!
Wir haben euer Gelöbnis vernommen. Ihr habt euch ein großes und edles Ziel gesetzt. Feierlich nehmen wir euch auf in die große Gemeinschaft des werktätigen Volkes, das unter Führung der Arbeiterklasse und ihrer revolutionären Partei, einig im Willen und im Handeln, die entwickelte sozialistische Gesellschaft in der DDR errichtet. Wir übertragen euch eine hohe Verantwortung. Jederzeit werden wir euch mit Rat und Tat helfen, die sozialistische Zukunft schöpferisch zu gestalten.

Source: Andreas Meier, *Jugendweihe – JUGENDFEIER* (Munich: dtv, 1998), p. 202.

Topics
FOR DISCUSSION / FURTHER RESEARCH

■ What do the 1968 GDR constitution (Document 7a) and the *Jugendweihe* oath (Document 7b) reveal about the SED's aims for GDR society?

■ Compare and contrast the political systems of the *Drittes Reich* and the GDR.

■ How dependent was the SED on the patronage of the Soviet Union?

■ How justified was the *Bundesrepublik* in commemorating 17 June 1953 as the *Tag der deutschen Einheit*?

■ What basis was there in the SED's claims that the Berlin Wall secured European peace during the Cold War?

■ Were economic or political factors more significant in weakening the GDR?

■ By what point was the GDR's fate sealed?

Two into one: uniting Germany, 1969–2000

Soviet–American relations were strained throughout the postwar era, despite periods of *détente* when both sides attempted to reduce tensions. However, the 1979 Soviet invasion of Afghanistan and the election of Ronald Reagan, inherently suspicious of communism, as American president in 1981 heralded a renewed arms race. Mikhail Gorbachev, the Soviet leader after 1985, recognised the USSR's inability to match western military expenditure. His reforms undermined communism, bringing the USSR's collapse in 1991 and removing postwar political and military structures. New states emerged across the former Soviet Union, the Czech Republic and Slovakia peacefully separated, and wars raged for control of Yugoslavia. Western Europe strengthened its institutions: the EC, renamed the European Union (EU), admitted Austria, Sweden and Finland and launched a common currency (the 'Euro'). Many eastern European countries joined NATO, and most instituted economic reforms to meet EU membership requirements. Russia, isolated from these developments and unsettled by its reduced status, viewed this process uneasily.

Having considered the separate developments of the two postwar German states, this final chapter studies their strained relations, and Willy Brandt's attempts to forge better links between the *Bundesrepublik* and the GDR. While the two German states remained antagonistic to one another during the 1970s and 1980s, the collapse of socialist rule in the GDR during late 1989 demonstrated that the bonds between them had remained strong. East Germans naturally looked to their larger West German neighbour for help in reconstructing their country, while many West Germans saw their republic's extension into the east as a natural development and the confirmation of the *Bundesrepublik*'s historical mission to embrace the entire German nation (excluding Austria) in a true democracy. The second part of this chapter shows how unification was managed in 1990, and how the enlarged *Bundesrepublik* met the challenges of its first decade. These included not only the enormous financial burden of restricting the east German economy to western standards, but also absorbing a population with very different traditions and expectations.

The two Germanies: strained relations

At their creation in 1949, both the *Bundesrepublik* and the GDR aspired to represent the whole of Germany, and each refused to acknowledge the other's legitimacy. For the GDR, the *Bundesrepublik* represented an Anglo-American puppet state, created as a bulwark against the peace-loving Soviet Union, and a restoration of the old power of militarists and monopoly capitalists. These forces, the SED argued, could not represent the mass of the West German people; only a state based on truly democratic principles, in which economic power was in the people's hands, could claim true legitimacy. That state was unambiguously the GDR; the inclusive nature of the *Volkskongressbewegung* and the election of May 1949 (see Chapter 5) were cited as evidence of the GDR's democratic origins.

The Bonn government took a diametrically opposed view, and for many years refused to recognise that the GDR was a true state at all, preferring well into the 1960s to refer to the entity as merely the 'Soviet occupied zone'. The absence of free elections, the constant flow of 'refugees' from east to west and finally the imprisonment of the East German population behind the Berlin Wall enabled the *Bundesrepublik* to dismiss the GDR as a Soviet imposition with no popular mandate. As such, Bonn could have no diplomatic relations with East Berlin.

Although some trade was conducted between the two Germanies in the 1950s and 1960s, the *Bundesrepublik* went to great lengths to avoid any sign of even tacit recognition of the GDR state. This was best illustrated by the emergence of the 'Hallstein Doctrine' in 1955, devised by Walter Hallstein, an official in Bonn's *Auswärtiges Amt*. The *Bundesrepublik*'s policy was to refuse to recognise any state which recognised the GDR. The doctrine was based on the logic that the presence of both West and East German embassies in the same foreign capital would imply Bonn's tacit acknowledgement of the GDR's existence. Consequently, Bonn had no relations during the 1950s and 1960s with the GDR's eastern European allies. There was only one exception: Bonn established relations with the Soviet Union in 1955 since it was one of the occupying powers which retained rights over Germany as a whole. This concession secured the release of the 30,000 German prisoners of war who had spent the previous ten years or more in the Soviet Union. Otherwise, lack of contact with eastern Europe was a relatively minor price to pay for the *Bundesrepublik*, as the Hallstein Doctrine had the great advantage of effectively isolating the GDR in world affairs: given a choice, most states preferred links with the richer *Bundesrepublik*. While the Hallstein Doctrine remained, the GDR's appearance of impermanence was heightened, not least among its own subjects.

The *Bundesrepublik* not only refused to accept the legitimacy of the GDR state, but also laid claim to the whole territory of the *Deutsches Reich* as it had existed in 1937, including the provinces to the east of the *Oder-Neiße-Linie* which had been placed under Polish or Soviet administration (but not finally handed to these countries) by the allies in the Potsdam Agreement of 1945. Until the early 1970s the *Bundesrepublik*'s official *Statistisches Jahrbuch* ('Statistical Yearbook') included figures and maps relating to both the 'Soviet zone' and the lost eastern provinces. There was a clear domestic political dimension to the *Bundesrepublik*'s continuing commitment to the whole of pre-1938 Germany, linked to the existence in West Germany of *Vertriebenenverbände*, organisations representing the many Germans who had been forced out of Silesia, Pomerania, East Prussia and the Sudetenland after the war. These groups tended to have close political links to the CDU/CSU and sustained the agenda of German national unity, supporting Adenauer's *Politik der Stärke* in their rejection of Soviet rule.

In short, with its democratic political system, and as by far the larger of the two postwar German states, the *Bundesrepublik* saw itself as the only legitimate representative of all Germans (albeit without extending this definition to include Austrians). The strictest interpretation of this *Alleinvertretungsanspruch* made it incompatible in the 1950s and 1960s for the *Bundesrepublik* to deal with the GDR, but also ensured that no separate West German citizenship law was ever introduced. Instead, the *Bundesrepublik* recognised only one, German citizenship, based on the traditional primacy of descent rather than place of birth, and refused to acknowledge the separate GDR citizenship laws introduced by East Berlin in 1967.

This principle allowed GDR citizens who were able to reach the west to settle there as 'German' citizens, and to obtain a western passport. Similarly, the logic of the *Bundesrepublik*'s position required the country to admit ethnic Germans from eastern Europe who arrived there. While the Cold War continued and emigration from eastern Europe was almost impossible, this made little difference, but the collapse of the Soviet Union and its satellite states in 1989–91 heralded the arrival of tens of thousands of immigrants, the majority from Russia or Kazakhstan, many of whom had little or no knowledge of the German language but who were descended from German settlers in previous generations. Conversely, German law denied citizenship to non-Germans even if they were born in the *Bundesrepublik*. The large number of children and grand-children of the first wave of *Gastarbeiter* found they had no automatic citizenship rights until a limited reform took force in 2000 (see p. 195).

By the early 1960s a stand-off had developed between the two German states. In 1955 both had been granted formal sovereignty by their respective occupation powers.

As we have seen, the Berlin Wall prevented the continuing westward haemorrhage of the GDR's population after 1961 and confirmed Germany's division as a lasting feature of the European map. From the late 1960s onwards the GDR insisted that unity would only come when the West German workers rejected the *Bundesrepublik* and joined the progressive, socialist German state. In the meantime, the GDR hoped to achieve full western recognition of its sovereign independence, and of the status of East Berlin as its legitimate capital. For its part the *Bundesrepublik* refused to consider GDR approaches, though some contacts were possible through informal channels.

Nonetheless, the Berlin Wall's construction initiated a process of reflection in the west, which partially provoked Adenauer's fall in 1963: his *Politik der Stärke* had been undermined in the eyes of those many who wished to preserve the reality rather than merely the rhetoric of a single German nation. Chief among these was the social democratic *Regierender Bürgermeister* (governing mayor) of West Berlin at the time of the Wall's construction, Willy Brandt. Brandt experienced at first hand the distress caused to Berliners who found themselves abruptly cut off from family and friends. Not only were GDR citizens no longer permitted to leave their country, but West Berliners were also forbidden access to the east.

Though not an SED sympathiser, Brandt believed that real progress could only be made by negotiating concessions with the GDR's authorities, rather than perpetuating the cycle of propaganda attacks and counter-attacks which had already contributed to a practically unbridgeable gulf between the two states. Brandt was concerned that the German nation would be irreparably undermined over time if steps were not taken to restore lines of communication (see Brandt's 1969 *Bundestag* speech in Document 6b).

Brandt set a precedent in 1963 by arranging visas for West Berliners to visit relatives in the east at Christmas, albeit without formal recognition of the GDR's state authority. The SED nonetheless claimed that the West Berliners who had accepted GDR visas had effectively acknowledged the GDR state. The diplomatic tightrope walk which accompanied even this minor and temporary concession emphasised the difficulties which would surround any wider agreement.

As *Außenminister* after 1966 and then *Bundeskanzler* from 1969, Brandt initiated a sea change in West German policy, generally termed *Ostpolitik* ('policy towards the east'). His aim was to accept the realities of postwar Europe – in particular that the Soviet Union's apparent strength would guarantee the continued existence of socialist states throughout eastern Europe – as the price for opening doors to the East German population. Brandt's policy was one of small steps (*Politik der kleinen Schritte*): by improving relations to the east he hoped to achieve concessions on human rights and travel restrictions, and to make available western aid which would improve East Germans' living conditions. Brandt was fortunate that his term of office as *Bundeskanzler* (1969–74) coincided with a period of lessened tensions in superpower relations. This era of *détente* had been ushered in by the Cuban missile crisis of 1962, when the world had stood for a few days on the brink of atomic war over the Soviet Union's apparent desire to station weapons in Cuba, uncomfortably close to America's borders. Both sides hoped to avoid further scares, and the United States wished to concentrate its efforts on the war in Vietnam rather than the perceived Soviet threat by the mid-1960s. The Soviet Union's willingness to make some concessions in return for a general recognition of the postwar status quo complemented Brandt's plans.

For the GDR authorities, *Ostpolitik* was a two-edged sword. On the one hand, despite Brandt's assertion on assuming the chancellorship in 1969 that 'Eine völkerrechtliche Anerkennung der DDR durch die Bundesregierung kann nicht in Betracht kommen' ('There can be no question of the federal government recognising the GDR in international law'), bilateral treaties between the two Germanies would in practice give the GDR the recognition it had long craved. On the other hand, Brandt commented in the same breath that: 'Auch wenn zwei Staaten in Deutschland existieren, sind sie doch füreinander nicht Ausland; ihre Beziehungen zueinander können nur von besonderer Art sein' ('Even if two states exist in Germany they are not foreign to one another; their relations must be of a special nature'). This remained the *Bundesrepublik*'s official stance for the remainder of the GDR's existence, deliberately leaving open the option of unification which would sweep away the SED's hold over the east, but which was Brandt's ultimate goal, and the constitutionally enshrined objective of the *Bundesrepublik*.

Brandt recognised that better relations with the GDR could only be achieved as part of a wider process which included other eastern European states, particularly the Soviet Union itself. As *Außenminister* he had already recognised Romania (then a somewhat independently minded member of the Soviet bloc) in 1967, an action which amounted to a renunciation of the Hallstein Doctrine.

In August 1970 the *Bundesrepublik* signed a new treaty with the Soviet Union, the *Moskauer Vertrag*. For the first time, the *Bundesrepublik* recognised the existing borders in Europe. The treaty made explicit reference to the *Oder-Neiße-Linie* and to the border between the *Bundesrepublik* and the GDR, effectively implying West German recognition of the East German state. Furthermore, both sides affirmed that they had no territorial claims of any kind – in other words, the *Bundesrepublik* would no longer claim the German provinces which had been incorporated into Poland and the Soviet Union after the Second World War. However, the federal government was careful to send a note to the Soviet foreign minister, the 'Brief zur deutschen Einheit' ('Letter on German unity'), in which the *Bundesrepublik* underlined that the *Moskauer Vertrag* did not alter West Germany's will to achieve German unity; both sides also emphasised that this treaty did not alter the rights of all four allied powers jointly to determine Germany's future at some future date in a peace treaty which would resolve the unanswered questions of 1945.

Better West German relations with the east also required an accommodation with Poland, since most of the former German territories east of the *Oder-Neiße-Linie* lay within Poland. Furthermore, a sign of German reconciliation was essential following the Nazi occupation of Poland and the extermination of so many Polish Jews. In December 1970 Brandt travelled to Warsaw to sign a treaty with Poland which contained renewed recognition of the postwar borders and, consequently, an abandonment of claims to the lost territories. More symbolic of the new era than the official paperwork was Brandt's spontaneous gesture of falling to his knees as a sign of German repentance in front of the memorial to the victims of the Warsaw Ghetto. Here, during the war, the German occupation authorities had confined more than 300,000 Jews to a small quarter of the city. Many of them died of starvation or disease in primitive conditions, and the remainder were shipped to the *Vernichtungslager* after a brave but ultimately unsuccessful uprising.

The treaties with Moscow and Warsaw were the key to establishing official relations with the GDR, and during their negotiation the first talks began between the SED and the Bonn government. The first meeting between the heads of the two German governments took place in Erfurt (GDR) on 19 March 1970. Despite the efforts of the *Volkspolizei*, Brandt was cheered by crowds of East Germans, clearly optimistic that *Ostpolitik* would open the borders to the west. The GDR *Ministerpräsident*, Willi Stoph, visited Kassel (FRG) for further talks in May. Though historic, these talks achieved little as the GDR remained cautious of making any concessions.

Instead, agreements between the four allied powers kickstarted German–German relations. A *Viermächte-Abkommen* ('Quadripartite Agreement') was signed between all four powers in December 1971 to regulate the status of Berlin, a step made necessary not least by the Berlin Wall, a development which had not been foreseen when the Potsdam Treaty was signed. The Berlin question was so controversial that the *Viermächte-Abkommen* did not even specifically define the geographical area under discussion. The treaty effectively confirmed the status quo: Berlin as a whole remained under allied jurisdiction, and West Berlin was not a part of the *Bundesrepublik*, though the special links between the two were recognised. The west did not, however, formally dispute that East Berlin constituted the *Hauptstadt der DDR*. In return, the east abandoned the claim that West Berlin belonged to the GDR and the Soviets guaranteed free transit along agreed routes between West Berlin and the *Bundesrepublik*.

The four allied powers left the two German states to agree between themselves and with the West Berlin government how free movement of people could best be implemented under the treaty. This led to the first formal agreements between the *Bundesrepublik* and the GDR in late 1971, with improved postal links and strict rules to cover travel from West Germany to West Berlin across GDR territory. A further agreement allowed West Berliners to visit the GDR for up to thirty days annually, precisely the human relations dividend to which Brandt aspired.

With these first agreements, the *Bundesrepublik* had unambiguously recognised the authority of the GDR government. But the whole *Ostpolitik* process had aroused conservative opposition in West Germany which had to be resolved before full diplomatic relations could be established with East Berlin. For many CDU *Bundestag* members, the eastern treaties represented a breach of the duty laid on the federal government in the *Grundgesetz* to strive for German unity. However, the CDU/CSU failed to unseat Brandt over the issue in the *Bundestag*, despite his small majority, by attempting a *konstruktives Misstrauensvotum*, the first in the country's history. With the Moscow and Warsaw Treaties ratified, and a Nobel Peace Prize under his belt, Brandt engineered early *Bundestag* elections which he won with an increased majority for the SPD–FDP coalition.

This clear public endorsement of *Ostpolitik* enabled the *Bundesrepublik* to press ahead with a full settlement with the GDR, the *Grundlagenvertrag* ('Basic Treaty') of

December 1972. Both sides recognised the inviolability of their borders, affirmed that they would not interfere in each other's internal affairs, and that neither would claim the right to speak for the other: for the GDR this meant formal recognition and an end to the *Bundesrepublik*'s *Alleinvertretungsanspruch*. There was a compromise over the form of diplomatic relations. As the *Bundesrepublik* insisted that the two German states were '*füreinander nicht Ausland*' (in Brandt's words of 1969), ambassadors could not be exchanged; instead, each side established a *Ständige Vertretung* ('permanent representation') in the other's capital. Brandt's aims were most clearly visible in the agreement to make progress on postal, telecommunications and travel links between the two states, along with educational and cultural exchanges. As with the 1970 *Moskauer Vertrag*, the *Bundesrepublik* appended a letter to the treaty in which it committed itself nonetheless to pursuing the ultimate goal of German unity.

Despite this codicil, the Bavarian CSU was still implacably opposed to treaties which appeared to sign away the *Bundesrepublik*'s rights over Germany's national interests and referred the matter to the *Bundesverfassungsgericht*. This ruled the treaties lawful: since the *Grundgesetz* did not specify how the goal of unity was to be achieved, it remained for the federal government to determine the precise policy.

Ostpolitik did not finally solve the 'German question': a peace treaty between 'Germany' and the wartime allies had still not been signed, and the *Grundgesetz* still committed the *Bundesrepublik* to unification. However, the situation had been normalised, and this enabled both German states to join the United Nations in 1973. Freed from the confines of the Hallstein Doctrine, the GDR quickly established diplomatic relations with most countries, including the western allies. The Soviet Union's hopes of a wider European settlement were also eased by *Ostpolitik*: a 'Conference on Security and Cooperation in Europe' (CSCE) brought together thirty-five European states from both sides of the continent, along with the USA and Canada. In the final CSCE agreements, signed in Helsinki in 1975, all participants recognised the existing European borders and agreed that these should not change unless all thirty-five states approved. The west had acknowledged the Soviet Union's hold on eastern Europe. In return the west insisted on the adoption of a range of human rights guarantees, including the freedom to travel across international borders. However, these agreements were generally not respected in the Soviet bloc states. The optimism which accompanied the Helsinki process in the GDR quickly turned to disillusionment with the SED government, as the Berlin Wall remained largely impermeable.

The *Grundlagenvertrag* fundamentally altered the climate in German–German relations. Whereas contacts between ordinary people in east and west had been almost impossible previously, West Germans could henceforth visit relations in the GDR with relative ease, and increasing numbers of East Germans were also allowed to travel west on important family business, such as close relatives' significant birthdays and funerals. In return for loans and other financial support, the GDR government further relaxed travel restrictions in the 1980s, notably allowing pensioners (whose loss would not damage the economy if they did not return) to travel to the west. Self-shooting devices along the border fortifications were also removed in 1983 in return for financial assistance. Despite the CDU/CSU's opposition to *Ostpolitik* in the early 1970s, Helmut

Kohl's government made no attempt to revert to Adenauer's *Politik der Stärke* after 1982 and presided over the high watermark of German–German relations, Erich Honecker's state visit to the *Bundesrepublik* in 1987. These general improvements should not obscure the fact that would-be escapers continued to be shot and killed by the GDR's border guards, and that East Germans' visits to the west still required the approval of unaccountable SED officials whose decisions were often arbitrary and politically motivated.

Despite the advances, official relations between the two states were often frosty, reflecting the ideological gulf, and particularly following the Soviet Union's invasion of Afghanistan in 1979, the crackdown on the independent Polish trade unions the following year and the resumption of the superpowers' arms race which dominated the early 1980s. Meanwhile, the GDR under Honecker embarked on a policy of *Abgrenzung* ('distancing') from the west which emphasised a separate GDR identity. This involved deleting references to a single German nation in a revised constitution of 1974, and renaming many institutions which had retained the attribute '*Deutsch*'. Westerners were dissuaded from visiting the GDR and bringing their potentially polluting ideology by the imposition of a *Zwangsumtausch* – a minimum sum of hard currency which westerners had to exchange into GDR marks at an unfavourable rate for each day they spent in the east.

While many East Germans remained interested in the west, and the number of applicants hoping to emigrate to the *Bundesrepublik* steadily grew, the normalisation of German–German relations contributed to a general apathy surrounding the 'German question' in the west. The West German '*Tag der deutschen Einheit*', commemorating the uprising of 17 June 1953 in the GDR, degenerated into a public holiday with little political significance for West Germans; by the late 1980s few had any real interest in achieving unification. Consequently, the *Wende* in the GDR came as a shock to many in the west for whom the *Provisorium* of 1949 had become a fixed landmark. The complexities which still surrounded the 'German question' became evident as the *Bundesrepublik*, the GDR, the four allies and the wider international community struggled to resolve the political, economic, diplomatic and military issues raised by the collapse of communist rule in the GDR and the rest of eastern Europe.

1989–1990: 'Wir sind ein Volk!' – the road to German unity

Two things were clear to all East Germans by the end of 1989. First, the revolutionary events of the autumn and the opening of the Berlin Wall had swept away the SED's power for ever. Second, the GDR was bankrupt and in desperate need of western credit. It was estimated that the East German standard of living would have to fall by a third if the GDR were to live within its means. *Bundeskanzler* Kohl was, however, only prepared to provide financial support in return for a fully reformed GDR with a functioning market economy and an end to socialist experiments. Soon after the fall of the Berlin Wall, Kohl announced his ten-point plan to achieve the confederation of the two German states; the GDR's stopgap SED–PDS premier Hans Modrow also accepted that the popular tide was turning to German unity, and that there seemed little reason for a separate GDR existence once the country's socialist identity had been abandoned.

The CDU coalition's victory at the March 1990 *Volkskammer* elections under the title *Allianz für Deutschland* was widely viewed as a vote for the *D-Mark*. Negotiations then began between the two states over the modalities of unification, even though no referendum was held to secure West Germans' agreement. The talks concerned not only the merger of the two states' internal political, social and economic mechanisms, but also united Germany's position in the international community and her legal status with respect to the Potsdam settlement of 1945. In international law, the four allies still retained their sovereign rights over Germany as a whole, and the two German states could not merge without the approval of the allies or the other CSCE states.

The initial task was to create the economic basis for renewal and investment in East Germany. This was achieved in a *Wirtschafts-, Währungs- und Sozialunion* (economic, currency and social union) between the two states which ended the GDR's planned economy and lifted restrictions on price setting, private economic initiative, the labour market, international trade and foreign investment. In their place the *Bundesrepublik*'s successful *soziale Marktwirtschaft* was introduced, with wide-ranging economic freedoms. The GDR's traditional safety net of social welfare measures was replaced with the West German equivalents. The Modrow government had already established a *Treuhandanstalt* ('trustee agency') to manage the GDR's state-owned economy. The *Treuhand*, placed under West German managers following the March elections, had the task of closing redundant, uneconomic state enterprises and privatising the healthy or salvageable companies. It was anticipated that the enormous receipts from this sale of such extensive state assets would finance many of the costs of unification, and perhaps provide GDR citizens with investment bonds.

The cornerstone of this first unification treaty was the abolition of the GDR's weak currency and its substitution with the *D-Mark*. Amid great controversy, *Bundeskanzler* Kohl determined to convert GDR marks to *D-Mark* at a rate of 1:1 for wages, pensions and savings accounts up to 4,000 marks (6,000 marks for pensioners, 2,000 marks for children). Remaining savings were converted at a rate of 2:1. As the true value of the GDR currency to the *D-Mark* was generally believed to be nearer 4:1 or 5:1, many observers believed that the *Bundesrepublik* was paying too high a price for economic unification, and weakening its currency. Politically, however, East Germans could not be asked to accept a conversion rate which would have impoverished them by comparison with West Germans. The *Wirtschafts-, Währungs- und Sozialunion* took force on 1 July 1990. Overnight the GDR's shops filled with western goods which had been held back until they could be sold for the new, strong currency.

Although the GDR had already surrendered any meaningful sovereignty to the west by placing its currency, and with it economic policy, under the auspices of the *Bundesbank*, formal unification was dependent on international agreement. *Bundeskanzler* Kohl was determined that the future united Germany should continue the *Bundesrepublik*'s tradition of *Westintegration* as a full NATO member. Kohl rejected the possibility of neutrality on the Austrian model as an infringement of German sovereignty. However, the eastward extension of NATO's borders was initially unacceptable to the Soviet Union. Kohl secured Gorbachev's agreement in July at the cost of some DM 21 billion in payments and loans to the bankrupt Soviet Union. In part this financed the departure of the large Soviet military presence in the GDR, to be achieved by 1994. During this interim period, Germany would be a full NATO member, but NATO would not extend its military structures into eastern Germany. Kohl also agreed to limit the *Bundeswehr* to 370,000 men.

While the British and French leaders, Margaret Thatcher and François Mitterrand, had reservations about the potential international dominance of a united Germany (both were indelibly influenced by the Second World War), neither could halt the growing German enthusiasm for unification. Talks between the two German states and the four wartime allies produced the *Zwei-plus-vier-Vertrag* of 16 September 1990. This lifted all remaining allied rights over Germany resulting from the unconditional surrender of 1945, and confirmed Germany's existing borders, despite complaints from conservative quarters that the eastern provinces were being finally yielded to Poland and Russia.

A further *Staatsvertrag* (state treaty) between the FRG and GDR of 31 August 1990 regulated a large number of outstanding, mainly technical issues, including the future of the GDR's public institutions, the application of law in united Germany and necessary alterations to the *Grundgesetz*.

> ### Unification and the Grundgesetz
>
> §23: Dieses Grundgesetz gilt zunächst im Gebiete der Länder Baden, Bayern, Bremen, Groß-Berlin, Hamburg, Hessen, Niedersachsen, Nordrhein-Westfalen, Rheinland-Pfalz, Schleswig-Holstein, Württemberg-Baden und Württemberg-Hohenzollern. In anderen Teilen Deutschlands ist es nach deren Beitritt in Kraft zu setzen.
>
> *N.B.: Württemberg-Baden and Württemberg-Hohenzollern merged to form Baden-Württemberg in 1952; despite the wording of the Grundgesetz, the four allies were agreed that no part of Berlin formed part of the Bundesrepublik and that the Grundgesetz was not applicable there.*
>
> §146 Dieses Grundgesetz verliert seine Gültigkeit an dem Tage, an dem eine Verfassung in Kraft tritt, die von dem deutschen Volke in freier Entscheidung beschlossen worden ist.

Controversy surrounded the legal mechanism for unification, since the *Grundgesetz* allowed two different possibilities (see box). Kohl's government had no desire or intention of sacrificing the established order of the *Bundesrepublik* by replacing the *Grundgesetz* as Article 146 proposed; nor was there widespread willingness in the GDR to delay unification while a new constitution was agreed. Instead, the *Volkskammer* resolved to declare the GDR's *Beitritt* (accession) to the *Grundgesetz* in accordance with Article 23, effective from 3 October 1990. Amid scenes of general celebration around the *Reichstag* building in Berlin, but somewhat mixed feelings about the future among many East Germans, the GDR simply ceased to exist on that date and power passed to the existing Bonn government. Formally, Germany was united as a takeover by the stronger state of its weaker neighbour rather than as the merger of equals. However, the work of integrating the two different economies, traditions and mentalities into one coherent country had hardly begun.

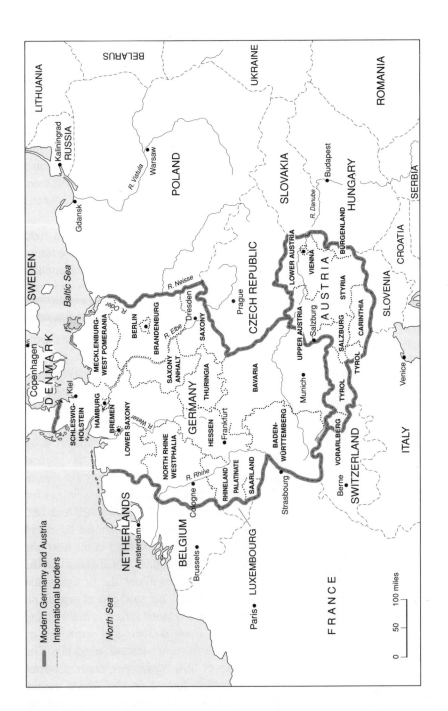

Map 8.1: *Central Europe, 2000*

1990–2000: United Germany?

As united Germany took the form of an enlarged *Bundesrepublik*, there was no change to the country's basic political structures. The *Bundestag* included members from eastern constituencies and the *Bundesrat* grew to include representatives from united Berlin and the five reconstituted east German *Länder*, Brandenburg, Mecklenburg-West Pomerania (Mecklenburg-Vorpommern), Saxony (Sachsen), Saxony-Anhalt (Sachsen-Anhalt) and Thuringia (Thüringen). Berlin also became *Bundeshauptstadt*, though Bonn retained its role as the seat of government until 1999.

On 2 December 1990 the first national elections confirmed the CDU/CSU–FDP coalition in government, following Kohl's triumphal achievement of unification. However, the *Fünfprozenthürde* was uniquely applied separately in the east and west, enabling the **PDS**, with 9.9 per cent of the vote in the former GDR but a national average of only 2.4 per cent, to enter the *Bundestag*. It was assumed that this reservoir of support for the reformed communists would ebb away as German unity and the *soziale Marktwirtschaft* took root. Instead, the PDS grew steadily in the east at elections during the 1990s, regularly taking 20 per cent of the vote and as much as 40 per cent in east Berlin, while remaining insignificant in the west. The party entered the *Bundestag* in both 1994 and 1998.

The PDS's success contributed to a widening gulf between the party political systems in east and west, despite the merger of the old GDR bloc parties with western partners during 1990. (The GDR's CDU and DBD joined the western CDU, while the LDPD and NDPD merged with the FDP.) In the west, the CDU and SPD remained dominant, while the FDP slowly declined and the *Grünen* maintained their small but solid core of support. In the east the SPD found it hard to build a party structure from scratch, and many of its natural constituency instead voted PDS. The alliance of GDR *Bürgerbewegungen* (citizens' movements) formed in the *Wende* period, *Bündnis 90*, became largely redundant and declined to the status of a splinter party despite its merger with the *Grünen* in 1993.

Partei des demokratischen Sozialismus (PDS)

As the SED's successor party, the PDS remains committed to a reformed socialism, albeit not clearly defined. Broadly speaking, the party opposes globalisation as a new form of international capitalist exploitation and favours fair trading with the Third World. It endorses radical democratisation and free internal party debate, as a complete break with the GDR and SED past; full societal equality, especially for women, the disabled and homosexuals; and full racial equality in sharp opposition to the rise of racist neo-Nazism (see pp. 194–5). During the 1990s the PDS built a loyal electorate by championing east German interests and traditions against incursions from the west. It benefited from anger at the high levels of unemployment which followed unification, and from the belated emergence of a distinct east German identity, constructed from the separate experience of the previous forty years rather than identification with the old SED version of socialism. However, the party membership is predominantly of pensionable age.

The eastern FDP also withered, reflecting the generally small number of private entrepreneurs in the new *Länder*.

Given the erosion of support for the FDP and *Grünen*, single-party governments, either CDU or SPD, or grand coalitions of the two parties have been common in the eastern *Landtage*. However, in the mid-1990s the eastern SPD became increasingly prepared to work with the PDS. The minority SPD government in Saxony-Anhalt endured thanks to its 'toleration' by the PDS; a similar arrangement enabled the SPD and *Grünen* to assume power in Berlin in June 2001. In Mecklenburg-West Pomerania the SPD preferred a formal coalition with the PDS to a *große Koalition* with the CDU after the 1998 regional elections. Such arrangements allowed the CDU to defame the SPD as communist sympathisers, and to raise the spectre of a new merger of the left-wing parties on the model of the SED's formation in 1946. Conversely, despite the PDS leadership's aspirations to enter national government in coalition with the SPD, many PDS members regretted their party's willingness to compromise with the SPD, a party which no longer propounded a radical socialist alternative.

The SPD reengineered itself as a mass party of the centre-left during the 1990s, more than ever committed to the market economy and the needs of business, and prepared to accept the shift from public to private ownership of key services and industries. This further departure from the SPD's ideological roots to become a more economically responsible 'lifestyle' party – albeit without dropping the party's commitment to its core constituency of blue-collar workers and trade unionists – transformed the party's electoral fortunes in national politics. The choice of the pragmatic and charismatic *Ministerpräsident* of Lower Saxony (Niedersachsen), Gerhard Schröder, as the party's *Kanzlerkandidat* (chancellor candidate) at the 1998 *Bundestag* elections enabled the SPD to secure enough seats for a majority coalition with *Bündnis 90–Die Grünen*, ousting the CDU-led coalition under Kohl which many believed had run out of steam after sixteen years in office. As *Bundeskanzler*, Schröder attempted to secure the SPD's hold over the political middle ground by claiming that the party now represented the *neue Mitte* (new centre). While the SPD presented itself as the natural party of government, the CDU became mired in corruption scandals in 1999 as it emerged that the party had not fully declared its sources of finance under Kohl's leadership.

The evolution of the party political system makes it unlikely that Germany will return to the traditional pattern of the CDU and SPD alternating in national government, supported by the permanent presence of the FDP. Much will depend on whether the FDP can rediscover a distinct political role, independent of the two major parties, and on whether the PDS can maintain its current level of support. During 2001 the SPD leadership again publicly rejected the possibility of a national agreement with the PDS at the 2002 *Bundestag* elections. For the established parties, any notion of conciliation with the reform communists endangers their standing with their core west German electorate, still highly suspicious of the eastern tradition. For the SPD and PDS, the divisions which emerged in socialist politics in the late nineteenth century and weakened the left in the *Weimarer Republik* were still present in the *Bundesrepublik* of the early twenty-first century. Yet the SPD may not always be able to rely on the *Grünen*.

The *Grünen* were somewhat discredited in their core constituencies after 1998 by their failure as a government party to achieve a quick end to nuclear power and the reprocessing and storage of spent nuclear fuel in Germany. The Green policy of increasing fuel taxes has also proved highly unpopular.

Though the increased attractiveness of the SPD was an important factor in the first ever national victory of a 'red–green' coalition at the 1998 *Bundestag* elections, the result principally represented a negative vote against the CDU/CSU–FDP coalition and reflected the Kohl government's enormous difficulties in mastering the economic challenges of German unification (see Document 8). Despite the rhetoric of the *Kanzler der Einheit* (chancellor of unity), east Germany's economy had not produced 'blühende Landschaften' (blossoming landscapes) after the end of socialism; nor had it been possible, despite Kohl's promises, to finance unity without tax rises.

Admittedly, the task of renewing and privatising the GDR's largely run-down state enterprises was huge. The attempt resulted in mass unemployment, as the overstaffed companies were slimmed down or went bankrupt. The failure of many east German businesses resulted, ironically, from the introduction of the *D-Mark* since the GDR's traditional export markets were centred in eastern Europe where hard currency resources were scarce. Equally, many east German products were uncompetitive once the home market was opened to higher quality western alternatives following the *Währungsunion*. By the time the *Treuhand* and its successor organisation had completed their work, the projected surplus from asset sales had been recalculated as a crushing deficit. The *Treuhand* was unable to secure the expected prices from private investors and instead had to invest large sums of public money in redundancy payments, reequipping industrial plant and ensuring that factories no longer produced unacceptable pollution levels. Anger grew in eastern Germany that the GDR's substantial assets had effectively been valued at less than nothing, that many firms had been sold to western competitors at knock-down prices, and that much of the working population had been dislocated, in many cases forced into long-term unemployment, early retirement or short-time working as the GDR's economy was restructured or, in the view of some, deconstructed. Meanwhile, the lower productivity of east German enterprises meant that even ten years after unification, east German workers received only around 80 per cent of the standard west German wage. East Germans also experienced high inflation on retail goods in the early 1990s and much higher bills for rent and basic services once the subsidised GDR system was dismantled.

Despite east German disgruntlement, the cost to the German taxpayer in west–east resource transfers was immense. Besides heavy investment in *Arbeitsbeschaffungs-maßnahmen* (short-term job creation schemes to alleviate the mass unemployment statistics) and public infrastructure projects such as improved road, rail and telecommunications networks, all under the heading *Aufschwung Ost*, the *Bundesrepublik* faced huge bills to cover unemployment benefits, extra pension costs and other social security benefits. This was financed partly by a special income tax, the *Solidaritätszuschlag*, and partly by reduced public spending in some areas (the *Sparpakete* went some way to reducing the social security burden), but also by a substantial increase in government debt, which almost doubled within ten years. After 1998, Kohl's SPD successors responded with still tighter controls on public spending to prevent the further growth of Germany's debt mountain.

Despite the problems, East Germans benefited greatly from unification. Besides the freedom to travel, they enjoyed improved access to modern technology (not least the western cars, computers and mobile phones which were soon visible in the *neuen Länder*) and a high degree of political freedom in a state based on the rule of law (*Rechtsstaat*). Yet these advantages were quickly taken for granted in the east as part and parcel of life in a normal state. Instead of gratitude to the west, a sense of injustice emerged over the way that *Wessis* (west Germans) had assumed the leading role in the economic and political structures of the east, while *Ossis* (east Germans) were written off as lazy and backward. Nostalgia, wittily dubbed *Ostalgie*, grew for GDR products, music and television programmes, swept away by the tide of convergence with western norms, while vigorous campaigns were successfully fought to preserve the distinctive east German *Ampelmännchen*, the figures on pedestrian traffic signals.

The west German parties' dogged condemnation of anything which remained of the old GDR as tainted with the legacy of the *Stasi* and the Berlin Wall provoked resentment among many *Ossis* of all political persuasions, who generally did not recognise this monochrome view of their former lives as the unwilling victims of a totalitarian dictatorship. The enthusiasm of former GDR citizens, especially those who had suffered political repression, to bring the old SED and *Stasi* elites to justice also encountered difficulties. The campaign to discredit the popular SPD *Ministerpräsident* of Brandenburg, Manfred Stolpe, a senior church official who had discussed church matters with the *Stasi*, arguably in the interests of religious dissidents, aroused much interest in the early 1990s. Despite the accusations, Stolpe increased his majority in the 1994 *Landtag* elections. Some members of the old *Politbüro* were tried over the policy of shooting to kill would-be escapers at the Berlin Wall and the German–German border but many of the cases collapsed as the elderly accused fell ill and died. Meanwhile the trial of Markus Wolf, the former head of *Stasi* foreign intelligence (spying), on treason charges provoked accusations of *Siegerjustiz* (victors' justice). The attempt by *Bundesrepublik* courts to review the actions of the old GDR government by a mixture of East German and 'natural' law provoked considerable disquiet and, arguably, held back the integration of the two halves of Germany.

Further controversy surrounded the status of east German property which was seized under the Soviet Union's occupation rights before 1949. So far, the government's inclination to restore the *status quo ante*, effectively reversing the *Bodenreform* and restoring the old *Junker*, has been resisted. In the case of property nationalised or expropriated after 1949 by the GDR, the Kohl government's general principle was to restore it to the original owners where possible and otherwise pay compensation. This enabled many who left the GDR before 1961 to reclaim houses and other assets, but created much confusion and uncertainty over ownership rights in the east. The emergence of competing claims from the descendants of those expropriated during the *Drittes Reich* further complicated matters. Much effort was also expended on untangling the rights to agricultural land which had been pooled in the LPGs (see p. 166), while maintaining east German farms as viable businesses.

German foreign policy was the focus of considerable interest and some concern after unification, since many expected Germany to play a more significant role in world affairs. In fact, the enlarged *Bundesrepublik* has essentially continued its pre-1990 traditions. Kohl was keen to emphasise that Germany posed no threat since it was fully integrated into wider European structures. Germany pursued greater European unity with dedication during the 1990s, stressing its commitment to include the eastern European states in an expanded Union. Germany also played a leading role in preparing the single currency, the Euro, which absorbed the *D-Mark* on 1 January 1999. However, the generally pro-European German public was unsettled by the new currency's weakness and reluctant to abandon the *D-Mark* which had underpinned the *Wirtschafts-wunder* of the 1950s and drawn East Germans to unification with the west in 1990.

The *Bundesrepublik*'s increasing importance in world affairs resulted more from an international desire for Germany to play a role commensurate with its size and economic status, than from any great power aspirations in Bonn or Berlin. In particular, German forces were deployed in United Nations peace-keeping missions in Somalia and former Yugoslavia during the 1990s, and participated within NATO in the Kosovo war of 1999. The use of German military forces outside the NATO area was opposed by the pacifist movement, a strong tradition since the defeat of 1945; participation in the Kosovo conflict, which saw NATO bombing Serbian targets, was a particularly divisive issue for *Bündnis 90–Die Grünen*, whose ministers took joint responsibility for German involvement despite the party's pacifist origins. Nonetheless, far from becoming a stronger military force, Germany reduced the size of the *Bundeswehr* following the end of the Cold War, partly to achieve savings in public expenditure, and is considering an end to conscription. There seems no possibility of a return to an independent, let alone aggressive, German foreign policy.

Concern was raised, however, by a dramatic rise in right-wing extremism following unification, characterised by violent attacks on asylum seekers' hostels and individual foreigners, some of whom were murdered. The violence was perpetrated by a small minority within a much larger movement, stronger in the east than the west. The far right benefited from anger at the increasing number of foreigners who entered Germany in the early 1990s and the problems of mass unemployment, particularly in the east. Some commentators have argued that young people in the east were especially vulnerable to the lure of the extreme right since it represented the clearest rejection of the socialist GDR, and provided a strong group identity for a generation dislocated by the disintegration of the state in which it grew up.

By 2001 the three principal far-right parties (*Deutsche Volksunion* (DVU), NPD and *Republikaner*) had not significantly threatened the political order. They were too divided to stand on a united ticket, and even their combined vote normally would not have been sufficient to surmount the *Fünfprozenthürde* (see p. 133). Where such a party won seats – the DVU spectacularly secured 12.9 per cent of the *Landtag* vote in Saxony-Anhalt in 1998 – its representatives generally proved incapable of exerting an effective political force. Following a terrorist explosion in mid-2000 which injured ten immigrants from the Soviet Union (six of them Jewish) in Düsseldorf, the government set in motion the procedure to ban the NPD. Despite the developments of the 1990s, the

Bundesrepublik's strong constitutional structures appear sturdy enough to contain any serious internal threat to democracy.

The late 1990s saw government attempts to lessen the attraction of the far right by reducing the number of foreigners entering Germany, but at the same time to build a wider sense of Germany as a multicultural society by strengthening the rights of long-standing foreign residents. Nonetheless, during 1999 the new SPD/Green government's plans to introduce German citizenship rights for the permanently settled *Gastarbeiter* and their families were weakened by firm CDU/CSU opposition in the *Bundesrat*. In its final form the law allowed easier naturalisation and enabled children born in Germany full citizenship rights if their parents had been resident for eight years. However, such children had to decide to adopt either German or another citizenship by the age of 23; dual nationality therefore remained generally banned.

Conclusion

The absorption of the communist GDR after 1990 has presented the biggest challenge yet to the *Bundesrepublik*, yet the system proved robust enough to withstand the severe economic cost, a post-communist movement with mass support and renewed right-wing extremism. Ten years on, much work remained before the unification project could be considered complete. Besides the ongoing investment requirements in the *neuen Länder*, the GDR heritage proved surprisingly durable as an alternative identity to that prevalent in the west. In the first decade after unification the west German establishment regarded the remnants of the GDR system with suspicion, lest they contaminate the reconstituted whole. As the twenty-first century opened, however, there was a greater willingness to consider the east's different experiences more even-handedly, and signs of a more critical approach to West German history, particularly the old *Bundesrepublik*'s handling of the Nazi past.

The start of a new century will not, and should not, draw a veil over the turmoil of Germany's twentieth century. It remains important to recall the consequences of, and to take steps to prevent any recurrence of, inadequate democracy, demagogy, state-sponsored lawlessness and national division. However, the *Bundesrepublik* has already outlasted any other German state form of the last two centuries and appears to be one of the most secure pillars of the European continent. Aspirations to territorial aggrandisement are the daydream of a small minority, and the *Bundesrepublik* seems as capable as any western European nation (more capable than some) of containing internal threats to stability. National unity within the European Union enables Germany to move forward as a 'normal' country at last.

Republik Österreich, 1990–2000

During the 1990s, the postwar Austrian consensus began to break down. This coincided with the changes in the wider European framework following the collapse of communism in eastern Europe. Hitherto Austria had prided itself on its neutrality between east and west, and (the Waldheim years notwithstanding) had built a reputation as a centre of diplomacy. With the Cold War certainties gone, and the EC's single market in force after 1993, Austria felt somewhat isolated. In a 1994 referendum, two-thirds of Austrian voters supported joining the EC, with effect from 1995. In 1999 the *Schilling* was absorbed into the new European single currency, the Euro. Though neutrality remained, by the late 1990s questions were raised about whether and how Austria could be incorporated into any future EU military role.

The opening of eastern Europe's borders and the wars in former Yugoslavia also brought far higher numbers of immigrants and asylum seekers to Austria (and other western European countries). This, and the perceived threat to Austrian sovereignty of EU membership, sparked reactions in domestic politics. The established SPÖ–ÖVP duopoly (still in power under SPÖ *Bundeskanzler* Franz Vranitzky as the decade began) was increasingly challenged by a revived FPÖ under the charismatic leadership of Jörg Haider. The FPÖ campaigned throughout the decade against EU membership and immigrants, and accused the SPÖ and ÖVP of corruption. In 1992–93 an FPÖ petition against foreigners declared that Austria would not be a land of immigration or multi-culturalism, and proposed specific restrictions on foreigners in the country.

Though only 7.4 per cent of the electorate supported the petition, the youthful Haider brought a breath of fresh air to the stale world of *Proporz*. The FPÖ made gains throughout the decade at national and regional elections, despite Haider's repeated controversial remarks about the supposedly positive or harmless aspects of the *Drittes Reich*. Conversely, the true liberals within the FPÖ reacted to this shift towards the far right by splitting away to form their own party, the *Liberales Forum* (LiF), under Heide Schmidt. The FPÖ petition was also countered by a mass demonstration against racism and xenophobia in Vienna in early 1993.

At the 1999 *Nationalrat* elections the FPÖ benefited greatly from public weariness with grand coalition politics and *Proporz*, and the often unclear policy distinctions between the ÖVP and SPÖ. The two major parties garnered just 60 per cent of the vote (compared with over 90 per cent twenty years earlier). With 26.9 per cent of the vote, Haider controlled as many seats as the ÖVP. *Bundeskanzler* Viktor Klima, Vranitzky's less charismatic SPÖ successor, was unable to renew the coalition with the ÖVP, which feared that its steady electoral decline reflected the compromises it had been forced to make in government with the SPÖ. Instead, the ÖVP leader, Wolfgang Schüssel, broke the Austrian political mould by agreeing a coalition pact with Haider's far-right FPÖ.

The FPÖ's entry into government caused consternation in Austria and abroad, particularly in Israel where the antisemitic utterances of some FPÖ leaders were viewed with alarm. Vienna witnessed mass demonstrations against racism, and *Bundes-präsident* Thomas Klestil (ÖVP) only formally appointed the new government after the ÖVP and FPÖ had issued an unprecedented declaration confirming Austria's commit-ment to full human rights including the equality of all races, religions and minority groups, and to European integration. Haider himself pragmatically remained outside national government, and even stepped down as FPÖ leader in May 2000 to lessen tensions, remaining, however, as *Landeshauptmann* (governor) of his stronghold, Carinthia (Kärnten). Nonetheless, the other EU states imposed a diplomatic freeze on Austria in protest at the FPÖ's involvement in government, reminiscent of the international reaction to Waldheim's election. This move provoked general resentment in Austria, where many believed the EU had no right to penalise a member state for its internal politics. Partly recognising that the policy was achieving the reverse of what was intended, partly acknowledging that the new Austrian government's human rights record met European standards, the EU lifted the sanctions in September 2000.

The shape of future Austrian politics is particularly uncertain. The inclusion of the FPÖ in national government may well initiate overdue renewal in the other main parties, yet it seems unlikely that the SPÖ will improve its position far enough to enable a coalition with the still small Green party on the German model. The FPÖ is arguably being tamed by its governmental responsibilities and the shock of the vociferous international reaction to its election; its share of the vote in regional elections fell during 2000 and early 2001. From the perspective of mid-2001, there seems little enthusiasm for the compromises and fudges of renewed grand coalition, but also no other clear alternative to the continued presence of the FPÖ in government, or a radical reform of the electoral system away from proportional representation.

Document 8: *Jahresbericht 1999 der Bundesregierung zum Stand der Deutschen Einheit*

Regierungserklärung von Bundeskanzler Gerhard Schröder in der 69. Sitzung des Deutschen Bundestages am 11. November 1999 in Berlin

Verehrter Herr Präsident! Meine sehr verehrten Damen und Herren!

. . . Durch die gewaltlose Revolution des Jahres 1989 ist Deutschland ein souveräner und gleichberechtigter Partner in einem zusammenwachsenden Europa geworden. Zugleich sind die Erwartungen an das vereinte Deutschland gestiegen, Verantwortung in Europa und darüber hinaus in der Welt zu übernehmen. . . . Inzwischen liegen zehn Jahre seit den bewegenden Ereignissen des Revolutionsherbstes hinter uns. . . .

Die erste und wichtigste Erkenntnis meiner Bestandsaufnahme lautet: Wir haben unbestreitbar große Erfolge beim Aufbau Ost erzielt. Diese Erfolge sind ebenso unbestreitbar zuallererst das Resultat der Leistungen der Ostdeutschen selbst.

Zweifellos waren und – ich füge hinzu – bleiben die Solidarität der Westländer und die Leistungen des Bundes weiter wichtig. Sie waren und sie sind oftmals Initialzündung und Katalysator; aber vollbracht wurde das bisher Geleistete vor allen Dingen von den Menschen in Ostdeutschland. . . .

Die Aufbausituation seit der Vereinigung stand unter einem ganz anderen Vorzeichen als die Zeit des Wirtschaftswunders in den fünfziger Jahren oder auch die Eingliederung des Saarlandes in den Jahren nach 1957. Es gab keine wirtschaftliche Sonderzone Ostdeutschland und kaum Übergangsregelungen oder Schutzklauseln für ostdeutsche Unternehmen. Unternehmer und Arbeitnehmer mussten sich über Nacht auf eine neue Wirtschaftsordnung einstellen. Die Märkte für ostdeutsche Produkte in Ost- und Mitteleuropa sind vielfach weggebrochen. An den westeuropäischen Märkten waren die Unternehmen unvermittelt einer starken westlichen Konkurrenz ausgesetzt.

Die zweite Feststellung zur Zwischenbilanz lautet deshalb: Die Revolution von 1989 brachte zwar allen demokratische Freiheiten und in der Folge vielen auch materiellen Wohlstand. Aber der Übergang von der sozialistischen Staatswirtschaft zur

Marktwirtschaft verlief nicht bruch- und auch nicht reibungslos. Für viele Menschen war er mit herben Einbußen und tiefen Einschnitten verbunden. Das betrifft vor allen Dingen den Arbeitsmarkt. Millionen von Arbeitsplätzen gingen verloren. Sie konnten durch die hohe Zahl der neugeschaffenen Arbeitsplätze bei weitem noch nicht ausgeglichen werden. . . .

Ebenso unbestreitbar ist aber, dass nach zehn Jahren in Ostdeutschland das Gefühl der Entfremdung und der Enttäuschung noch immer sehr deutlich zu spüren ist. Diese Empfindungen werden auch von Menschen geteilt, die vom Schicksal der Arbeitslosigkeit verschont wurden und ihren privaten und beruflichen Weg unter neuen Verhältnissen erfolgreich gegangen sind. Dafür lassen sich objektive wie subjektive Ursachen ausmachen, die allesamt zu tun haben mit 40 Jahren getrennter, aber auch mit zehn Jahren gemeinsamer, aber unterschiedlich erlebter Geschichte.

Zu den objektiven Ursachen gehören die einschneidenden und alle Lebensbereiche umfassenden Veränderungen im persönlichen Umfeld. Die Veränderungsleistung, die den Ostdeutschen nach der Vereinigung abverlangt wurde, war ohne Frage ungleich größer als die ihrer westdeutschen Landsleute. Mit der Industrie- und Gewerbestruktur ging häufig die soziale und auch die kulturelle Infrastruktur verloren. Aber vor allem wurde mit dem Verlust der Arbeit für viele der wichtigste soziale Bezugsrahmen zerstört. Mit den sozialen Strukturen und den gesellschaftlichen Bindungen ging wiederum ein Teil des Identitätsgefühls verloren.

Viel schwerer wiegen darum die subjektiven Ursachen: Viele Ostdeutsche schmerzt das als zu gering empfundene Interesse der Westdeutschen an ihrer Geschichte und auch an ihrer Heimat. Sicher ist: Mehr Neugier auf Ostdeutschland, seine Geschichte und seine Menschen würde das Verständnis zwischen Ost und West fördern. . . . .

Source: Presse- und Informationsamt der Bundesregierung, *Bulletin*, No. 79: 18, November 1999 (CD-ROM edition).

Topics
FOR DISCUSSION / FURTHER RESEARCH

■ Was Brandt's *Ostpolitik* or Adenauer's *Westintegration* more instrumental in creating the prerequisites for German unification?

■ How fairly did Gerhard Schröder's 1999 *Bundestag* speech (Document 8) reflect west and east Germans' experiences of the unification process?

■ Were east Germans justified in considering themselves second-class citizens in the first decade after unification?

■ Did the relative weakness of the east German economy in 1999 result principally from SED policy in the GDR period or from the policies pursued during and after the unification process?

■ Compare and contrast the extreme right in Germany and Austria in the 1990–2000 period.

Further reading

The study of German (and to a lesser extent Austrian) history has produced a rich and detailed literature in both English and German. The suggestions below represent only a very small sample of the works which will enable readers of this introduction to extend their knowledge and understanding of the field, and are not intended as a comprehensive bibliography of the texts consulted by the author. Incidentally, not all of the works listed are still in print.

General overviews

Among the best are Mary Fulbrook's *Concise History of Germany* (Cambridge: Cambridge University Press, 1994) and William Carr's *History of Germany 1815–1990* (London: Arnold, 1991, shortly to be revised and updated). A. J. P. Taylor's *Course of German History* (London: Routledge, latest reprint 2001) is now somewhat outdated (it first appeared in 1945) but presents an interesting interpretation of the pre-1945 period. Hajo Holborn's *History of Germany* (Princeton: Princeton University Press, 3 vols, latest reprint 1982) remains a formidable, yet accessible resource on Germany from Luther to Hitler. The development of German national identity is interestingly explored in a cohesive series of essays edited by John Breuilly, *The State of Germany* (London/New York: Longman, 1992).

Other essential texts cover shorter periods in greater detail. Highly recommended are James Sheehan's *German History 1770–1866* (Oxford: Clarendon Press, 1989), David Blackbourn's *The Long Nineteenth Century* (London: HarperCollins, 1997), and Gordon Craig's *Germany 1866–1945* (Oxford: Oxford University Press, 1981). In German there are Thomas Nipperdey's three volumes entitled *Deutsche Geschichte*, one on the 1800–66 period, two on 1866–1918 (Munich: C. H. Beck, 1983–93). For an overview of the twentieth century, the standard work is Mary Fulbrook's *Divided Nation 1918–1990* (London: HarperCollins, 1991). Two collections of essays, *Nineteenth-Century Germany*, edited by John Breuilly, and *Twentieth-Century Germany*, edited by Mary Fulbrook (both London: Arnold, 2001) are particularly recommended as solid guides to current knowledge and debate.

Other key works to be consulted in association with the chapters of this book are suggested below. Particularly recommended titles are asterisked.

Prologue/Chapter 1 (Germany before 1871)

Manfred Botzenhart, *Reform, Restauration, Krise. Deutschland 1789–1847* (Frankfurt am Main: Suhrkamp, 1985)

William Carr, *The Origins of the Wars of German Unification* (London/New York: Longman, 1991)

Ernst Engelberg, *Bismarck. Urpreuße und Reichsgründer* (Berlin: Siedler, 1985)

Heinrich Lutz, *Zwischen Habsburg und Preußen. Deutschland 1815–1866* (Munich: btb/Goldmann, 1998)

Hagen Schulze, *Der Weg zum Nationalstaat* (Munich: dtv, 1985)

* Brendan Simms, *The Struggle for Mastery in Germany, 1779–1850* (London: Macmillan, 1998)

Michael Stürmer, *Die Reichsgründung* (Munich: dtv, 1984)

Chapter 2 (the *Kaiserreich*)

V. R. Berghahn, *Imperial Germany 1871–1914* (Providence/Oxford: Berghahn, 1994)

Ernst Engelberg, *Bismarck. Das Reich in der Mitte Europas* (Munich: dtv, 1993)

Wolfgang J. Mommsen, *Imperial Germany 1867–1918* (London: Arnold, 1995)

John C. G. Röhl, *The Kaiser and his Court: Wilhelm II and the Government of Germany* (Cambridge: Cambridge University Press, 1994)

Volker Ullrich, *Die nervöse Großmacht 1871–1918* (Frankfurt am Main: Fischer, 1997)

* Hans-Ulrich Wehler, *The German Empire 1871–1918* (New York/Oxford: Berg, 1985)

Chapter 3 (the *Weimarer Republik*)

Paul Bookbinder, *Weimar Germany. The Republic of the Reasonable* (Manchester: Manchester University Press, 1996)

John Hiden, *Republican and Fascist Germany* (London: Longman, 1996)

* Eberhard Kolb, *The Weimar Republic* (London: Routledge, 1988)

* A. J. Nicholls, *Weimar and the Rise of Hitler* (London: Macmillan, 4th edn, 2000)

Panikos Panayi (ed.), *Weimar and Nazi Germany* (London: Longman, 2000)

Hagen Schulze, *Weimar* (Berlin: Severin und Siedler, 1982)

Chapter 4 (the *Drittes Reich*)

Martin Broszat, *The Hitler State* (London: Longman, 1981)

* Karl Dietrich Bracher, *The German Dictatorship* (London: Penguin, 1991)

Michael Burleigh, *The Third Reich* (London: Macmillan, 2000)

Philippe Burrin, *Hitler and the Jews* (London: Arnold, 1994)

Conan Fischer, *The Rise of the Nazis* (Manchester: Manchester University Press, 1995)

* Martin Gilbert, *The Holocaust* (London: Collins, 1986)

Neil Gregor (ed.), *Nazism* (Oxford: Oxford University Press, 2000)

* Ian Kershaw, *The Nazi Dictatorship* (London: Arnold, 4th edn, 2000)

* Ian Kershaw, *Hitler* (London: Penguin, 2 vols, 1999–2000)

* Jeremy Noakes and Geoffrey Pridham (eds), *Nazism: A Documentary Reader* (Exeter: Exeter University Press, 4 vols, 1983–1998)

Richard Overy, *War and Economy in the Third Reich* (Oxford: Oxford University Press, 1995)

Chapters 5–8 (post-1945 Germany)

Mark Allinson (ed.), *Contemporary Germany* (London/New York: Longman, 2000)

* Dennis L. Bark and David R. Gress, *A History of West Germany* (Oxford: Basil Blackwell, 2 vols, 2nd edn, 1991)

David Childs, *The GDR. Moscow's German Ally* (London: Allen & Unwin, 1982) – though this title appeared before the *Wende*, it remains a useful reference source

* Mary Fulbrook, *Anatomy of a Dictatorship: Inside the GDR 1949–1989* (Oxford: Oxford University Press, 1995)

* Mary Fulbrook, *German National Identity after the Holocaust* (Cambridge: Polity Press, 1999)

* Mary Fulbrook, *Interpretations of the Two Germanies, 1945–1990* (Basingstoke: Macmillan, 2nd edn, 2000)

Lothar Kettenacker, *Germany since 1945* (Oxford: Oxford University Press, 1997)

Christoph Kleßmann, *Die doppelte Staatsgründung. Deutsche Geschichte 1945–1955* (Göttingen: Vandenhoeck & Ruprecht, 5th edn, 1991), and *Zwei Staaten, eine Nation. Deutsche Geschichte 1955–1970* (Göttingen: Vandenhoeck & Ruprecht, 1988)

* A. J. Nicholls, *The Bonn Republic* (London: Longman, 1997)

Peter Pulzer, *German Politics 1945–1995* (Oxford: Oxford University Press, 1995)

Klaus Schroeder, *Der SED-Staat. Partei, Staat und Gesellschaft 1949–1990* (Munich: Carl Hanser, 1998)

Dietrich Staritz, *Geschichte der DDR* (Frankfurt am Main: Suhrkamp, 1996)

* Hermann Weber, *Geschichte der DDR* (Munich: dtv, 1999)

Austria

Barbara Jelavich's *Modern Austria: Empire and Republic 1815–1986* (Cambridge: Cambridge University Press,1987) and Gordon Brook-Shepherd's *The Austrians* (London: HarperCollins, 1996) – chattier but just as incisive – are good starting points. On the decline of the Habsburg Empire, see John W. Mason's *The Dissolution of the Austro-Hungarian Empire 1867–1918* (London: Longman, 1985), Edward Crankshaw, *The Fall of the House of Habsburg* (London: Longman, 1963), and A. J. P. Taylor, *The Habsburg Monarchy* (most recently London: Penguin, 1990). In German see the two-volume collection of introductory essays and documents, *Österreich im 20. Jahrhundert*, edited by Rolf Steininger and Michael Gehler (Vienna: Böhlau, 1997), and the two volumes entitled *Handbuch des politischen Systems Österreichs* covering the First and Second Republics respectively (Vienna: Manz, 1995 and 1997).

Historiographical debates

Gerhard Botz and Gerald Sprengnagel (eds), *Kontroversen um Österreichs Zeitgeschichte. Verdrängte Vergangenheit, Österreich-Identität, Waldheim und die Historiker* (Frankfurt am Main/New York: Campus, 1994)

Dan Diner (ed.), *Ist der Nationalsozialismus Geschichte? Zu Historisierung und Historikerstreit* (Frankfurt am Main: Fischer, 1993)

* Richard J. Evans, *Rereading German History 1800–1996* (London: Routledge, 1997)

James Knowlton and Truett Cates (eds), *Forever in the Shadow of Hitler?* (Atlantic Highlands, NJ: Humanities Press, 1993)

* Charles S. Maier, *The Unmasterable Past: History, Holocaust, and German National Identity* (Cambridge, MA: Harvard University Press, 2nd edn, 1998)

Useful internet sites for historians of Germany and Austria

The internet now offers a wealth of useful resources for those with interests in German and Austrian history. Its particular strengths are collections of historical documents and 'virtual' museums; you will also find articles about particular events or personalities, and overviews of historical periods, but here some caution may be required in judging a site's worth. In general, books and journals (and their web-based editions if available) remain far more reliable sources for historical narrative and interpretation than web sites posted by individuals or interest groups. The list below is far from comprehensive, and please bear in mind that as sites come and go, and URLs change, this information (accurate in November 2001) may quickly be outdated.

One of the best German sites is operated by the Deutsches Historisches Museum in Berlin. Visit its virtual museum, an excellent and visually stimulating quick reference source, at *http://www.dhm.de/lemo/home.html*. This currently concentrates mainly on the post-1900 era, but past and present exhibitions on a variety of periods and themes can be visited at *http://www.dhm.de/ausstellungen/*.

The German Studies Web (*http://www.dartmouth.edu/~wess/*) is an important resource for Germanists in all areas, providing links to worthwhile sites covering history and politics, but also literature, German language and the law. There are also links to newspapers and broadcasters in the German-speaking world, though a more comprehensive list can be found at the University of Exeter's Media Index (*http://www.ex.ac.uk/german/media/index.html*). History links are at: *http://www.lib.byu.edu/~rdh/wess/germ/hist.html*. There are other useful link catalogues at the Virtual History Library (*http://www.phil.uni-erlangen.de/~p1ges/heidelberg/gh/gh.html*), and at the site offered by the Univeristy of Dortmund (*http://www-geschichte.fb15.uni-dortmund.de/links/*).

Collections of primary documents across a number of different periods are linked from the Brigham Young University (*http://library.byu.edu/~rdh/eurodocs/germany.html*) and documents with a legal or constitutional bias for the period since 1800 are being collated by a project in Chemnitz (*http://www.documentarchiv.de/*). PSM Data also has a growing list of resources, with both primary documents and secondary literature (*http://www.psm-data.de/*). There is a good collection of maps for the period covered by this book at *http://www.fortunecity.de/lindenpark/caesarenstrasse/69/grenzen/index.htm*.

For the nineteenth century, the Virtual History Library has an extensive list of links at *http://www.erlangerhistorikerseite.de/heidelberg/gh/e6.html*, and you will find documents of the 1848 revolution at *http://zaurak.tm.informatik.uni-frankfurt.de/ 1848/index.html*. The *Weimarer Republik* is well represented at *http://home.t-online.de/ home/d.nix/weimar/*, and there is useful and detailed information about election results in the 1919–33 period at *http://www.gonschior.de/weimar/*.

The national socialist era has produced a number of sites by extremists or sympathisers, some with an antisemitic focus, but there is a carefully chosen set of links on all aspects of Nazi rule at *http://www.nationalsozialismus.de/*. Meanwhile, *http:// www.thirdreichpages.com/* focuses particularly on Hitler. For a considered view of different aspects of the Holocaust, try the United States Holocaust Memorial Museum site (*http://www.ushmm.org/*), or the site at *http://www.shoah.de/*, which has a very good links collection. Propaganda, in both the *Drittes Reich* and the GDR, is the focus at the German Propaganda Archive (*http://www.calvin.edu/academic/cas/gpa/*).

For the postwar era, see '50 Jahre Bundesrepublik Deutschland' at *http:// koep3og.virtualave.net/* (though this site carries a lot of advertising); there is basic information at '50 Jahre Deutschland' (*http://www.b.shuttle.de/rz1002/rap2000/*). The GDR is increasingly well represented on the internet, including a number of nostalgia and satirical sites. The site '40 Jahre DDR' at *http://home.ptt.ru/ego/* has a good collection of links, as does *http://www.ddr-suche.de/*; *http://ddr-im-www.de/* is an increasingly useful site in its own right. The Berlin Wall is given full treatment at *http://www.chronikdermauer.de*, and there is detail on the GDR's collapse during 1989-90 at *http://www.chronik-der-wende.de*. The *Stasi* is documented by the German government agency now responsible for its files at *http://www.bstu.de/home.htm*.

For Austrian history, the best site is the comprehensive *http://www.aeiou.at/*. There are useful primary documents on twentieth century Austria at *http://zeit1.uibk.ac.at/. goes20_ger.html*, and an overview of Austria since 1945 at *http://www.oefrei.at/*.

On modern Germany and Austria, apart from using the links at the German studies web (see above), *www.bundesregierung.de* and *http://www.austria.gv.at/* will take you to the official German and Austrian government sites respectively. There are comprehensive sets of links to political parties and other institutions at *http:// www.politicalresources.net/germany.htm* and *http://www.politicalresources.net/ austria.htm*. Germany's Bundeszentrale für politische Bildung also has excellent online resources about political structures and issues, as well as many of the historical periods covered in this book, at *http://www.bpb.de*. Particularly recommended at this site is the series 'Informationen zur politischen Bildung' under 'Online Publikationen'.

Academics, teachers and professionals in particular will be interested by H-German at *http://www2.h-net.msu.edu/~german/*, H-Net Habsburg at *http://www2.h-net.msu.edu/ ~habsweb/*, and by the 'Nachrichtendienst für Historiker' (*http://www.crispinius.com/ nfh3/index.shtml*), which includes a daily review of press items on German and other history.

Index/Glossary

Bold references indicate a text box.